Edward Albee
A Critical Introduction

Edward Albee (1928–2016) was a central figure in modern American theater, and his bold and often experimental theatrical style won wide acclaim. This book explores the issues, public and private, that so influenced Albee's vision over five decades, from his first great success, *The Zoo Story* (1959), to his last play, *Me, Myself & I* (2008). Matthew Roudané covers all of Albee's original works in this comprehensive, clearly structured, and up-to-date study of the playwright's life and career: in Part I, the volume explores Albee's background and the historical contexts of his work; Part II concentrates on twenty-six of his plays, including *Who's Afraid of Virginia Woolf?* (1962); and Part III investigates his critical reception. Surveying Albee's relationship with Broadway, and including interviews conducted with Albee himself, this book will be of great importance for theatergoers and students seeking an accessible yet incisive introduction to this extraordinary American playwright.

Matthew Roudané is Regents' Professor of English at Georgia State University. He has published widely on various aspects of American drama, particularly the theater of major figures including Tennessee Williams, Arthur Miller, and Edward Albee. He is editor of *The Cambridge Companion to Tennessee Williams* (1997) and of *The Cambridge Companion to Sam Shepard* (2002).

Edward Albee
A Critical Introduction

MATTHEW ROUDANÉ
Georgia State University

CAMBRIDGE
UNIVERSITY PRESS

CAMBRIDGE
UNIVERSITY PRESS

University Printing House, Cambridge CB2 8BS, United Kingdom

One Liberty Plaza, 20th Floor, New York, NY 10006, USA

477 Williamstown Road, Port Melbourne, VIC 3207, Australia

4843/24, 2nd Floor, Ansari Road, Daryaganj, Delhi – 110002, India

79 Anson Road, #06-04/06, Singapore 079906

Cambridge University Press is part of the University of Cambridge.

It furthers the University's mission by disseminating knowledge in the pursuit of education, learning, and research at the highest international levels of excellence.

www.cambridge.org
Information on this title: www.cambridge.org/9780521898294
DOI: 10.1017/9781139034845

First published 2017

Printed in the United States of America by Sheridan Books, Inc.

A catalogue record for this publication is available from the British Library.

ISBN 978-0-521-89829-4 Hardback
ISBN 978-0-521-72695-5 Paperback

For Jim Fox

Contents

Preface

The title of this book, *Edward Albee: A Critical Introduction*, suggests its scope and emphasis: a study aimed at introducing the works of Edward Albee to theatergoers, readers, and a newer generation of students, many of whom are perhaps discovering Albee's plays for the first time. This book will explore the public and private issues that so inform Albee's vision, from his first great success, *The Zoo Story* (1959), through his last play before his death, *Me, Myself & I* (2008). This book traces Albee's artistic vision and his major subjects as reflected in twenty-six original plays.[1]

Part I, "Albee's Life and World," begins with Chapter 1, "Life," a brief introductory biographical chapter concerning Albee's life and world, while Chapter 2, "Overview: The Theater of Edward Albee," provides an overview of Albee's dramatic theory of art and what so preoccupied him over his legendary career. Chapter 3, "Contexts," presents an historical background focusing mainly on Albee's formative years in the later 1940s through 1962, the breakthrough year when he made his Broadway premiere with *Who's Afraid of Virginia Woolf?* Readers will get a sense of the ethos of Broadway when Albee entered that world.

Part II, "The Plays," concentrates on twenty-six Albee plays. Chapter 4, "Ritualized Forms of Expiation," explores the early plays from *The Zoo Story* through *The American Dream*, plays that first attracted us to a new, young playwright. Chapter 5, "Challenging Broadway," considers the rest of the plays from the 1960s, from *Who's Afraid of Virginia Woolf?* through the companion plays, *Box* and *Quotations from Chairman Mao Tse-Tung*. Albee, indeed, found an ossified Broadway "challenging" in many ways, with its aversion to experimentalism at odds with Albee's world view, and "challenging" in the sense that Albee with laser-like precision confronted Broadway with life and death matters in the profoundest ways. The title of Chapter 6 – "The greatest sin in living is doing it badly – stupidly, or as if you weren't really alive" – comes from one of Albee's lesser known plays, *Listening*, but stands as a touchstone into all of his plays; this is a chapter devoted to the plays from the 1970s. Chapter 7,

"A Quest for Consciousness," concentrates on the problematic plays from the 1980s, from *The Lady from Dubuque* through *Marriage Play*. Chapter 8, "As I Lay Dying," examines the plays from the 1990s through the early 2000s, such as *Three Tall Women* and *The Goat or, Who Is Sylvia?*, works that reinvigorated Albee's career. The last chapter devoted to the plays, Chapter 9, "A Theater of Loss," considers the last four plays of Albee's career, from *Occupant* through *Me, Myself & I.*

Part III, "Dialogues," features Chapter 10, "Critical Reception," a discussion of selected major critical studies published on Albee. I end the book with an epilogue, "Final Curtain," a brief coda regarding this extraordinary American dramatist. This is followed by "Further Reading," which gives readers a primary and secondary bibliography on Albee, one that points to excellent critical studies.

I have used *The Collected Plays of Edward Albee* in three volumes (Woodstock, NY: Overlook Duckworth, 2004–5), unless otherwise noted, to quote from the plays; I cite volume and page number parenthetically throughout this book.

* * *

There is no shortage of Albee scholarship. From the early books on Albee by Gilbert Debusscher (1967) and Christopher Bigsby (1969) through the more recent work by Stephen Bottoms (2005), Toby Zinman (2008), Anne Paolucci (2010), Rakesh Solomon (2010), and David Crespy (2013), Albee's plays have attracted much critical debate. Indeed, this *Critical Introduction* rests on the work of those (many of whom I know) who have written so impressively on Albee over the years. The sheer number of studies – books, book chapters, collections of critical essays, interviews, theater reviews, scholarly articles, and so on – make it increasingly challenging for students and the general reader to find a current and concise assessment of Albee, whose plays for some sixty years have engaged (and occasionally enraged) audiences globally. *Edward Albee: A Critical Introduction* addresses precisely such a challenge.

By exploring all of Albee's major works, I hope to show something of the range and versatility of his imagination. In an ideal world, one should see an Albee play live; the special kind of collective experience the audience shares with the actors and the multivalency of live theater simply cannot be reproduced fully in the text version. That said, it is sometimes a challenge to find a theater company producing every Albee play. Hence, somewhat surprisingly, Albee himself points to the value of seeing and hearing the play as literature: "I would rather have a person who knows how to read a play *read* a play of mine and see a good production in his mind than see a bad production." As Albee explains, "Ideally, a superb production is to be seen, but given a bad production – well, I'd prefer a good reading anytime. You just have to learn how to read and be able to *see* and *hear* the play out loud while you are reading it."[2] In light of Albee's remarks, I have written the book so that one can use it whether approaching the text as performance or viewing the actual spectacle. Finally, I hope that *Edward Albee: A Critical Introduction* will help theatregoers or readers better appreciate one of America's most important dramatists, one who reinvented as he re-invigorated the American theater.

On Friday, September 16, 2016, Edward Albee died. We have lost a titan of contemporary theater. With his passing, though, we can celebrate his life by enjoying his remarkable and distinguished contributions to the American stage. This book, I hope, is a humble and modest way to partake in that celebration.

Acknowledgments

I would like to thank a number of colleagues and friends who have been so supportive over the years. So a grateful thanks to Kate Brett, Victoria Cooper, Sarah Stanton, and their colleagues at Cambridge University Press. I am also grateful for the anonymous external referee whose suggested revisions were so valuable. Thanks, also, to some of my colleagues at Georgia State University: Rasha Alabdullah, Gina Caison, Stephen Dobranski, Isabel Durán, Lynée Gaillet, Audrey Goodman, Randy Malamud, Cristina Piaget, Elena Del Río Parra, Sara Rosen, and Carol Winker.

I've learned much from members of the Edward Albee Society, especially John Clum, Lincoln Konkle, and David Crespy. Thanks also to Michael Bennett, Natka Bianchini, Maija Birenbaum, Linda Ben-Zvi, Norma Jenckes, and Philip Kolin.

I've also had the benefit of working with various colleagues and friends over the years on American drama and Albee both here and abroad. Among them are Susan Abbotson, Tom Adler, Ana Antón-Pacheco, Christopher Bigsby, Stephen Bottoms, Jackson Bryer, Joseph Chaikin, Sydney Alice Clark, Nathalie Dessens, Ana Fernández-Caparrós, Karen Finley, Christopher Innes, Emeline Jouve, Leslie Kane, Steve Marino, Martin Middeke, Brenda Murphy, Anne Paolucci, David Popoli, Boróka Prohászka Rád, Ilka Saal, June Schlueter, Peter Paul Schnierer, Fabio Vericat, and Katherine Weiss. A special thanks to Susan Ashley and Nickolas Roudané.

Finally, a profound thanks to the late Edward Albee, who first welcomed me into his home in 1980 and whose many conversations about his theater and American drama I thoroughly enjoyed.

Part I

Albee's Life and World

Chapter 1

Life

In "*Exorcism* – the Play O'Neill Tried to Destroy" (2012), Edward Albee reflected on the start of his playwriting life.

> *The Zoo Story* was my first play – and there it sits in all definings: Edward Albee's first play. And I think of it that way. The only possible complication here is that I wrote three or four plays *before* I wrote *The Zoo Story* – before I wrote my first play – before I wrote my Opus 1 … In the case of *The Zoo Story*, it *was* a lot better than the stuff I wrote before it, rather as if my talent – such as it was – had matured enough to have it examined seriously. We separate our student work from our theoretically mature work, and we're usually right.[1]

Six decades later, Edward Albee betokened to the theater world a body of work whose impact animates as it energizes the American stage. Bringing to the stage, as he did, the ironist's sense of balance, the absurdist's sense of futility, and the poet's sense of loss, Albee staged original, challenging productions that define selected public issues of the nation as reflected through the private anxieties of the individual. When he died on September 16, 2016 at the age of eighty-eight, we lost one of *the* great forces of the American stage.

The early work of Edward Albee began when he knew he wanted to be a writer when he was only six years old. He continued writing poetry and fiction for the next twenty years, without much success. Realizing his limitations as a poet, he once told me, "I never felt like a poet; I felt like someone who was writing poetry. I attempted the novel twice, in my teens, once when I was fourteen – a novel of some 1,800 pages – and again when I was sixteen, when my energies were either depleted or elsewhere, a second novel of only 900 pages."[2] The form of the novel, like poetry, was not in accord with his artistic instincts.

The legendary playwright Thornton Wilder mentored, briefly, the twenty-something-year-old future playwright. As Albee remembers in a *New York Times* video (circa 2007), *The Last Word: Edward Albee,*

> We went to a tiny little lake in New Hampshire, sunset, with a bottle of bourbon and my poetry. And as we discussed my poems, he kept

throwing them, gently setting them in the water. And when we finished, all of my poems were floating in the water. He said, "I read all these poems – (pause) – have you ever thought about writing plays?" I don't think [Wilder] saw the incipient playwright because it's not there in the poetry. I think he was trying to save poetry from me![3]

Wilder had a great influence on the young Albee, as Lincoln Konkle reminds us in *Thornton Wilder and the Puritan Narrative Tradition*. Moreover, Konkle suggests that "For Albee, Thornton Wilder was important to American drama attaining the status of literature (an achievement usually credited to Eugene O'Neill alone), as opposed to the tradition of commercial entertainment that was a legacy of the nineteenth-century American theater for which Albee continuously criticized theater owners, producers, and playwrights."[4] Having tried his hand at poetry, the novel, and the short story, Albee thus attempted playwriting. He wrote *Aliqueen*, a three-act sex farce, when he was twelve and, in his teens, *Schism*, a one-act piece whose protagonist, Michael Joyce, becomes alienated from Catholicism and finally from his own sense of humanity. But it was not until the late 1950s that Albee found his *daemon* while composing *The Zoo Story*. "Something very, very interesting happened with the writing of that play. I didn't discover suddenly that I was a playwright; I discovered that I had *been* a playwright all my life, but didn't know it because I hadn't written plays … And so when I wrote *The Zoo Story*, I was able to start practicing my 'nature' fully." With this play Albee quickly established himself as an adamantine voice in contemporary American literature. *The Zoo Story*, Albee enjoyed recalling fifty-three years later,

> had its world premiere in West Berlin, Germany, at the Werkstatt of the Schiller Theater on September 28, 1959 – in German! – on a double bill with Samuel Beckett's *Krapp's Last Tape*. (How fortunate can a young playwright be!)
> The U.S. premiere was (in English!) on the same double bill at the Provincetown Playhouse in New York City's Greenwich Village on January 12, 1960. The evening was well reviewed and *The Zoo Story* ran for nearly three years.[5]

Thus Albee progressed from his "student work" to his "mature" work, and for six decades that maturation process has continued. An indefatigable writer, Albee was working on *Laying an Egg*, his newest play, at the time of his death.

Albee was abandoned by his natural parents soon after his birth on March 12, 1928 in Washington, D.C. Louise Harvey gave her son up for adoption two weeks later – after the father (name unknown) abandoned both the mother and the son. Albee would never meet his natural birth parents. Fortuitously, millionaires Reed and Frances Albee of Larchmont, New York, took into their mansion the infant on March 30, and he was formally adopted on February 1, 1929. Mel Gussow in his excellent *Edward Albee: A Singular Journey* (1999), the only biography of the playwright, writes that "Albee later referred to himself as 'tiny me, a little twig of a thing.' 'They bought me,' he said. 'They paid $133.30,' explaining that was the cost for 'professional services.'"[6] They named him Edward Franklin Albee III after his adoptive grandfather. Albee was thus taken in by a family with theatrical background, for his grandfather co-owned, with B. F. Keith, a profitable chain of vaudeville theaters. Indeed, it was the largest and most vibrant vaudeville circuit in the United States, and in 1928 Edward F. Albee II sold his shares of the theater to Joseph P. Kennedy, father of the thirty-fifth president of the United States. Albee's new mother was nearly a foot taller than her husband and, apparently, was the domineering wife who remained emotionally distant and finally estranged from her newly adopted son. In the mid-1980s, Frances Albee, unbeknownst to her son, changed her will – and cut her son out of much of the inheritance. In any event, as a young man Albee found himself in a family bereft of love (except for his grandmother) and within the wealthy community of Westchester, New York. As a child he motored around in a Rolls Royce and the family sometimes traveled in their private train car to Florida. As he grew older, he met in his home such writers as Thornton Wilder and W. H. Auden.

A rebellious youth, Albee and school did not mix well. After being expelled from three preparatory schools and a military academy, Albee somehow managed to graduate from Choate, a Connecticut prep school. His two-year stay at Choate influenced his literary aspirations, for he received the kind of support that any young writer needs: his work – poems, short stories, essays, and one play – was accepted for publication in the *Choate Literary Magazine*. When Albee was in his eighties, he credited his adoptive parents with giving him what he called an excellent high school education because there he found teachers who encouraged him to pursue the creative arts. He attended Trinity College in Connecticut, lasting only one-and-a-half years before being asked to leave for not attending certain required classes and chapel. As Albee later reminisced, "I didn't write *Catcher in the Rye* and *End as a Man*; I lived them."[7]

After working at various odd jobs from 1948 to 1958, Albee felt increasingly desperate because he might not succeed in any profession. A modest trust fund, established by his grandmother, did not allay his uneasiness as a young man in his twenties in New York City. Apparently out of a sense of youthful *Angst*, then, Albee once again committed himself to serious playwriting; in a self-consoling effort he penned *The Zoo Story*, a "sort of a thirtieth birthday present to myself."[8] In 1981, Albee recalled the creative process he experienced while composing what would be his first public success:

> One evening, twenty-three years ago, I borrowed a hundred sheets or so of poor quality yellow typing paper from the Western Union office where I was employed as a messenger boy, brought it back to my Greenwich Village walk-up and placed it on the rickety kitchen table next to my battered non-portable typewriter. Three weeks later, some fifty sheets of yellow paper had become a play, and I had become a playwright.[9]

When Albee launched his career, he was unknown. However, suddenly in the earlier 1960s Albee found himself in the very epicenter of the American theater world. Essentially an Off-Broadway dramatist, he found his plays being staged on the Great White Way. The theater critics often took issue with Albee; he often took issue with the critics. Controversy and Albee made good bedfellows. In any event, this relatively unknown newcomer found himself on the cover of *Newsweek Magazine*. He traveled to the Soviet Union with John Steinbeck, who had just won the Nobel Prize in literature in 1962. *Who's Afraid of Virginia Woolf?* (1962) was a sensational hit on Broadway, while the Hollywood 1966 film version, staring Elizabeth Taylor and Richard Burton, catapulted Albee into the midst of popular culture. Regardless of his growing fame, he always challenged his audiences. He was the fresh, new, exciting voice of American drama. But many felt that, after the Pulitzer Prize winning *A Delicate Balance* (1966), Albee's language, once the source of heated repartee, became more brittle and abstract. After *Seascape* (1975), which won him his second Pulitzer Prize, he fell out of favor with many critics and the theatergoing public. As Christopher Bigsby put it, "Edward Albee also visited the outer planets of the critical world for several decades."[10] *Three Tall Women* (1991), however, signaled his return, earning him his third Pulitzer, and since then Albee's reputation, it seems, has been restored. He ultimately survived the critical ambuscades gracefully, never compromising artistic probity for commercially safe plays.

Not only had Albee become a playwright of the first rank in the early 1960s, but he also began a lifetime of helping, encouraging, promoting other, younger playwrights such as Terrence McNally, Sam Shepard, Amri Baraka, and Adrienne Kennedy. He influenced Tony Kushner, David Mamet, Paula Vogel, Suzanne Lori-Parks, and, among many others, Karen Finley. Surely such newer voices such as Lynn Nottage, Amy Herzog, Sarah Ruhl, Katori Hall, Francis Ya-Chu Cowhig, Tracy Letts, and David Lindsay-Abaire saw Albee as an inspiring model. In the 1980s and 1990s, he taught playwriting at the University of Houston and, afterwards, was a central participant in the Last Frontier Theatre Conference, held each summer in Valdez, Alaska, a conference in which he challenged new playwrights to achieve dramatic excellence. Albee also increasingly directed his own plays well into the twenty-first century, exerting authorial control over his work and receiving praise for his directorial skills. Indeed, no major American dramatist has directed so many of his own original plays as has Albee. Further, he has worked the college circuit over the decades, lecturing throughout the country. Honorary doctorates, here and abroad, have been bestowed upon him. For decades he oversaw the William Flanagan Memorial Creative Persons Center, an artist colony in his second home in Montauk, New York. This was part of his lifetime commitment to supporting new writers and artists. Albee was also a skilled essayist, as evidenced in his collection *Stretching My Mind* (2005). Many of the essays are vigorous in their plain style and perspicuity.

Albee lived for most of his adult life in New York City (Tribeca) in a beautifully renovated warehouse filled with original art that he began purchasing in the 1960s. He was with his lifetime partner, sculptor Jonathan Thomas, from 1971 until his death in 2005. Once a notorious drinker, Albee had been on the wagon since the mid-1980s, and in 2012 he marveled how, after five years of grieving over the loss of Thomas, he turned an emotional corner for the better. In 2012 he underwent open heart surgery, an operation that left the then eighty-four-year-old understandably frailer, but as helpful, sharp, and opinionated as ever. Albee was pleased to learn that in 2013 a group of dedicated American drama scholars established the Edward Albee Society, housed at the Cherry Lane Theatre.

Some two dozen original plays, three Pulitzer Prizes, and numerous other dramatic accolades later, including an Obie Award for Sustained Achievement in the American Theatre (1994), a National Medal of the Arts (1996), and a Tony Award for Lifetime Achievement (2005), Albee rightfully stood side by side with such other major shapers of the American stage who came before him, most notably Eugene O'Neill, Tennessee Williams, and Arthur Miller. With the passing of Miller in 2005, Albee was, until his death in 2016, considered the elder statesman of American theater, one who commanded worldwide acclaim for his incredible body of work. Today he is considered, simply put, one of America's preeminent playwrights.

Chapter 2

Overview: The Theater of Edward Albee

The theater of Edward Albee is a theater of rebellion and recovery, confrontation and expiation. His plays provoke and incite, engage and surprise. His interest lies not in surface banalities – though indeed many of his characters seem mired in just such a prosaic world – but in various disputatious zones, zones in which his characters' indifferent or uncomprehending masks of imperturbability are shattered by a coming to consciousness about the self, the other, and the culture they inhabit. What's left by curtain's end is often rough stuff. Typically a married character, sleepwalking through much of his life, is shocked by some epiphany, some key point in which he realizes that much of his life has been wasted. Often Albee + Marriage = Trouble. There is, to be sure, a sense of hope, even guarded optimism embedded in the earlier plays, but Albee tempers such affirmation with an increasing emphasis in the later plays on death and dying, on wasted opportunities, on loss, and on the individual dwelling in an absurdist universe. Albee very much believes in the primacy of consciousness. But gaining such consciousness comes with a penalty: what is gained, to paraphrase Jerry in *The Zoo Story*, is loss. If one looks back at six decades of Albee's career, one hears Albee echoing precisely such thoughts – in the plays, foremost, but also in interviews, prefaces, articles, and other commentaries. As Steven Price astutely notes, "Albee is, in a crude sense, a more repetitive playwright than his contemporaries: he returns obsessively to particular images, patterns, structures, and ideas."[1] Loss, dying, death, pain, betrayal, abandonment, and anesthetized individuals leading death-in-life existences have long been the central subjects of his theater.

Ever since Jerry fatally impaled himself on the knife in *The Zoo Story*, Mommy and Daddy recounted their spiritual dismemberment of their child in *The American Dream*, and Martin reveals he is in a love relationship with a farm animal in *The Goat or, Who Is Sylvia?*, Albee has been recognized for his focus on confrontation and death. Indeed, verbal dueling and death – real and imagined, physical and psychological – pervade the Albee canon. His plays typically address such issues as betrayal, abandonment, illusionary children, and withdrawals into a death-in-life existence by white upper-middle class articulate married couples – hardly issues appealing to the commercial world of Broadway. And yet, even after reluctantly making a successful transition to a commercially based and family-friendly Broadway in 1962, Albee continued to stage morally serious plays, imbued with a kind of absurdist density, often with surprising twists and turns that baffle as they astonish.

Albee's plays may be, generally speaking, divided into three periods. The first, the Early Plays (beginning in 1959–66), are characterized by gladiatorial confrontations – Jerry impales himself on a knife at the end of *The Zoo Story*; we learn about the (metaphorical) dismemberment of a baby in *The American Dream*; there is the bloodied action (actual) within *The Death of Bessie Smith*; and, of course, George and Martha fight to the (metaphorical) death in *Who's Afraid of Virginia Woolf?* Ever one to follow his artistic instincts rather than commercial formulas, Albee's voice, tone, and frenzied action began to change – slightly at first, but with more clarity as the years went on – as early as 1964 with the baffling *Tiny Alice*, continuing in 1966 with the beautiful *A Delicate Balance*, and culminating in 1968 with the experimental *Box* and *Quotations from Mao Tse-Tung*.

Certainly after 1971, Albee entered what could be called the Middle Plays (1971–87), which extend roughly from 1971 with *All Over* (1971) and *Seascape* (1975) and through the 1980s with *The Lady from Dubuque* (1980), *The Man Who Had Three Arms* (1982), *Finding the Sun* (1983), and *Marriage Play* (1987). During this period, Albee lost favor with the theatergoing public and critics alike, and he himself turned his back on Broadway and began premiering his plays in regional theaters in the United States and in various European cities, notably Vienna and London.

Regarding the long trajectory of his career, Albee shifts his writing style while staying true to his world view. The frenzied action of *The Zoo* Story or *Who's Afraid of Virginia Woolf?* gives way, in many of the later plays, to a more rarefied, abstract theatrical spectacle. Albee, many theatergoers felt, had fallen prey to the mimetic fallacy. Frenzied action yields to linguistic games in which the various meanings of a word are debated and dissected by bewildered characters. Actors sensed a difference. That is not how someone *speaks* in a performance; that is how someone *writes*. Audiences sensed the difference, too. Given such issues and charges of self-destruction, it is hardly surprising to discover both students and critics labeling Albee a pessimistic or even nihilistic writer, a dramatist whose plays are single-mindedly fixed on presenting the demonic, the destructive. Beginning in 1991–2, Albee staged what could be called the Later Plays (1991–present). He enjoyed a remarkable comeback with *Three Tall Women*, and since then most Albee plays – especially *The Goat or, Who Is Sylvia?* (2002) – have been watched by appreciative audiences and critics the world over.

There is, then, a beauty, a resonance to Albee's plays that still have a purchase on our consciousness. One way to appreciate more fully Albee's theater is to consider his world view. A careful viewer or reader will discover that the plays embody, on the one hand, a palpable sense of loss. On the other hand, underneath the external action, aggressive texts, and obvious preoccupation with death lies an inner drama that discloses the playwright's compassion for his fellow human beings.

A Full, Dangerous Participation

This sense of compassion becomes easier to understand when one listens to the playwright. Albee outlines what has for six decades engaged his imagination:

> I am very concerned with the fact that so many people turn off because it is easier; that they don't stay fully aware during the course of their lives, in all the choices they make: social economic, political, aesthetic. They turn off because it's easier. But I find that anything less than absolutely full, dangerous participation is an absolute waste of some rather valuable time. ... I am concerned with being as self-aware, and open to all kinds of experience on its own terms – I think those conditions, given half a chance, will produce better self-government, a better society, a better everything else.[2]

Albee's observation provides a key to understanding all of the plays. Alluding to a spiritual malaise that may psychologically anesthetize the individual, Albee suggests that "full, dangerous participation" in human intercourse is a necessary correlate to living authentically. His remarks also suggest something of his underlying hope or optimism for his fellow human beings. The Albee play, in brief, becomes equipment for living. As the Woman in *Listening* recalls her grandmother saying, "We don't have to live, you know, unless we wish to; the greatest sin, no matter what they *tell* you, the greatest sin in living is doing it badly – stupidly, or as if you weren't really alive" (2: 489). Her reflection could well serve as a touchstone of the ethical problem with which every Albee hero deals. In plays as different in dramatic conception as *The Zoo Story*, *Box*, *Seascape*, and *Occupant*, Albee consistently implies that one can choose consciously to intermix the intellect and the emotions into a new whole, measured qualitatively, which is the aware individual. The tragic irony, of course, lies in the fact that too often his characters become aware – after it is "all over."

While the plays appear consistent in artistic purpose, they are quite varied in method. Albee uses a wide range of theatrical styles and technical devices to present naturalistic and satiric images as well as expressionistic and absurdist images of the human predicament. The plays range from fourteen-minute sketches to full-length Broadway productions. Occasionally Albee presents social protest pieces or domestic dramas staging imbalances within relationships. He has borrowed from others, with less than satisfying results, in the adaptations: *The Ballad of the Sad Café* (1963), *Malcolm* (1966), *Everything in the Garden* (1967), and *Lolita* (1981); he also worked on the script for a musical adaption of Truman Capote's *Breakfast at Tiffany's* (1966). But he remained steadfastly drawn to innovative plays whose musical quality complements the visual spectacle. A technically versatile dramatist, Albee demonstrates – often at the cost of commercial if not critical success – a willingness to take aesthetic risks, a deliberate attempt to explore the boundaries, the essences of the theater. As Albee writes in his prefatory remarks to the interrelated plays *Box* and *Quotations from Chairman Mao Tse-Tung*, two of his most structurally experimental works, "Since art must move – or wither – the playwright must try to alter the forms within which his precursors have had to work" (2: 262). Each play demonstrates Albee's ongoing efforts to reinvent dramatic language and contexts, his awareness of the modern dramatic tradition, and his individual talents. Such experiments invite Anne Paolucci to observe: "Albee's arrogance as an innovator is prompted by profound artistic instincts which are constantly at work reshaping dramatic conventions. He does not discard such conventions, but restructures them according to the organic demands of his artistic themes."[3]

Audience

Albee always challenges the audience. He delights in inviting the audience to partake in a complex spectatorial process, one that may prove entertaining, astonishing, tedious, depressing, life-affirming, and anxiety-inducing. In his experiments with dramaturgic boundaries, he places much faith, and responsibility, in his audience. It is a faith predicated on Albee's conviction that the ideal audience approaches a play unencumbered by preconceptions or distorting labels, with the capability to suspend disbelief willingly, and to immerse itself fully within the three-dimensional essence of the stage experience. Albee rejects the audience as voyeur. He courts the audience as active participant. Of course, Albee does not direct characters to assault the audience physically, as Judith Malina and Julian Beck of the Living Theatre had performers do to their audience. But the structure and language of an Albee play conspire to assault the audience's individual and collective sensibility. Regarding the spectators, Albee explains that in many of his plays:

> actors talk directly to the audience. In my mind, this is a way of involving the audience; of embarrassing, if need be, the audience into participation. It may have the reverse effect: some audiences don't like this; they get upset by it quite often; it may alienate them. But I am trying very hard to *involve* them. I don't like the audience as voyeur, the audience as passive spectator. I want the audience as participant. In that sense, I agree with Artaud: that sometimes we should literally draw blood. I am very fond of doing that because voyeurism in the theater lets people off the hook.[4]

Albee's reference to the French actor, director, and aesthetician Antonin Artaud is important. In 1938 Artaud, founder of the Theater of Cruelty, wrote *The Theatre and Its Double*, a study which Robert Brustein calls "one of the most influential, as well as one of the most inflammatory, documents of our time."[5] In this seminal study Artaud discusses, among many other issues, the civic function of theater: the dramatic experience should "disturb the senses' repose," should unleash "the repressed unconscious," should produce "a virtual revolt."[6] Cruelty, for Artaud, was the primary ingredient that could generate an apocalyptic revolt within the audience – an audience which Artaud viewed as the bourgeois Parisian who expected realistic performances. But it is important to recognize that his theories extolling aggression and violence were grounded more in the cerebral and metaphysical than in the merely physical. His aesthetic imagination focused on religious, metaphysical experiences. Artaud felt that the cruelty he wished to deploy was more of a cosmic and metaphysical kind, a kind that worked to sever individual freedom. Albee, of course, does not stage the kind of theater Artaud envisioned, but Artaud's influence on Albee is unmistakable in terms of the use of physical, psychological, and metaphysical violence on stage. Albee emphasizes the value of staging Artuadian militant performances:

> All drama goes for blood in one way or another. Some drama, which contains itself behind the invisible fourth wall, does it by giving the audience the illusion that it is the spectator. This isn't always true: if the drama succeeds the audience is *bloodied*, but in a different way. And sometimes the act of aggression is direct or indirect, but it is always an act of aggression. And this is why I try very hard to involve the audience. As I've mentioned to you before, I want the audience to participate in the dramatic experience.[7]

Albee's theatrical strategy ideally minimizes the actor/audience barrier. As active participants within the play, the audience contributes to the ritualized forms of confrontation and expiation that characterize much of Albee's work. This is why Albee sees the violence and death as, finally, and paradoxically enough, life-giving:

> If one approaches the theater in a state of innocence, sober, without preconceptions, and willing to participate; if they are willing to have the status quo assaulted; if they're willing to have their consciousness raised, their values questioned – or reaffirmed; if they are willing to understand that the theater is a live and dangerous experience – and therefore a *life-giving force* – then perhaps they are approaching the theater in an ideal state and that's the audience I wish I were writing for.[8]

Language

In 2016, playwright Terrence McNally, who lived with Albee for some six years in the 1960s, rightly noted that Albee "invented a new language – the first authentically new voice in theater since Tennessee Williams. He created a sound world. He was a sculptor of words."[9] Indeed, Albee animates his "life-giving" theater through language. In fact, language stands as the most conspicuous feature of his dramaturgy as well as his major contribution to American drama. Albee's verbal duels, some of which seem analogous to musical arias, are now a well-known part of American dramatic history. In both text and performance, his technical virtuosity emanates from an ability to capture the values, personal politics, and often limited perceptions of his characters through language. Christopher Bigsby characterizes Albee's work thus: "By turns witty and abrasive, and with a control over language, its rhythms and nuances, unmatched in the American theater, he broke new ground with each play, refusing to repeat his early Broadway success."[10] Although the language from *A Delicate Balance* onward becomes more stylized, elliptical, even obscure, Albee's repartee – when he is at his best – still generates a compelling energy within each play. One of the chief tenets of the Living Theatre, writes Julian Beck, was to "revivify language," and through language the playwright might realize the civic and religious powers of the art of drama: "*to increase conscious awareness, to stress the sacredness of life, to break down the walls.*"[11] Although Albee was in no way associated with the Living Theatre, the language of his early plays captured the "kinetic" energy which Judith Malina and Beck felt so necessary for the stage.

Few American playwrights use language as effectively – and as precisely – as Albee. His is a multifoliate diction, often with detailed references to food, animals, and even grammar. His stage directions at times function as mini prose-poems within the text, accentuating for the actor and reader the emotional intensity during particular scenes. No other American playwright, moreover, uses italics for *more nuanced* deliveries of lines, lines that embody heightened emotional tensions thanks to those strategically placed italics.

Albee's theater, for many, reflects the sweep and play of a nation thinking in front of itself, of a culture seeking to locate its identity through the ritualized action implicit in the art of theater. Albee, it seemed, was the new Angry Young Man, a decidedly sociopolitical dramatist who anticipated, and subsequently became a part of, the social eruptions in the United States during the 1960s. Such a play as *The Death of Bessie Smith* only cemented his reputation as a "political" writer, one whose rage existed in equipoise with his moral seriousness.

Consciousness

Despite his experiments with dramatic language and structure, and such seemingly political works as *Bessie Smith*, Albee presents a kind of intuitive *existentialist* apprehension of experience. Throughout his career, in plays, college lectures, and private conversations, Albee alludes to the influence the existentialist movement exerts on his artistic vision. Indeed, once while visiting Albee in his Tribeca home, he told me – over a cup of freshly brewed coffee and with his cat meandering about – "I would say that I'm an optimistic existentialist. I'm interested in exploring self-awareness and the healthy isolation of the individual. But consciousness is all, for heaven's sake! And what bothers me so much is that many people are sleeping, are wasting their lives – not participating."[12] In an early interview, moreover, he discussed the impact of this movement on the literary artist:

> The existentialist and post-existentialist revaluation of the nature of reality and what everything is about in man's position to it came shortly after the 2nd World War. I don't think that it is an accident that it gained the importance in writers' minds that it has now as a result of the bomb at Hiroshima. We developed the possibility of destroying ourselves totally and completely in a second. The ideals, the totems, the panaceas don't work much anymore and the whole concept of absurdity is a great deal less absurd now than it was before about 1945.[13]

Such a "revaluation of the nature of reality" has since become the unifying principle within Albee's aesthetic. Not surprisingly, he often alludes to Albert Camus's influence on his thinking. Thus Albee reaffirms the importance of one of his most compelling subjects, consciousness:

The single journey through consciousness should be participated in as fully as possible by the individual, no matter how dangerous or cruel or terror-filled that experience may be. We only go through it once, unless the agnostics are proved wrong, and so we must do it fully conscious. One of the things art does is to not let people sleep their way through their lives. If the universe makes no sense, well perhaps we, the individual, can make sense of the cosmos. We must go on, we must not add to the chaos but deal honestly with the idea of order, whether it is arbitrary or not. As all of my plays suggest, so many people prefer to go through their lives semiconscious and they end up in a terrible panic because they've wasted so much. But being as self-aware, as awake, as open to various experience will produce a better society and a more intelligent self-government.[14]

The confluence of public issues and private tensions – the civic as well as personal functions of the theater – is wedded to Albee's sense of consciousness. The preeminence of consciousness necessarily generates within his heroes primal anxieties, dissociations, imbalances. Certainties yield to ambivalences. If his heroes demonstrate gracelessness under pressure, if their deadening routines prompt lifelong friends to respond to each other as uninvited guests, Albee still maintains faith in the regenerative powers of the human imagination. Animating the imaginative faculties, of course, is consciousness, and Albee celebrates Albert Camus's views concerning self-awareness. "Weariness comes at the end of the acts of a mechanical life," writes Camus in *The Myth of Sisyphus*, "but at the same it inaugurates the impulse to consciousness. It awakens consciousness and provokes what follows ... For everything begins with consciousness and nothing is worth anything except through it."[15]

Physical, psychological, and spiritual forces – these stand as the elements that so often converge within Albee's characters. Such an intermixture, moreover, precipitates an elemental anxiety, what Albee calls "a personal, private yowl" that "has something to do with the anguish of us all."[16] Accordingly, the power of Albee's plays emanates not from their philosophical content but from their powerful narratives that dramatize humankind's struggle with the complex and messy business of living. If his heroes are to "burst the spirit's sleep," as Saul Bellow writes in *Henderson the Rain King*[17] (a novel that appeared when Albee's first plays were mounted), such epiphanic moments are not realized through the process of philosophic intellection but, as Bellow's hero discovers, through the process of concrete immersion into a cosmos which seems exciting yet hostile, reliable yet puckish, life-giving yet death-saturated. Underneath his characters' public bravado lies an ongoing inner drama, a subtext presenting characters' quest for consciousness. The profound irony stems from the characters' inability to understand the regenerative power of consciousness.

For Albee, the play becomes the hour of consciousness. During this fleeting but illuminating hour, Albee's vision underscores the importance of confronting one's self and the other, without O'Neill's "pipe dreams" or illusions. If O'Neill's, Ionesco's, Mamet's, or Beckett's characters seem aware of suffering, they also accept an attitude that precludes any significant growth. In contrast, Albee's heroes suffer, dwell in an absurd world, but realize the opportunity for growth and change. Of course, Albee ironizes such opportunities, for it is often too late for his characters to recover from their spiritual inertia. Or, as Toby Zinman aptly observes, "Many of his characters make the fundamental human discovery that they have tried bravely and failed miserably, but that there was nothing, finally, to be done, life being what it is, they being who they are."[18] Still, they sometimes experience a coming to consciousness that draws them – to allude to an important metaphor in *Who's Afraid of Virginia Woolf?* – toward "the marrow": toward the essence, the core of their relationships. Stripped of illusions, Albee's protagonists stand naked. And once naked, they begin rekindling those forces which may profoundly alter their stance towards human encounters. Of course, Albee offers no guarantee of order, comprehension, survival, or love. Whether each character takes advantage of powers of consciousness varies from play to play. Or if indeed it is too late for his characters, perhaps the audience or reader, through the process of engagement with each Albee play, can become more honest with both their own inner and outer worlds. Hence there is a powerful civic dimension to Albee's work.

Throughout his career, Albee defines in dramatic terms, to use his own words, "how we lie to ourselves and to each other, how we try to live without the cleansing consciousness of death."[19] To experience the "cleansing" effects of such self-awareness, the Albee hero necessarily questions the nature of his or her values, predicaments, and relationships. To live honestly is a liberating quality that frees the mind, even at the risk of facing a grimly deterministic world in which one suddenly feels the utter precariousness of existence. That certain characters fail to take advantage of this capacity to bear a world so conceived, that certain audiences seem unwilling to accept experiments with dramatic language and structure, that sometimes the plays themselves cannot always sustain the dramaturgic burdens placed upon them, does not negate the significance, Albee suggests throughout his theater, of such self-perception.

Chapter 3

Contexts

The energy, anger, and intense verbal battles of so many Albee plays reflect the playwright's rebellion against a culture whose identity radically transformed during his youth. In the late 1940s and through the 1950s, the young Albee took measure of, and became disenchanted with, the rapidly shifting industrial, social, and political climate of the United States. A young man in his teens and twenties during this period, Albee felt as perplexed with American culture as would Jerry, his first antihero in *The Zoo Story*.

From 1945 through much of the 1950s and early 1960s, an optimism, buoyed by economic growth, confirmed the United States's a priori belief in the beauty of self-reliance, hard work, and democracy. Suddenly America, it seemed, found itself fulfilling its self-created prophecy as the watch keepers of the entire free world, a position certified by military and technological triumphs in World War II and sustained by unheard-of economic recrudescence. While Albee was being expelled from one prep school after another, soldiers returned from the war, increasing college enrollments to record-breaking numbers as the G. I. Bill of Rights picked up the tuition tab. Harry Truman sanctioned military assistance to any free nation challenged by communism. George C. Marshall ushered in a plan to reconstruct war-ravaged Europe – Axis and Allied countries alike. The United Nations was established, meant to underscore a transnational hope for world peace, even as the iron curtain divided Berlin and Mao Tse-tung subjugated China to his tyranny. Indeed, as Albee's career first took off, it was not for nothing that John F. Kennedy launched the Peace Corps. During these and of course countless other geopolitical developments, the teenage Albee struggled as a novice writer, trying his hand at poetry, the short story, and the novel while growing up in or near New York City. There he witnessed, in retrospect, the Golden Age of Broadway.

A dramatist who would animate the American alternative theater world *and* the mainstream Broadway world from the 1960s onward, Albee's unease with his culture was fermenting in the 1950s. On one level, the 1950s seemed a complacent period, surely a cultural response to the Great Depression

of the 1930s and World War II in the 1940s, an anodyne for the two decades of cataclysms that rocked the country. While Albee left the privileged
if troubled and troubling home of his millionaire family for the bohemian
life in Greenwich Village during his twenties (largely possible because of
a generous trust fund set up by this grandmother), the country spawned
a "silent generation" of conformist students, subdivision housing, and the
Eisenhower era. Recent biographers of Ike paint a portrait of a far more
complex, clever president, but his public image, in memory, remains an
emblem for a sleepy, pipe-and-slippers world many Americans elevated
to new heights. While Albee felt alone, out of place, a cosmic waif drifting
through the 1950s with little discernible purpose, he witnessed the homog-
enization of America. Television and the first fast-food restaurants, suburbs
and barbecues, shopping centers (and later malls) and Little League seemed
to dominate the geographical as well as moral landscape. The Interstate
Highway System, the most audacious public-works project in US history,
further contributed to cultural homogenizing. As incomes for many families
increased to new levels, matched, it seemed, by the height of the high-finned
Cadillacs, many Americans celebrated their new wealth and recrudescence
through conspicuous consumption. For the first time car ownership lay
ahead for many. Then home ownership. Television too. Indeed, television,
first black and white, then color, enraptured as it anaesthetized the country – think of the flickering blue light emanating from Dodge's television in
Sam Shepard's *Buried Child* (1978) – and television not only joined people
of differing regions and racial backgrounds with an electronic immediacy,
but quickly outdistanced radio and the theater as a source of cultural education and entertainment. The increasing influence of popular culture was
not lost on Albee, who would soon become part of the iconography of that
culture. While the youthful Albee grew more introspective, Hula-Hoops and
3-D movies were great fads. Soon after he was expelled from Trinity College
in Hartford, Connecticut, Albee would see an American college population
stuffing one another into phone booths, among other pranks.

Of course the 1950s were exceedingly more problematic and complex than
the banal and monologic world implied above. The decade, in fact, appeared as
divided and confused as the characters in Albee's first plays. For Albee would
read about the Korean War and America's ambivalent response to the "conflict." Foreshadowing the social eruptions of the 1960s, the 1950s and early
1960s that form an ideological backdrop to many of Albee's works gave rise to
civil rights protests and the contemporary Civil Rights Movement first precipi-
tated, in part, by such nineteenth-century activists as Louis Charles Roudanez,
founder of the first African American daily black newspaper in America.

Identity politics, then as now, informed Albee's reading of the American cultural landscape. In the 1950s Chief Justice Earl Warren altered the judicial
system as the Supreme Court sought to alleviate racial injustice in public
schools. Albee would read newspapers filled with reports of federal troops in
Little Rock, Arkansas, under Eisenhower's orders, trying to enforce desegre-
gation; of Rosa Parks's defiant and definitional act of keeping her seat on the
bus; and of Martin Luther King, Jr's subsequent organization of the boycott
of Montgomery, Alabama's public bus system. There was also a bothersome
skirmish brewing in Vietnam in the 1950s, which was such a formative decade
for Edward Albee. The Soviets invaded Hungary and Nixon held court with
Khrushchev in the "kitchen debate."

When Albee was still in his twenties, he lived through McCarthyism
and would hear about Clifford Odets, Elia Kazan, Lillian Hellman, Arthur
Miller and countless other writers, actors, and "subversives" brought before
the House of Un-American Activities Committee. Surely Arthur Miller was
"traveling" (the term used in the 1950s), some authorities thought, with communists. Indeed, fear of Alger Hiss, the Rosenbergs, and communist spies
assumed, many felt, hysterical proportions. And while many important
American writers were establishing themselves in the 1950s – J. D. Salinger
and Saul Bellow, Adrienne Rich and Lorraine Hansberry – the conservative
social ambiance put a damper even on those writers valorized by their past
glories. While Little Richard and Elvis Presley entranced the nation with
rock and roll in 1956, Arthur Miller endured hostile questioning during the
McCarthy "witch hunt" trials; while a consumer society elevated material
acquisition to an exalted position; and while many Americans reveled in a
cultural memory that more often than not elided history from reality, Allen
Ginsberg howled, James Baldwin exiled himself, and Jack Kerouac hit the
road – all while the writer within Albee yearned to create art. During the
1950s, Albee said, he felt uneasy because he might not succeed in any profession, including a profession in the often-crazy world of the theater. Before
the decade was out, he would compose *The Zoo Story*, a brilliant debut, as a
thirtieth birthday present to himself.

A Search for the Real

On October 4, 1957 – Albee was twenty-nine years old – the Soviet Union
stunned America. With the launching of Sputnik, the Russians conquered
space, an achievement hailed as the most significant technological feat since the
Americans developed the atomic bomb. Sputnik mystified. The sphere-shaped

object flew faster, higher, and was much larger than any American space-craft: 18,000 m.p.h. speed, 560-mile altitude capability, mysterious in its tightly guarded contents – these were incredible facts. While US scientists labored with tiny, yet-to-be launched space probes, the Russians basked in what was perceived by the world as mastery of earthly and outer-space affairs. Suddenly America's unquestioned position as the world's super-power was undermined technologically and psychologically.

The moment affected writers as well. Few other events "so deeply influenced contemporary thinking as the launching of the first Sputnik," writes Mas'ud Zavarzadeh in *The Mythopoeic Reality*. Even the very methods of fiction-making were radicalized "since about 1957 – the very year the Soviet Union's Sputnik shook America and almost overnight changed the cold war of ideological opposition between the two postwar super-powers into a planetary polarization between Man and Machine."[1] Zavarzadeh theorizes about the postwar American nonfiction novel, but the point is that, for Albee, the certainties, the reliabilities of past notions of objective reality were no longer safe guides. Such destabilizations, of course, manifested themselves in the earlier twentieth century too. An expectation of the new, the unpredictable animated the Century of Progress. But Albee, writing throughout his career in context of the nuclear age and anxiety, Sputnik, and other geopolitical changes, presents characters who are dimly aware of the precariousness of their existences, and who are searching for the Real within an American culture whose unreality baffles the individual. In other words, Albee's career began in the context of the nuclear age, the Space Race, and many other historical changes, and he wrote and continues in the twenty-first century to write with a great sense of the utter precariousness of human existence. As Albee said in 1963, the existentialist revaluation of the nature of objective reality gained importance as a result of the bomb at Hiroshima. More recent world events such as the 9/11 attacks on the World Trade Center (Albee lived minutes from Ground Zero) and other locations, the wars in Iraq, Afghanistan, and Syria, and the rise of global terrorism in the twenty-first century surely have done little to change Albee's observations from decades ago.

Indeed, in the months before Albee took Broadway by storm with *Who's Afraid of Virginia Woolf?*, US–Soviet relations headlined the news. For six uneasy days in October 1962, as the cast went through final rehearsals of the play, Khrushchev and Kennedy brought us to the brink of nuclear war. The Soviets had shipped missiles to Cuba, America threatened military intervention, and Khrushchev blinked – the crisis was diffused when the Soviets agreed to ship the missiles back to the USSR. After Korea, Sputnik, the Bay of Pigs debacle, and Khrushchev's victory in the Vienna summit meeting with Kennedy, the diffusion of the Cuban missile crisis was, for Americans at least, both a relief and a triumphant stand against the communists during the height of the Cold War. And yet, as new-frontier optimism swept the land, Kennedy also authorized sending American troops and military advisors to Vietnam, and race relations continued to press Americans to rethink cultural memory and the mythicized solidities on which American nationhood was based. A country inspired by its democratic ideals and culturally constructed notions of national perfectionism, America was becoming more aware of its imperfections. Yet America, despite its faults, still seemed energized by a naive ebullience and unwavering faith in the myth of the American Dream. The pot of gold at the end of the rainbow surely loomed just beyond the horizon, many Americans felt, even as the primal family unit itself was under increasing pressure. American exceptionalism animated the cultural poetics of the United States. Albee would limn precisely such public issues and private tensions throughout his theater. Until November 22, 1963, at noontime – when an assassin's bullets shattered Camelot – America reveled in its idealism, although with such early plays as *The American Dream*, especially, Albee began interrogating America, its ideals, its ironies, its myths, its dreams, and its inhabitants. In Albee's world, the space between the mythologized ideal and the depleted reality precipitates emotional havoc. The space between often proves to be unbridgeable. A sense of loss pervades the Albee canon.

As his career developed, Albee also benefited from other European absurdists. Three Nobel Prize winning playwrights would become inspiring models: an Italian, an Irish, and a British. Indeed, Luigi Pirandello, Samuel Beckett, and Harold Pinter especially influenced Albee. There is, in the plays he writes, more than a hint Pinter. A Pinteresque sense of tragicomedic menace, of terror in the common, and of the exploration of memory and desire lurk within so many Albee plays. When I saw the New York premiere of Pinter's *Ashes to Ashes* in 1999, I felt like I was watching a vintage Albee play. Like Luigi Pirandello, Albee is not afraid to call attention to the artificiality of the theater, allowing him to move more readily from the real to the dream, from the familiar realistic props and settings to a symbolic and even mythic stage. Indeed, one sees a Pirandellian playfulness that darkens as his own postmodern characters search for their identities. At times it was as if he drew from Antonin Artaud the power of the sacred, the violent, and the myth. Albee called Samuel Beckett the greatest dramatist of the twentieth century, and the Beckettian influence on his theater is unmistakable. These were among the many international figures Albee turned to for inspiration. As a young, emerging artist living in the

Village, he could hardly help but be imbued with international artistic cross-currents. When I asked him which artists might influence his work, Albee told me:

> I read voluminously. I see and read hundreds of plays. I listen to classical music as much as I can. I read novels, poetry, go to museums and galleries constantly. I'm flooded with aesthetic information and I like to surround myself by art. I would like to think that I'm being influenced one way or another, my aesthetic is being honed, in one fashion or another, by every aesthetic experience I have. Selection: you learn what and what not to do; what to like and dislike. I do know that when I'm writing a play, I'm as close to composing music as I am to anything else. Music influences me as much as anything else. But if I had to list specific playwrights, I admire Chekov, Sophocles, Beckett – those guys I think of as producing experiences. Magnificent plays. I think the experience of seeing O'Neill's *The Iceman Cometh*, a play I don't like that much anymore, but one which *Who's Afraid of Virginia Woolf?* is a response to. Then there is Williams's *Suddenly Last Summer*. I think of my first experience with Beckett and Genet as being *authentic* experiences for me. But those are just educated guesses![2]

The Theatrical Landscape

When Albee made his Broadway debut, in 1962, the theatrical landscape of America was as divided as the culture dramatized by its playwrights. A volatile mix of theatrical forces – economic, social, political, aesthetic, historical – conspired to make Albee's Broadway debut particularly timely. "To many people," writes Christopher Bigsby, "the American theatre seemed threatened with imminent collapse, while the great dramatists who had sustained the international reputation of American drama for so long were no longer in evidence."[3] In other words, Broadway had reached a low point by the time *Who's Afraid of Virginia Woolf?* made its epochal premiere that Saturday evening, October 13, 1962. Broadway audiences were seeking some sort of original American play that could rekindle the excitement and moral seriousness generated by Susan Glaspell's *Trifles*, Eugene O'Neill's *Long Day's Journey into Night*, Tennessee Williams's *A Streetcar Named Desire*, and Arthur Miller's *Death of a Salesman*. Audiences were also looking for a dramatist who could match the technical precision of the European playwrights. Simply put, Albee suddenly found himself anointed to be the one to carry on the legacies of the earlier great American dramatists who commanded worldwide respect for their work.

Albee Enters Broadway

Despite the troubled and troubling state of Broadway, there were some extremely popular plays staged during the 1962–3 Broadway season – the year Albee staged *Who's Afraid of Virginia Woolf?*, which was his first experience dealing with the ethos of Broadway. Sumner Arthur Long's comedy *Never Too Late*, Richard Sheridan's eighteenth-century comedy *The School for Scandal*, and *Oliver*, a musical adaptation of Charles Dickens's *Oliver Twist*, attracted sizable and largely supportive audiences. The Actors' Studio Theatre staged two well-received revivals – O'Neill's *Strange Interlude* and George Bernard Shaw's *Too Good to Be True*. Further, several commanding holdovers from other seasons still drew enthusiastic crowds during the 1962–3 season. *The Sound of Music* still attracted appreciative audiences after 1,424 performances while *Mary, Mary* weighed in next with 977 showings. Several other major productions that finally closed during this season were *My Fair Lady* – after six years and 2,715 shows; *Camelot* – after 873 performances; and *Carnival* – after 719 shows. Clearly, then as now, on one level Broadway exhibited a degree of vitality.

But as much of this sampling of the early 1960s Broadway fare suggests, mainstream American theater in New York City proved resistant to truly innovative, politically and morally charged theater. Producers were cautious. While theaters across Europe were typically staging plays imbued with ethical import and political textures, many Broadway shows (not all, of course) tended to produce superficial works. The political and social issues addressed by such important European dramatists as Adamov, Ionesco, Genet, Brecht, Pinter, and others, were not to be found in the commercially based Broadway aesthetic. If a play were "safe" – it would not offend too many and would sell at the gate – it might see a healthy stage life. Experiments in performance theory and practice, politically extreme works, highly experimental works, plays that deliberately challenged the conservative tastes of Broadway when Albee came along were to be found beyond the Great White Way – in Off- and then Off-Off-Broadway venues, in university theaters, in regional theaters. From a purely business standpoint, such "alternative" productions did not earn profits – and nor did they ever aspire to. Thus, paradoxically enough, while Broadway audiences were eager to discover the Great New Playwright, they also preferred *Mary, Mary* to *Waiting for Godot*. A Broadway play's vitality often seemed measured in commercial value than aesthetic achievement; a play's worth, after all, directly corresponded to its ratings at the gate. True, there were always revivals of masterpieces of world drama, but predictable works – plays appealing those paying for entertainment – diluted Broadway, especially when Albee got his start. A prominent American dramatist partially explains the limitations on Broadway. "If you hand a producer a piece that offends a significant portion of the Broadway audience, not to speak of the critics," Arthur Miller observes,

> he'll think two or three times before putting it on. You are in that way bound to one level of consciousness. It's not a new thing; my argument with our theater on that level is that it's constricted to a degree greater than I have ever known in my lifetime. It's very important that people not have to pay … [a lot] to get into the theater, because if they pay … [a lot], they're probably not going to want what I am writing … [An expensive] ticket brooks no philosophies, tends toward trivialities.[4]

So when Albee packed up his talents from Off-Broadway and journeyed, as Jerry would put it in *The Zoo Story*, a very long distance out of his way to Broadway in 1962, plays "bound to one level of consciousness" were saturating the market. And even the "safe" plays were often beset by financial disaster. Over $6 million (in 1962–3) dollars were lost on Broadway flops. Nor were such failures confined to avant-garde experiments or even sentimental musicals. Tennessee Williams's *The Milk Train Doesn't Stop Here Anymore* (sixty-nine shows in the 1962–3 season); Sidney Kingsley's *Night Life* (sixty-three shows); Bertolt Brecht's *Mother Courage and Her Children* (fifty-two shows); William Inge's *Natural Affection* (thirty-six shows); and Lillian Hellman's *My Mother, My Father, and Me* (only seventeen performances) all "failed" at one of Broadway's chief gauges of "success": the box office. In other words, the year Albee debuted on Broadway was a terrible year from both an artistic and monetary viewpoint.[5]

The uneasy state of Broadway that Albee would have to confront was in many respects not new. Indeed, its decline in the 1960s was part of a larger, dismal pattern harkening back to the earlier twentieth century. Broadway enjoyed its best days from the 1899–1900 season, when there were eighty-seven new productions, through the 1927–8 season, which spawned an all-time high of 264 new shows. However, with the Great Depression, and then World War II, the number of new productions in New York City persistently diminished. Three decades before *Who's Afraid of Virginia Woolf?*, there were 174 new productions in New York City; two decades before, eighty; one decade earlier, fifty-four. Two seasons before Albee entered Broadway, only forty-eight new productions were staged, an all-time low to that point.[6]

The Decentralization of Broadway

American playwrights since 1970 have moved their way toward the center of the national creative consciousness. The best have done so by making significant contributions to the rhetoric of nationhood, to the languages that define the "Americanness" of American drama, and to the symbology of the self. Of the numerous forces affecting the cultural production and reception of texts and performances, perhaps one of the most distinguishing shifts in recent American drama concerns its relationship to Broadway. When Eugene O'Neill, Susan Glaspell, and Alice Gerstenberg first conferred upon the American stage its modernity, Broadway in New York City was the Great White Way. Then, Broadway was the site of dramatic originality. Broadway was the launching site for playwrights who, with uneven achievements, defined the scope and emphasis of American drama. Broadway somehow mattered. Its stages mirrored the circulation of social *energia*. When O'Neill's *The Hairy Ape* (1922) premiered, the Mayor of New York City, troubled by the play's themes, tried to close the show. The public, in response, flocked to see one of the first successful expressionistic plays staged by an American. When at mid-century Lillian Hellman, Tennessee Williams, Arthur Miller, and Lorraine Hansberry extended as they refurbished notions of American theatrical modernity, Broadway was still a vibrant source of theatrical energy. Four plays in a four-year span confirm the point: *The Glass Menagerie* (1945), *A Streetcar Named Desire* (1947), *All My Sons* (1947), and *Death of a Salesman* (1949) together ran for 2,466 performances. By contrast, Williams's last Broadway play staged prior to his death, *Something Cloudy, Something Clear* (1981), closed after only fifty-one shows to indifferent reviews. Miller simply chose to premier selected recent plays outside of Broadway, *The Ride Down Mt. Morgan* opening London in 1991 and *Broken Glass* premiering in New Haven, then London, and finally New York City in 1994.

As the twenty-first century unfolds, Broadway has changed. If the earlier Broadway was an initiating theater, where key plays received their premieres, today many of the best American playwrights open their shows both geographically and symbolically well beyond Broadway. Its decentralization process is unmistakable. Albee opened *Counting the Ways* (1976) in London and *Marriage Play* (1987) and *Three Tall Women* (1992) in Vienna. David Mamet staged *Glengarry Glen Ross* (1983) and *The Cryptogram* (1994) in London. Sam Shepard waited two decades before staging a play, *A Lie of the Mind*, on Broadway (1985). Further, these three playwrights, along with an increasing number of fellow dramatists, began directing their own works, an exercise of authorial control rarely seen during the mid-century glory days of such directors as Elia Kazan and José Quintero. In some respects, Albee's point in a 1962 article, "Which Theatre Is the Absurd One?" – in which he calls Broadway the true theater of absurd because of its cultural production of and insistence upon superficial work – remains true today. For many cultural and ideological reasons, Broadway now is a receiving theater. Broadway, a showcase theater, is a place where musicals, classics, or guaranteed contemporary sensations find their way to the stage. It is scarcely astonishing that works by "major" playwrights featuring entertainment stars, who ensure packed houses, occasionally open on Broadway, as was the case with Mamet's *Speed-the-Plow* (1988), which starred Madonna, or the 1988 revival of Beckett's *Waiting for Godot* (1952), which featured the comedic talents of Steve Martin and Robin Williams.

Well into the twenty-first century, Albee's Broadway revivals are now warmly received. Ironically, Broadway, despite being a largely showcase theater, somehow survives: in 2015, 13.1 million people attended Broadway shows whose gross revenues for that year were $1.36 billion.[7] Within such a context, the complexities of which can hardly be fully explored in this brief chapter, emerged one of the most influential American dramatists: Edward Albee.

Part II

The Plays

Chapter 4

Ritualized Forms of Expiation

The Zoo Story

> Writing, itself, taking the trouble, communicating with your fellow
> human being is valuable, that's an act of optimism. There's a positive
> force within the struggle. Serious plays are unpleasant in one way or
> another, and my plays examine people who are not living their lives
> fully, dangerously, properly.[1]
>
> When I wrote the play ... I was making a living delivering telegrams,
> and I did quite a bit of walking. I was always delivering telegrams to
> people living in rooming houses. I met all those people in the play in
> rooming houses. Jerry, the hero, is still around. He changes his shape
> from year to year.[2]
>
> —Edward Albee

When Norman Mailer saw *The Zoo Story*, he "announced it as 'the best fucking one-act play' he had ever seen."[3] Mailer, indeed, captures the excitement
and emotional response the play evokes. *The Zoo Story*, first produced at the
Schiller Theater Werkstatt, West Berlin, Germany, on September 28, 1959,
embodies many of the qualities that have since come to characterize vintage
Albee. The necessity of ritualized confrontation, the primacy of communication, the paradoxical mixture of love and hate, the cleverly abrasive dialogue,
the religious and political textures, the tragic force of abandonment and death,
the felt awareness of a gulf between the way things are and the way things
could be, and the penalty of consciousness all coalesce in Albee's first composition. The play remains an exemplary achievement, one reflecting what John
Barth identifies as "passionate virtuosity," the writer's ideal fusing of intellect
and emotion.[4] Perhaps the most remarkable feature of *The Zoo Story* is its compelling presentation of a particular series of events which suddenly broaden to
encompass universal experiences: Jerry and Peter emerge as essentially tragic
figures, in the specifics of whose confrontation Albee sets forth nothing less
than the general tragedy of modern existence itself.

Albee generates much of the play's tragic tension by yoking opposites together. Peter, the passive listener, lives on the East Side of New York City, and his world seems conspicuously well ordered. He represents the successful businessman, the contented upper-middle-class family man in late 1950s America. Few issues bother Peter because he shuts out any experience that might upset his cushioned life. On the other hand, Jerry is the active speaker, lives on the West Side, and dwells in a world of attenuated possibilities. He appears as the battle-fatigued, alienated cosmic waif, the loner who searches for meaning within public issues and private values which seemingly negate themselves. Moreover, the sociopolitical dimensions of the play seemed to cast Albee as a consummate civic protester, a playfully demonic social jester, the new angry young playwright blasting societal schisms which separate the haves from the have-nots. Finally, an American playwright had arrived whose aesthetic instincts existed in equipoise with his political impulses, something audiences were accustomed to expect in such great continental works as Bertolt Brecht's *Mother Courage* (1939) or Jean Genet's *The Balcony* (1957), for instance. Until *The Zoo Story*, it seemed, audiences had not witnessed such bold, socially engaged American drama since Elmer Rice's *The Adding Machine* (1923), Clifford Odets's *Waiting for Lefty* (1935), and Arthur Miller's *The Crucible* (1953). And yet, while *The Zoo Story* clearly invites sociopolitical analysis, its real emphasis lies elsewhere: Albee focuses much more on the inner reality of Peter and Jerry, on the quality of their respective sensibilities, and on the fundamental choices each person makes. Crimes of the heart, not the state, stand out in *The Zoo Story*.

Albee accentuates Peter's and Jerry's differing sensibilities by contrasting their worlds. Peter's world is comfortable. A publishing executive, he is married, has two daughters, pets, and a fashionable home. Every aspect of Peter's well-ordered environment seems predictable, safe. Lacking individuality and cast as the conformist in an Eisenhower era, Peter is, for Albee, a representative type of a bourgeois American. Conditioned by a culture prizing language largely devoid of genuine meaning, Peter reduces external experience to prescribed formulas, unconscious that he substitutes derivative thought for original insight. Anne Paolucci captures the quality of Peter's consciousness when observing that he moves "monotonously on the surface of life, pushed on by a kind of inertia which is mistaken for intention."[5] Although Peter is a thinly sketched figure, as Albee admits,[6] his presence is vital because, among other factors, he acts as a foil. With his banal responses and attendant emotional paralysis, Peter accentuates Jerry's frenetic stage movements and dialogue/monologue. Peter emerges as an emblematic figure, the representative of an upper-middle-class world which Albee will explore often throughout his career. The audience is struck by the path-of-lesser resistance characterizing Peter's life, a point Albee reinforces not only through dialogue but through stage descriptions as well: "*A man in his early forties, neither fat nor gaunt, neither handsome nor homely*" (1: 14). By describing Peter in negatives, Albee suggests something about Peter's non-participatory stance toward meaningful human encounters. Like Tobias in *A Delicate Balance* and Charlie in *Seascape*, Peter prefers to withdraw from confrontation, engagement – indeed any form of communication predicated on honest commitment. This is why, until physically (and, by extension, morally) pushed regarding the park bench, Peter tries avoiding Jerry, a strategy of avoidance that occurs on a verbal as well as non-verbal plane. Peter's body gestures – the constant turning away during the opening exchanges, the pretending not to hear, raising a hand to object, the winces, the forced smile – serve as ways of deflecting social engagement. Jerry, of course, challenges such an attitude. Jerry emerges as a rebarbative presence in the play.

Jerry's world is troubled, an environment filled with suffering humanity and with a disarming mixture of love, hate, and squalor. His neighbors – a "colored queen" who plucks his eyebrows, the Puerto Rican family, the invisible crying woman, the landlady – function as constant reminders of those whose lives are ontologically different from Peter's. In many respects, Jerry's present environment is merely a terrible extension of his past world: his mother ran away, had numerous affairs, and wound up dead; soon after, a city bus crushed his drunken father; Jerry then moved in with his aunt, only to witness her death on his high school graduation day. Emotionally buffeted in his youth, Jerry feels abandoned on all fronts, any youthful innocence or opportunity for community subverted by a naturalistic universe. His present condition offers little sense of resolution, boundaries, and solace. In fact, Jerry's relentless questions, the rapidity of speech, the quickness of breath, reveal a man in the midst of emotional collapse during what turns out to be the last hour of his life. His hypnotic overacting plainly suggests a man on the brink.

For Jerry, however, near-insanity nurtures lucidity. His baffling remark – "sometimes a person has to go a very long distance out of his way to come back a short distance correctly" (1: 21) – throws telling light on his confrontations with an unsuspecting Peter. For one perversely expiative scene, when Jerry sacrifices himself on the knife for Peter's sake, Jerry finds meaning to his existence through the ultimate form of communication: death. He has taken thirty-odd years to experience a minute of fulfillment, a tragic point where, for once, he has not depended on the kindness or cruelty of strangers – or dogs or pornographic playing cards – but has helped another human being. When Jerry impales himself, he has finally "come back a short distance correctly." As

Albee observes, "Peter's made too many safe choices far too early in his life, and Jerry has to shock him into understanding the tragic sense of being alive."[7]

Because he possesses an acute insight into his own condition, Jerry is capable of elevating a merely pathetic situation to the tragic and, through the catharsis of tragedy, is able to find some coherence in what hitherto has been a meaningless existence. Such an elevation is not always present in the works of, for instance, O'Neill. A figure such as Yank in *The Hairy Ape* (1922) struggles to understand his place in an industrialized, dehumanizing cosmos, but he ultimately never changes. O'Neill presents a Yank who, from the opening curtain to scene 8, remains caught within the dismal patterns of his life, one who remains the same: a pathetic naturalistic victim, an object among objects, a bothersome stoker symbolizing the helplessness of those trapped within a grimly deterministic universe. The play's closing image, set at the zoo where the gorilla crushes an utterly bewildered Yank, confirms the tragic legacy of Yank's noble yet ineffectual struggle "to belong." In such plays as *Desire Under the Elms* (1924), *Long Day's Journey into Night* (1956), and *The Iceman Cometh* (1940), O'Neill told the truth as he felt it: that the individual is victimized by his hubris as well as by a cajoling, beguiling external world which promotes a reliance on illusions as the only way to cope with life's absurdities and personal betrayals. Albee, beginning with Jerry in *The Zoo Story*, modifies (some would say rejects) O'Neill's vision.

In fact, Albee's world view differs from the visions of his two greatest American contemporaries after O'Neill, Arthur Miller and Tennessee Williams. In *Death of a Salesman* (1949) and *A Streetcar Named Desire* (1947), both Miller and Williams, like O'Neill before them, relied on a naturalistic vision of experience as the broader social and psychological canvas on which they placed their characters' struggles. Albee, of course, does not deny the presence of the naturalistic universe; indeed, *The Zoo Story* and *The Death of Bessie Smith* show an Albee acutely aware of the pervasive influence of a Zolaesque world. Albee retains the buffeting forces of naturalism within his imaginative terrain, but he also gives his characters the opportunity to transcend the limitations and horrors of naturalism. Jerry's and Peter's sense of consciousness ultimately enables them to go beyond Willy Loman's or Blanche Dubois's worlds.

Despite the degree of heightened awareness Albee bestows on Peter and Jerry, and despite the obviously contrasting realities of the two, Albee presents them as *sharing* a profound sense of isolation. The forced communication between the two underscores the point. Peter fails in human intercourse because of a withdrawal into comfortable, bourgeois life, a life of denying the tragic. Legally Peter will not be accountable for Jerry's death, but, Albee implies, after this Sunday afternoon's events he will feel accountable in a spiritual sense. Peter will no longer be able to remain isolated. Jerry fails because of his inability to maintain lasting relationships in his world, a world that courts the tragic. Accountability means little to Jerry, for he would rather die than perpetuate his desperate life. Thus both characters' experiences of isolation, although prompted by seemingly opposite predicaments – Jerry is too aware of felt isolation, Peter too anesthetized to discern separateness – dovetail within a broader context of aloneness.

Jerry violates Peter's isolation through communication. Exceeding the limits of expected propriety for a chance first encounter, Jerry bombards Peter with a disarmingly shrill and frank account of his private life. But he does this because Peter's initial indifference prompts Jerry to rely on the powers of invention, the weaving together of fact and fiction, a method of sorting through his fragmented experience and keeping Peter transfixed. Christopher Bigsby makes a useful point regarding Jerry's inventiveness: "When simple conversation is subverted by Peter's inability to engage in language on any but the most superficial level, he resorts to parable, telling the story of his relationship with his landlady's dog, a relationship which parallels that between Peter and himself."[8] Jerry's compelling parable about the dog reveals an active, if confused, mind, a consciousness eminently capable of self-awareness and eagerly willing to make, as Jerry puts it, "contact." While Peter has not succumbed to a willful surrendering of the spirit to the extent certain future Albee protagonists shall, his initially indifferent responses to Jerry nonetheless imply that, at least on an unconscious plane, his ethical judgments have been dulled by a withdrawal from any experience that does not fit within his limited set of values. Jerry, on the other hand, rebels against those very patterns of withdrawal. Although obviously in a different fictional context, Jerry's lovingly hateful stance toward Peter is prompted by precisely that sense of the excluding other, by those who ostracize the Jerrys of the world.

The public and private schism dividing Jerry's world from Peter's is terribly confirmed in the dog story. Albee established his technical virtuosity, an uncanny ability to weave the tragic and the comic, in the well-known story within a play, which Jerry titles "THE STORY OF JERRY AND THE DOG!" (1: 27). The passage, which Albee told me was inspired partially by Tennessee Williams's *Suddenly Last Summer*,[9] is the nerve center of the play. The passage not only violates Peter's enameled self but allows Jerry the chance to clarify the nature of his self-torment, a necessary clarification which prepares him for death. The story within a play also allows the audience to view Jerry in a broader context, as something more than a neurotic misanthrope, for we see him emerging as a complex antihero. The dog parable, in symbolic terms, serves as Jerry's paradigm for the human condition, its intensely private narrative expanding to include a lament for all suffering humanity. With the dog story, moreover, Jerry becomes an artist. In presenting a "factual" account of his sordid past, Jerry creates a "fiction" rivaling, perhaps surpassing, objective circumstances. His imaginative faculties enable him to blur the distinctions between fact and fiction while also enabling the audience to see more clearly facts presented as fiction. Although it is never known if Jerry's account of his past life is accurate, the audience has little reason to doubt its veracity. But the exactitude of his story's content becomes irrelevant; of concern is what Jerry's fictional account reveals about his present physical, psychological, and spiritual makeup. In the dog story, Jerry highlights the quality of his sensibility and his desperate condition.

Rejected by family and all others, Jerry enters into a relationship with the dog, for "where better to make a beginning ... to understand and just possibly be understood ... a beginning of an understanding, than with ... (*Here Jerry seems to fall into almost grotesque fatigue*) ... than with A DOG" (1: 30). Unlike people with whom Jerry interacts, the dog was not indifferent: he stalked; he attacked. Through a relationship with the dog Jerry gains some insight into the paradoxical links between love and hate that will plague so many future Albee heroes: "I have learned that neither kindness nor cruelty by themselves, independent of each other, creates any effect beyond themselves; and I have learned that the two combined, together, at the same time, are the teaching emotion" (1: 31). The "teaching emotion" will find its full expression only through Jerry's ritualistic murder/suicide.

Jerry uses Peter as an emotional sounding board largely because he senses the pervasive lack of communication and felt sense of estrangement entrapping the individual in a "zoo," the shaping metaphor of the play. As Jerry explains:

> I went to the zoo to find out more about the way people exist with animals, and the way animals exist with each other, and with people too. It probably wasn't a fair test, what with everyone separated by bars from everyone else, the animals for the most part from each other, and always the people from the animals. But, if it's a zoo, that's the way it is. (1: 34)

As the shaping metaphor, the zoo, with its bars and cages, symbolizes the disconnectedness of one human being from another which fuels Jerry's *Angst*. Like the fence in Robert Frost's "Mending Wall" (1914) and in August Wilson's *Fences* (1987), the cages function, not as a social gathering place, but as psychological dividers between people.

Despite Jerry's parables, Peter rejects his narrative. But in rejecting a thinly disguised plea for contact, Peter rejects not only a crazed man but, Albee suggests, all experience associated with the visceral, mysterious, non-rational. Representing a consciousness unwilling to reexamine one's milieu, Peter cannot understand or accept those like Jerry, as his outburst indicates: "I DON'T WANT TO HEAR ANY MORE" (1: 32). Sensing Peter's rejection – not of the bizarre content of the dog story but of what he is, his total *being* – Jerry feels compelled to escalate his assault. Here Albee strengthens the parallels between Jerry's encounters with the dog and with Peter. For example, as Jerry and the dog challenged each other over territory, the entrance to the rooming house, so Jerry and Peter battle over territory, the park bench. As the dog tried to keep Jerry from his world, so Peter tries to screen Jerry from his. Finally, as Jerry and the dog engaged in physical skirmishes, so the tension between the two men builds, the tragic and comic uniting:

> PETER (*Furious*): Look, you; get off my bench. I don't care if it makes any sense or not. I want this bench to myself; I want you OFF IT!
> JERRY (*Mocking*): Aw ... look who's mad.
> PETER: GET OUT!
> JERRY: No.
> PETER: I WARN YOU!
> JERRY: Do you know how ridiculous you look *now*?
> PETER (*His fury and self-consciousness have possessed him*): It doesn't matter. (*He is almost crying*) GET AWAY FROM MY BENCH!
> (1: 36–37)

As with so many of Albee's subsequent plays, *The Zoo Story* stages a profound sense of engagement between two individuals, a felt militancy between characters that precedes the cathartic ending. From this point onward Peter appears aroused, angered, ready to define himself through concrete deeds rather than false compromises. Within the closing febrile scenes of the play, Peter experiences Albert Camus's "definitive awakening,"[10] a moment in which he comes to consciousness wherein he can apprehend the world external to the self in qualitatively new terms.

When he impales himself on the knife, Jerry not only gains his expiation but also shatters all of Peter's predictable patterns. Face to face, Jerry forces Peter into the "contact" he seeks throughout the play. Jerry finds his ultimate mode of engagement and communication; but paradoxically, it is the knife that gives meaning to his world while at the same time severing his contact with that world. Whether interpreting Jerry as psychopath, Christ-figure, or shaman, critics generally acknowledge Albee's chief thematic point regarding the play's climax: to present a Peter who, through "the cleansing consciousness of death,"[11] progresses from ignorance to awareness through Jerry's self-sacrifice. His howl – "OH MY GOD!" (1: 40) – transcends his previously banal responses.

Markedly altered by internalizing the force of death, Peter will never return to routine habits, what Samuel Beckett, who greatly influenced the young Albee, calls "the great deadener" within human experience.[12] The prescribed formulas and labels around which Peter once forged his safe, middle-of-the-road personal politic, Albee implies, will no longer work. Peter, like his adversary, is suddenly on "the precipice."[13] The ending of *The Zoo Story*, despite its ambiguity, suggests that Peter's subsequent language and action will be founded within a more expansive humanistic context, one in which Jerry's "teaching emotion" will forever temper his every gesture. In discussing the necessity of the stabbing, Albee suggests that death is the only way Jerry can break through the well-ordered world of Peter to educate him: "Had Peter understood, had he not refused to understand, then I doubt the death would have been necessary. Jerry tries all the way through the play to teach and fails. And finally makes a last effort at teaching, and I think succeeds."[14] Paradoxically enough, implicit in Albee's remarks is the muted but palpable sense of optimism.

The Zoo Story is a life-affirming play. Subordinating pessimism to the possibility that the individual can communicate honestly with the self and the other "during the precious time of our lives,"[15] Albee presents the potential for regeneration, a source of optimism which underlies the overtly aggressive text and performance. Perhaps, for some, Jerry discovers a degree of religious fulfillment by giving his life. Even the setting reinforces the religious overtones of the play. The backdrop of "foliage, trees, sky" (1: 14), the presence of light and warmth, the verdant lushness and vibrant aliveness of a sun-drenched park, and above all the day of the week, the Christian Sabbath, Sunday – surely these details, while not purely Edenic, complement the possibility of repose and inner peace, of resurrection and salvation. His death liberates him from an impossible present and also confirms the presence of the "teaching emotion" he had discovered earlier. Jerry's death gives way, in brief, to nothing less than Peter's rebirth, a recharging of the spirit. Albee even suggests that "Peter has become Jerry to a certain extent."[16]

The regenerative spirit of *The Zoo Story* is not limited to the actors. Albee also directs the benevolent hostility of the play toward the audience. When Jerry dies and an absolved Peter exits, Albee would like actor and audience to become one within a collective stage experience. By mixing pity, fear, and recognition within the play's closure, Albee transfers the tragic insight Peter gains to the audience. For Albee, communication shatters isolation.

The Zoo Story embodies both the civic function and aesthetic richness which Albee envisions as essential to the art of drama. The play, which made its debut in the United States at an Off-Broadway theater, the Provincetown Playhouse, in New York City on January 14, 1960, re-energized American theater. The dialogue in *The Zoo Story* rekindled an excitement in American theater not seen since Miller and Williams and, before them, O'Neill. *The Zoo Story* was one of the first American plays to sensitize audiences to the explosiveness of Off-Broadway. On a personal level the American debut of *The Zoo Story*, even before Peter and Jerry took to the stage that winter evening in 1960, must have been a fabulous inspiration to the unknown, young Albee. After all, his play was one half of a twin bill, the other play being *Krapp's Last Tape* (1958), written by none other than the world's foremost modern dramatist, one whom Albee always admired, Samuel Beckett. Albee's next compositions, *The Death of Bessie Smith*, *The Sandbox*, and *The American Dream*, only enhanced his reputation.

The Death of Bessie Smith

After *The Zoo Story* announced the arrival of a young, fresh, and dynamic new American playwright, Albee once again returned to Berlin, Germany, where *The Death of Bessie Smith* premiered at the Schlosspark Theater on April 21, 1960. The first American performance of the play was at the York Playhouse in New York City on January 24, 1961. He wrote it in 1959 – when he was only thirty-one years old. Although it is infrequently performed in the twenty-first century, the play foreshadows what would eventually be regarded as classic Albeean features. The precise use of language, accentuated with Albee's fondness for deploying a strategically placed italicized word for a more *nuanced* delivery; heated repartee between the characters that both sparkles and anticipates the verbal explosiveness of *Who's Afraid of Virginia Woolf?* and *The Goat or, Who Is Sylvia?*; and a fear of "*abandonment,*" as the Nurse puts it (1: 74; Albee's italics), a word, broadly defined, that informs so many of his plays.

Structurally, *The Death of Bessie Smith* is a one-act play featuring eight fast-paced scenes. The set of the play is fairly simple: the central part of the stage is the admissions room of a hospital. Theatergoers see a desk, a few chairs, a bench, and along the rear a slightly elevated platform. There are two doors on stage left and right. The hospital scenes dominate, though Albee places us briefly in a hotel bar and, later, in the screened-in front porch of the Nurse and her Father. Albee specifies that he wants an open play space, "*for the whole back wall of the stage is full of the sky, which will vary from scene to scene: a hot blue; a sunset; a great, red-orange-yellow sunset. Sometimes full, sometimes but a hint*" (1: 44). The visual effects of such Tennessee Williams-esque lighting complement the emotional state of affairs of each particular scene, as does the music the audience hears periodically throughout the play. With regard to the

music, it is slightly surprising that, for a dramatist famous for exerting authorial control over his work, he does not specify what particular songs should be
played, only that there should be music. Sensible directors, of course, would
have little trouble creating an appropriate playlist. Finally, the play is set in
and around Memphis, Tennessee, during the afternoon and early evening of
September 26, 1937 – the date when Bessie Smith died in a car accident.

   Albee claims to have long enjoyed jazz and Bessie Smith for years. As he told
Mel Gussow:

> I had loved gospel music and early jazz for a long time … I'd also
> been listening to Bessie Smith's records. An LP had come out and
> I happened to read on the album cover that the story of how she died,
> the automobile accident outside of Memphis, her arm outside the
> window of the car, her arm almost cut off, how she was taken to a white
> hospital and was refused admission and died on the way to a second
> hospital. That generated the play. How long after I became aware of
> that information did I write it? It can't have been very long. I made the
> necessary additional step, the gift of the dead Bessie Smith to the second
> hospital. That was totally my invention. But those facts prompted the
> play.[17]

An inspired Albee decided to write *The Death of Bessie Smith*, using as his
source of inspiration what he read on the album cover. Fair enough. However,
his source of information, it turns out, was based on hearsay and inaccuracies.
But it was those hearsay and inaccuracies that became part of the popular culture's version of her death.

   Bessie Smith was a passenger in her Packard. She and a long-time friend
Richard Morgan drove south from Memphis through the Mississippi evening.
Her best days as a singer behind her, Smith was launching a comeback, touring
much of the south. They were on Route 61 near Clarksdale when the Packard
crashed into a truck on the highway. Thompson, who was behind the wheel,
survived. Smith did not. Shortly thereafter Smith's record producer, John
Hammond, published an article in *downbeat* magazine entitled, "Did Bessie
Smith Bleed to Death While Waiting for Medical Aid?", which raised questions
for years about the singer's fate. Hammond claimed that Smith did not necessarily have to die – even though an arm was nearly severed and her body suf-
fered massive trauma. She received medical attention from a local doctor who
happened on the horrific accident, he said, then bled to death in a Memphis
hospital, where she was denied medical emergency treatment because she was
African American. The myth was born.

   In fact, Smith was taken by ambulance to a Clarksdale black hospital, but
she was dead upon arrival. For years questions lingered: was she turned away

at Clarksdale's white hospital or driven directly to the small city's African American hospital? Eventually Hammond conceded that he created his narrative based on rumors that proved to be inaccurate. Toby Zinman does an outstanding job of sorting through fact and fiction, noting many discrepancies and, among many other points, that "Hammond was expecting to make a handsome profit on her records when he reissued them."[18]

Just as Arthur Miller takes artistic liberties with historical facts in *The Crucible* (1953), so, Albee, it turns out, takes artistic liberties with the actual facts surrounding Smith's demise. Still, Miller informs his readers of such liberties in his preface, "A Note on the Historical Accuracy of this Play." Either Albee did not research Smith's death more vigorously, or perhaps in the late 1950s no corrective article existed. It seems he takes the blurb on the record album at face value. After all, that narrative makes for much more engaging *drama*. And both he and Miller are playwrights, not reporters or historians.

Despite the title of the play, we never see Bessie Smith. Nor do we learn much about her death. This technique of never having the central figure of the play take the stage was pioneered in American drama by Susan Glaspell in *Trifles* (1916), whose Minnie Foster Wright is noticeable by her absence. Albee deploys this approach to suit both his cultural and thematic interests. For this is less a play about the legendary blues singer, though Albee greatly admires her music. Rather, Albee seems more interested in recreating the racist ethos and the institutions denying fundamental human rights to African Americans in the Jim Crow South of 1937, and the affect such systemic racism has on the spirit and values of the Intern, the Orderly, the Father, the Second Nurse, and, above all, the Nurse. Interestingly, except for the light-skinned Orderly, only the African American figures in the play have first names: Bessie Smith, Jack, and Bernie. They have names within a white world that prefers they remain nameless, silent, invisible.

The Death of Bessie Smith embodies an important dialectic that would inform Albee's playwriting for nearly six decades, for this is a play that reflects selected public issues of a nation as reflected through the private anxieties of the individual. That public/private dialectic gives this play its theatrical power – as does its bracing language. The play opens with Bernie, a slender African American, enjoying a beer and music in a bar when Jack, a *"dark-skinned Negro, forty-five, bulky, with a deep voice and a mustache"* (1: 43) enters, and the two men talk. We learn that Jack will be driving Bessie Smith to New York City. Scene 2 takes place in the home of the Nurse and her racist Father; for Albee, their hostile exchanges underscore, beyond father/daughter recriminations and tensions, that the old aristocratic white South is in terminal decay. Scene 3 showcases Jack, who urges Bessie to get ready for their long road trip.

Albee alludes to animals and uses animal imagery in nearly all of his plays, and, here, he ironizes a bird allusion, for Jack enthusiastically refers to Bessie as a woman who surely is "free as a bird. Free as a goddamn bird" (1: 53). Of course neither Jack nor Bessie would enjoy such freedoms in the Deep South in 1937. The rest of the scenes are set in the hospital (and, briefly, in a second hospital) and spotlight the Nurse and all those who come within her orbit: the Father, the Orderly, the Intern, and, near play's end, Jack and a Second Nurse. The play reaches its climax when Jack drives up to the hospital, and the Intern defies the Nurse's orders to turn away Bessie Smith only to discover that the singer is already dead. Albee heightens the emotional impact by having the sunset blazing at the final curtain.

The Father, a historian, emerges as an irritable racist whose decline in heath stands, again, as a metaphor for the decline of the Old South and its troubling past. He apparently drives to the ironically named Democratic Club, surrounding himself, his daughter claims, "with that bunch of loafers" whose conversations surely have nothing to do with democracy for African Americans (1: 49). He cannot stand his daughter, the Nurse, playing "those goddamn Nigger records full blast," especially since he has a headache (1: 47). Albee describes him as a thin and balding man in his mid-fifties. He brags that he is friends with the mayor, but his daughter mocks him because, as she puts it, "you going to pretend you're something more than you are, which is nothing but ... a hanger-on, flunky" (1: 49). Albee devotes only one scene to the Father, but it is clear that this father–daughter relationship is fraught with bitterness and anger. Love is nowhere in evidence. Both are mean-spirited, frustrated, and, in the case of the Father, physically weak.

The Orderly acts as his name suggests: he is a respectful, polite twenty-eight-year-old, "*a light-skinned Negro*" who is "*clean-shaven, trim, prim*" (1: 43). He behaves as he should within the culturally proscribed racist world. He tries, with uneven results, to keep his own world in order. He is intelligent, ambitious, and subservient to the Nurse, who orders him around one moment, only to deride him the next. She attacks him for using for using the word "condone" – "My! Aren't you the educated one?" (1: 55). Reminding him of his race, she warns him that if he wants to keep his job, he must act in a servile manner: "You just shut your ears ... and you keep that mouth closed, too" (1: 57). The respectful Orderly is no match for the Nurse's racial diatribes, who jeers and maliciously taunts him because, in part, he has "Uncle Tom'd" himself (1: 59). The Nurse thinks he is no more than "a genuine little ass-licker, if ever I saw one" (1: 58). It is scarcely surprising, then, when a distraught Jack pulls up to the hospital with his dead companion, the baffled Orderly mirrors more of the white Southern world of 1937 values and responses when bringing the play to a close: "I never heard of such a thing ... bringing a dead woman here like that ... I don't know what people can be thinking of sometimes ..." (1: 81).

The Intern emerges as one of the more complicated characters. Albee describes him as "*a southern white man, blond, well put-together, with an amiable face; thirty*" (1: 43). He yearns to travel to Spain during its civil war, thinking he could put his medical talents to much better use by healing those fighting against the fascist Franco. Instead, he is consigned to do his internship at a small-town hospital in his home state. He has amorous designs on the Nurse, who teases him along but ultimately refuses his entreaties. He wants to enjoy sex with her where, he pleads, he could plunge strait into her "lovely vortex" (1: 63). He asks the Nurse if she has told her father about his supposed love for her, even alluding of his nightly erection he has when thinking about her: "Have you told him [her father] that at night the sheets of my bed are like a tent, poled center-upward in my love for you?" (1: 63). He professes his love to her, though it is clear to the audience or reader that he just wants to get laid. But the light banter between the two darkens when the Intern claims she is promiscuous and surely has slept with every man in two counties but himself. His comment triggers an unexpectedly vicious response from the Nurse, her body language – Albee's stage direction denotes that she brims with rage – bolstering her verbal attack; she vows to end his career at the hospital.

If there is a protagonist in the play, it is not Bessie Smith but the Nurse. Albee describes her as "*a Southern white girl, full blown, dark or red-haired, pretty, with a wild laugh. Twenty-six*" (1: 43). She is the most fully developed of the characters, one in the prime of her womanhood, but she emerges as the embodiment of sexual desire and frustration. On the one hand, she enjoys her suitor's attention but never consummates her relationship with the Intern. Perhaps it is her emotionally charged sexual desire and frustration, never satisfied, that triggers her scathing attacks on the others. Further, she feels trapped at home. She works full-time at a hospital, only to come home to take care of a father who chastises her. This is also a father who mocks her for flirting in the car with the Intern late at night. The Father refuses to loan her his car so she can drive herself to work, a refusal borne out of spite. Hence the Nurse lashes out at her father. Gilbert Debusscher even claims there may be a hint of incestuous love between father and daughter, though such a claim seems questionable for many.[19]

The Nurse, very much a product of the Old South, reinforces racial segregation and discrimination throughout the play. The point is nowhere better seen than in the climatic ending of the play. Scene 8 is as kaleidoscopic as it is frenetic, with the Nurse at the center of racial epitaphs, vicious verbal attacks, and, tragically, the one who asserts her racist authority. When a drunk and terrified Jack pulls up, the Nurse refuses to admit Bessie Smith to the all-white hospital. There will be no mercy within the Nurse's hospital or the second one to which Albee alludes, the ironically named Mercy Hospital. Albee emphasizes the point earlier in brief (less than one page) Scene 7 when Jack's frantic pleas for help are dismissed by the Second Nurse because Jack and Bessie are, of course, black. The audience watches as the Nurse unloads on the Orderly, the Intern, Jack, and, finally, herself. In an astonishing shift, the Nurse defends her Father, calling him an important man, and a knowledgeable historian – a racial reminder to the Orderly that she will uphold the mores and values of the Old South. Further, hers is a complete emotional meltdown. The Nurse by play's end is a woman savagely divided against herself. She acts like an increasingly demented figure. She in effect blots out her outer world and inner self. Albee's writing here sparkles, and, as we see in many of his subsequent dramas, there is a hint of T. S. Eliot's *The Hollow Men* (1925) in her lines: "Well, let me tell you something ... I am sick of it! I am *sick*. I am sick of everything in this hot, stupid, fly-ridden *world*. I am sick of the disparity between things as they are, and as they should be!" Albee is at his best when he first concentrates on the Nurse's outer, physical world, then deepens her breakdown by presenting her as experiencing a psychological implosion, the very collapse of her being in the world:

> I am sick of this desk ... this uniform ... it scratches ... I am sick of the sight of *you* ... the *thought* of you [the Orderly] makes me ... *itch* ... I am sick of *him* [the Intern]. *(Soft now: a chant)* I am sick of talking to people on the phone in this damn stupid hospital ... I am sick of the smell of Lysol ... I could die of it ... I am sick of going to bed and I am sick of waking up ... I am tired ... I am tired of the truth ... and I am tired of lying about the truth ... I am tired of my skin ... I WANT OUT! (1: 74)

The above scene, moreover, foreshadows the theatrical power of Albee's language that would become a singular feature of his future dramas.

Albee's theater, for many, reflects the sweep and play of a nation thinking in front of itself, of a culture seeking to locate its identity through the ritualized action implicit in the art of theater. Albee, it seemed, was the new Angry Young Man, a decidedly sociopolitical dramatist who anticipated, and subsequently became part of, the social eruptions in the United States during the 1960s. *The Death of Bessie Smith* only cemented his reputation as a "political" writer, one whose rage existed in equipoise with his moral seriousness. But to regard *The Death of Bessie Smith* as a thesis play, a play about racism, a social protest piece, does not fully account for its power. Such an assessment is not meant to discount the political dimensions of the play; clearly Albee tackles racism, then as now one of America's most controversial social, historical, and moral issues. However, the play's real subject lies less in its analysis of bigotry and prejudice than in its treatment, ultimately, of internal forces – psychological, ethical, spiritual – which negate the possibility of the individual coming to terms of the self. *The Death of Bessie Smith*, to be sure, pinpoints a broader social malaise but it also charts private crimes of the heart. The Nurse's outburst near the end presents an existential crisis, a kind of sickness unto death, confronting all of the main characters. The Nurse's is a kind of ontological sickness, a world-weariness which precipitates her violent attacks, defensiveness, and sense of entrapment. The Nurse's condition is, moreover, emblematic of the kind of frustration and self-betrayals afflicting the Orderly and, to a lesser extent, the Intern. Bessie Smith is clearly a victim of racial hatred. Black lives, in this play, do not matter. But to Albee, the Nurse, the Father, the Intern, and the Orderly may also be seen as victims, individuals unable to accept personal and social responsibilities that go with being human. Of course the Intern finally stands up the Nurse, defies her order to not help Bessie Smith, but his gesture becomes ironic, as he – and we – learn that singer is already dead.

The play's final moments confirm the sense of *loss* that permeates, not only *The Death of Bessie Smith*, but virtually all of Albee's plays. The last image of the Nurse is of a woman on the verge of a nervous breakdown, her racial insults intermixing with her perverse singing and laughing, a singing that is a keening, a laughter that borders on crying. As a great sunset blazes, the final curtain falls. Albee's apocalyptic ending brings the play to a satisfying close.

The Sandbox

The well-respected Italian-American composer and librettist Gian Carlo Menotti invited the largely unknown Albee in 1959 to submit a brief play for possible inclusion in the Festival of Two Worlds at Spoleto, Italy, a festival which at the time showcased some of the leading European absurdist playwrights of the late 1950s. In response, Albee set aside his work on *The American Dream* and composed a play using the principal players from *Dream*, and recast them in *The Sandbox*, a fourteen-minute playlet squarely in the absurdist tradition. This play, it turns out, was not staged in Spoleto, but in New York City, on April 15, 1960, at the Jazz Gallery.[20] Satiric in tone, absurdist in texture, *The Sandbox* is, for its author, one of his favorite pieces, what he calls " 'an absolutely beautiful, lovely, perfect play.' "[21]

Plot, action, and setting of *The Sandbox* are relatively simple, if non-realistic. Mommy and Daddy bring Grandma to sandy beach, where they abruptly dump her into a child's sandbox – complete with a toy pail and shovel. It is, Albee describes, a bare stage with two simple chairs in which Mommy and Daddy sit while waiting for Grandma to die. On the other side of the stage is another chair and music stand; on cue the Musician plays, the music composed by William Flanagan, Albee's early lover who very much influenced the young playwright. Completing the cast is the Young Man. Today theatergoers or readers familiar with Albee will recognize these characters, who are more fully developed in *The American Dream*, one of Albee's best-known plays. Mommy, fifty-five years old and well-dressed, is "*an imposing woman*" (1: 85). She is also clearly a portrayal of Albee's domineering and mean-spirited adoptive mother. Daddy at sixty is equally familiar: the weak, emasculated figure who Albee simply calls "*a small man*" (1: 85), an emotional portrait of the playwright's wealthy, whining, and detached adoptive father. The Musician delivers no lines but his sounds add an aural touch to the performance that, as the music does in *The Death of Bessie Smith*, complements the unfolding action of the play. The Young Man, a twenty-five-year-old, is "*a good-looking, well-built boy in a bathing suit*" (1: 85). He performs calisthenics throughout the entire play until the very end, fluttering only his arms because, Albee writes in a prefatory note, he is "*the Angel of Death*" (1: 86). A vacuous wannabe actor from Southern California, the Young Man embodies the superficial world inhabited by all the Mommys and Daddys in Albee's world. *The Sandbox*, we see, contains the anger, frustration, and sarcasm of a young playwright rejected by his own adoptive parents. Hence Mommy, especially, treats all who come within her orbit with callous disrespect. As Grandma nears death, she feigns bereavement. For Mommy, Grandma is a mere object. Mommy sees the world only in relation to herself; she is a woman who communicates with a language drained of authentic meaning. Not surprisingly, Mommy and Daddy, who view the sandbox more as a coffin, delight in infantilizing Grandma in her final moments on earth.

As *The Sandbox* commences, audiences are immediately taken by Albee's use of language. Whereas in *The Zoo Story* and *The Death of Bessie Smith* he deploys a fairly realistic dialogue, in *The Sandbox* Albee presents a non-realistic style in which dialogue and action are rendered in exaggerated, satiric, non-logical forms. The artificiality of the language, Grandma's direct address of the audience, and the overall metatheatrical quality of the performance stand out. In context of an ongoing narrative history of the American stage, Albee's experimentation ushered into the American theater what Martin Esslin, one year after *The Sandbox* appeared, called "the theater of the absurd,"[22] a movement which challenged traditional realistic dramatic conventions while exploring an angst-ridden world in which the individual is thrust into a meaningless universe over which he has little or no control. Logic, cause and effect, and language itself are called into question during a series of existentialist crises. For many, *The Sandbox* and *The American Dream* represent the first successful American contributions to the decidedly European absurdist theater movement. Indeed, Albee in *The Sandbox* emulates the likes of Samuel Beckett, Harold Pinter, Eugene Ionesco, Jean Genet, Arthur Adamov, and, among others and one from an earlier generation, Luigi Pirandello. Albee was in 1960 imbued with the full philosophical and aesthetic power of the absurdist movement.

All the figures in *The Sandbox*, save Grandma, are caricatures, which heightens the absurdity of their performance. In prefatory notes to the play, Albee pulls no punches: he names Mommy and Daddy so because "these names are of empty affection and point up the pre-senility and vacuity of their characters" (1: 85). Within such a context, Mommy is in a sense a director of this production. Albee presents her as the domineering wife of Daddy and the scornful daughter of Grandma. She speaks declaratively, always obtaining what she wants. As she says at the start, "Whatever I say [goes]" (1: 87). Compassionless as she is crass, she is an emasculating figure Albee delights in satirizing. Daddy, of course, is subservient, timid, even fearful of his wife. As he repeatedly (and vaguely) replies, "Whatever you say, Mommy" (1: 87). Mommy and Daddy pretend to care about Grandma, but the audience knows otherwise. In this play, authentic human relationships are nowhere in evidence. Understanding and compassion yield to selfishness and insensitivity. This is a young Albee exposing the illusion of sincerity and love, his way of attacking what Tennessee Williams would call the mendacity plaguing the modern American family circa 1960. Within the inverted logic of this play, the daughter thinks she suffers more than her dying mother.

The central figure of the play is, of course, Grandma. Albee dedicates the play to his beloved grandmother. She genuinely loved Albee in a home in which his adoptive parents privileged hostility, indifference, and spite. As Albee's biographer Mel Gussow observes, "*The Sandbox* was written for (and about) his grandmother, Grandma Cotter, his closest relative, the one member of the family with whom he had formed a lasting attachment. A crotchety and very amusing woman, she considerably brightened Albee's childhood and was a natural ally against his mother (her daughter) – and everyone else. When he left home, his one regret was having to leave Grandma Cotter behind."[23]

Grandma is the only character with substance – and a clear sense of objective reality. At eighty-six years old, she appears as "*a tiny, wizened woman with bright eyes*" (1: 85). Disrespected by Mommy and Daddy, Grandma nonetheless maintains her sense of humanity. We learn she married at seventeen, was widowed at thirty, and, in reference to Mommy, had to "raise that big cow over there all by [her] lonesome" (1: 90). Although treated like a dog at home, she rises above the mistreatment and vacuity around her. With a sense of grace, and relief, Grandma accepts her own death by play's end. In a play mainly devoid of sympathetic characters, Grandma impresses by maintaining her own grace under pressure, and thus earns the audience's respect.

The ending, for some of the early critics of the play, is "mawkish"[24] and "degenerates into tearful melodrama."[25] Admittedly the play veers toward sentimentality in its treatment of Grandma's death; perhaps it is Albee's artistic farewell to his grandmother (1876–1959), who had recently died. When Grandma says to the Young Man, "You're ... you're welcome ... dear," it is less a response to his preceding lines – "Oh ... thank you, thank you very much ... ma'am" – as it is her expression of relief that it is "all over"; she now accepts of her own death (1: 94). Long aware of the duplicity, hypocrisy, and illusions which surround her, Grandma goes to her death, Albee implies, with her dignity intact. It is not too fanciful to suggest that, had his Grandma Cotter lived to see the play, she surely would have had a felt understanding of the familial dynamics unwinding on the stage. With the completion of *The Sandbox*, Albee eagerly returned to working on *The American Dream*, a play now considered one of the classics in the Albee canon. But first he would stage *Fam and Yam*, a brief play.

Fam and Yam

In 1960 Albee staged a sarcastic piece, *Fam and Yam*, subtitled *An Imaginary Interview*, a fourteen-minute sketch about a young American playwright, named Yam, who interviews Fam, an older, famous American playwright. An unremarkable playlet, one that Albee elected not to include in the definitive edition of his works, *The Collected Plays of Edward Albee* in three volumes, *Fam and Yam* is, if nothing else, engaging within context of Albee's emerging presence on the contemporary stage. For many of the hallmarks of Albee's signature style – the acerbic wit, the attention to language, the use of italics, the attacks on tradition and institutions, and the delight in the absurd adumbrate features that will sparkle in the mature plays that follow. *Fam and Yam*, published in the September 1960 issue of *Harper's Bazaar*, was first performed on August 27, 1960, at the White Barn Theatre in Westport, Connecticut.

The simplicity of the narrative allows Albee to cut to the chase: the young playwright, thin, in need of a haircut, but willing to spend his limited money on a copy of the *Evergreen Review*, ostensibly is a huge fan of the older playwright, whose well-appointed Manhattan apartment, with its views of New York City, impresses the young artist, as do the plays of the famous man. Fam, after all, is carrying on the legacies of "Miller, Williams … Thornton Wilder, and … uh … (*Shrugs*) … Inge …"[26] All is a ploy, it turns out, for Yam (a thinly disguised Albee, most would concede) in his youthful idealism and enthusiasm, attacks the theater establishment, whose key members – theater owners, producers, directors, critics, agencies, and other "pin-heads" (94) – do not nurture and support the younger generation of new playwrights. Fam, who in all likelihood is a thinly disguised William Inge, begins to realize he is part of that very establishment, and admits: "the new generation's knocking on the door. Gelber, Richardson, Kopit … (*Shrugs*) … Albee … (*Mock woe*) You youngsters are going to push us out of the way …" (89). The strategically placed stage direction, "*Shrugs*," before the name Inge and then repeated before the name Albee reinforces the connection between the two playwrights. Inge, indeed, seems to have been the model for Fam, for in his efforts to mount a first production of *The Zoo Story*, Albee circulated that script to several artists, including the composer Aaron Copeland, who thought well enough of the script to send it to William Inge, whose *Picnic* (1953), *Bus Stop* (1955), and *The Dark at the Top of the Stairs* (1957) made him "one of the top Broadway playwrights of the moment. A word from him to a producer, director, or agent would have made a great difference." Although Inge read the script, and called it "a very good play," he returned the manuscript offering no specific help. His letter to Albee sounded "like a thank-you note for an unwanted gift."[27]

If Yam, author of a successful Off-Broadway play entitled *DILEMA, DERECLICTION AND DEATH*, is part Albee himself and part Jerry, Fam is part Inge and part Peter, a denizen of that well-ordered world that shuts out, in context of this play, new theatrical voices. So it is only fitting that Yam wants to title the essay he is supposedly going to write (hence the interview with Fam) "In Search of a Hero." But in the traditional Broadway theater world, such a search leads to a "list of villains," as Yam sarcastically tells an increasingly tipsy Fam, who downs several glasses of sherry: "The theatre owners … the producers … the backers … the theatre parties … the unions … the critics … the directors … and the playwrights themselves … That's the list. (*Smiles*)" (92).

The action ends when Fam, bellowing with laughter and knocking over tables, encourages Yam to attack the theater establishment in his article. Yam thanks his famous counterpart, leaves, but telephones from the lobby of Fam's swank apartment to thank him one last time for "the interview" (96). Suddenly realizing that he will be quoted as attacking his fellow well-established theater colleagues, understanding that he has just mocked his own self, an ashen Fam closes the play with the anguished lines, "THE

INTERVIEW!!! THE INTEVIEW!!!!!" as the famous paintings hanging on his walls signal their disappointment: "*One of the Modiglianis frowns ... the Braque peels ... the Kline tilts ... and the Motherwell crashes to the floor*" (96). Fam has, after all, just named names. He has betrayed those who supported him. When Yam implicates other playwrights as part of the villain list, he is attacking selected older, well-known dramatists who did not reach out to the newer generation of theatricians, as Albee himself experienced. Although Albee knew W. H. Auden and Thornton Wilder, and somehow found a way to contact Aaron Copeland, no established dramatists *mentored* Albee, who instead found his first play soundly rejected by producers in the United States.

This surely is why Albee throughout his life committed himself to encouraging new artists. As the decades went by, Albee emerged as an inspiring model to generations of younger playwrights. With his producers Richard Barr and Clinton Wilder, Albee established in the early 1960s the Playwrights Unit in an effort to offer just such support. Soon after he established the Edward Albee Foundation, whose website today reads:

> The Edward F. Albee Foundation exists to serve writers and visual artists from all walks of life, by providing time and space in which to work without disturbance. Using only talent and need as the criteria for selection, the Foundation invites any and all artists to apply.
>
> Founded in 1967 by Edward Albee, after proceeds from his play *Who's Afraid of Virginia Woolf?* proved abundant, the Foundation had maintained the William Flanagan Memorial Creative Persons Center (better known as "The Barn") in Montauk, on Long Island in New York, as a residence for writers and visual artists.

So it is hardly surprising that Albee would soon provide encouragement for such new talent in the early 1960s as Sam Shepard and, among many others, Adrienne Kennedy. Albee's support for his fellow artists (the kind Yam never received from the Fams of the world) would continue well into the twenty-first century. Newer voices of the American theater, Albee insists, will be heard. And Albee's own voice was certainly heard when he returned to finishing *The American Dream*.

The American Dream

The myth of the American Dream permeates American literary texts. Arthur Miller, for one, explained his views concerning this animating myth and the way in which objective reality, coupled with the individual's fallibility, too often subverts its alluring promise:

> The American Dream is the largely unacknowledged screen in front of which all American writing plays itself out – the screen of the perfectibility of man. Whoever is writing in the United States is using the American Dream as an ironical pole of his story. Early on we all drink up certain claims to self-perfection that are absent in a large part of the world. People elsewhere tend to accept, to a far greater degree anyway, that the conditions of life are hostile to man's pretensions. The American idea is different in the sense that we think that if we could only touch it, and live by it, there's a natural order in favor of us; and that the object of a good life is to get connected with that live and abundant order. And this forms a context of irony for the kind of stories we generally tell each other. After all, the stories of most significant literary works are of one or another kind of failure. And it's a failure *in relation* to that screen, that backdrop. I think it pervades American writing, including my own. It's there in *The Crucible*, in *All My Sons*, in *After the Fall* – an aspiration to an innocence that when defeated or frustrated can turn quite murderous, and we don't know what to do with this perversity; it never seems to "fit" us.[28]

The sense of innocence implicit in the myth of the American Dream collapses in Albee's *The American Dream*. Mommy and Daddy's dismemberment of their first son is a fitting gesture of perverse defiance, the unabashed response to a satisfaction-guaranteed market and mentality. In the play Albee used the ideological and mythic "screen" of the American Dream as the "ironical pole of his story." The then thirty-two-year-old Albee directed his satiric, ironic assault not against an American work ethic, but against a culture that placed its faith in a consumerist, materialist cosmos, a point he clarified nearly three decades after writing the play:

> There's nothing wrong with the notion of making your own way. What is wrong with the myth of the American Dream is that notion that is all that there is to existence! The myth is merely a part of other things. Becoming wealthy is OK, I suppose, but it is not a be all to end all. People who think that the acquisition of wealth or property or material things or power; that these are the things in life; the conspicuous consumption of material things is the answer; this creates a problem. The fact that we set arbitrary and artificial goals for ourselves is a problem, not the hard work ethic *per se*.[29]

A post-Eisenhower America, its unfettered enthusiasm for wealth and security an anodyne for the horrors of the Depression and World War II, a country flaunting its recrudescence through such conspicuous material acquisitions as the high-finned Cadillacs of the late 1950s, prompted the young Albee to rethink cultural values and assumptions, and finally, in this play, to generate combative imbalances. Satiric in tone, absurdist in technique, American in cadence, *The American Dream* was Albee's attack on what he saw as American complacency. For Albee, the humorous anger was necessary. For when he wrote the play, America's post-World War II optimism had yet to be undermined by its modern versions of regicide, the Kennedys' and King's assassinations. The Beatles, the Rolling Stones, and Jimi Hendrix, the Vietnam War and the revolutionary 1960s, were yet to come. The myth of the American Dream was still a talismanic force, a fanciful lie of the mind sustained by unprecedented free enterprise and unlimited hopes. Optimistic nationalism – emblematized by the "right stuff" attitude of the Space Race, technological and military prowess, an enthusiastic renewal of faith in science, youth, American exceptionalism, and, above all, money – infiltrated the American consciousness. The American Adam was now transformed into a postlapsarian figure, his youthful innocence tempered (and corrupted) by a blatantly self-reliant consumerism.

Such a cultural milieu invited the ironizing of experience, as Miller suggested. But for Albee the social climate, which greatly crippled Broadway, gave rise in *The American Dream* to absurdist satire. "The play is an examination of the American Scene," Albee emphatically announces in the preface to an earlier edition of the play, "an attack on the substitution of artificial for real values in our society, a condemnation of complacency, cruelty, emasculation and vacuity; it is a stand against the fiction that everything in this slipping land of ours is peachy-keen."[30]

Albee stages his attack through language. Receptive to such influential European absurdists as Beckett, Genet, Ionesco, and Pinter, Albee experimented with the absurdist technique of devaluing language, his often illogical, cliché-ridden repartee signifying the characters' banality. He quickly establishes the absurdist texture of the play when Mommy discusses the color of her hat. The length, detail, and obsession with which she analyzes the hat appears ridiculous and boring, Albee's method of capturing the superficiality of her values, the way that important energy of authentic communication is wasted on trite, meaningless expression. Like Ionesco's *The Bald Soprano* (1950), *The American Dream* continually parodies language and definition, substitutes cliché for genuine comprehension, mocks social convention and audience expectation. "A curious feature of Albee's work," writes Anne Paolucci, "is his early experimentation ... along the lines of Beckett and Ionesco – the defleshed abstract stage where language becomes an irritating puzzle and familiar conventions are struck down harshly, without any effort at salvaging some measure of our experience."[31]

Albee stages Mrs. Barker's entrance as a parody of etiquette and social discourse. Mrs. Barker (often referred to as "they") introduces herself only to witness Daddy's comically repetitious forgetfulness. Albee exaggerates social awkwardness moments after her entrance, first by having Daddy announce the unexpected – "Now that you're here, I don't suppose you could go away and maybe come back some other time" (1: 112) – and then by having Mrs. Barker make herself too much at home:

> MOMMY: … Are you sure you're comfortable? Won't you take off your dress?
> MRS. BARKER: I don't mind if I do. (*She removes her dress*).
> MOMMY: There. You must feel a great deal more comfortable.
> MRS. BARKER: Well, I certainly *look* a great deal more comfortable.
> DADDY: I'm going to blush and giggle.
> MOMMY: Daddy's going to blush and giggle.
> MRS. BARKER: (*Pulling the hem of her slip above her knees*): You're lucky to have such a man for a husband.
> MOMMY: Oh, don't I know it!
> DADDY: I just blushed and giggled and went sticky wet. (1: 114–115)

Throughout *The American Dream*, Albee employs this kind of dialogue, the overstated or unexpected outbursts underscoring the pettiness of the characters' lives, the smallness of vision, the ludicrousness of a world filled with empty platitudes. The overall image is one of social and spiritual entropy. Individuals are reduced to caricatures. Mommy and Daddy's directing force in life is monetary satisfaction, a goal attainable because of their belief in the myth of the American Dream. Their innocence long ago corrupted, however, Mommy and Daddy again at the play's close place their faith in a consumerist America which can deliver happiness and fulfillment through Mrs. Barker, the Bye-Bye Adoption Service agent who delivered their first son two decades earlier. That Mommy and Daddy respond exactly the same way to Mrs. Barker twenty years later highlights the stasis of their world, the lack of any intellectual or moral growth.

In this satire, Albee concentrates on Mommy and Daddy's relationship. The power of love which Jerry tried to understand in *The Zoo Story* vanishes in this play. Love never enters in Mommy and Daddy's non-marriage. At first they reduced love to the merely physical: "I have a right to live off of you because I married you, and because I used to let you get on top of me and bump your uglies" (1: 106). Presently, even sexual intercourse seems beyond possibility, Daddy's impotence objectifying the physical separation of man and wife. But their physical separateness is simply emblematic of their spiritual aridity, which, perhaps because he too was an adopted child, the young Albee saw as an ubiquitous condition in American culture. Most discernible by its absence, love collapses under the pressure of Mommy's domination and Daddy's acquiescence, with hatred and indifference filling the vacant spaces. Like Mommy in *The Sandbox*, Mommy is the badgering manipulative female, the controller and castrator of a defenseless and emasculated Daddy. And Daddy is one of several Albee male characters who earn Mommy's wrath, in part because his primary social and personal strategy is one of withdrawal, non-engagement, his path-of-least-resistance attitude leading toward isolation and an ossified spirit. Daddy embraces a sense of Nothing by leading a death-in-life existence: he just wants "to get everything over with" (70). Thus in *The American Dream*, Albee exposes the inertia paralyzing this family. This is Albee's staging of the absurdist apprehension of human experience, what Susan Sontag deems "the prototypically modern revelation: a negative epiphany."[32]

Grandma is the one source of vitality in the play. Alive, articulate, Grandma neither participates in nor is entrapped by the absurdism of the dialogue. Her observations are accurate, free from the banalities of the others. Dignified though treated with disrespect, clear-sighted though elderly, Grandma represents for the author the singular source of caring, an admittedly sentimental character based on Albee's grandmother, one harkening back to an era supposedly closer to innocence. She neither acquiesces to ridicule nor makes excuse for herself. She understands and accepts her condition, her eighty-six years of experience creating an adaptability in the midst of verbal indignities.

Mommy and Daddy, living in a self-created world of diminished possibilities, are so absorbed with material "satisfaction" and external façades that even the slightest awareness of public responsibility appears to be beyond their ken. But Grandma is unique in her capacity to remain apart from the deadening conformity which renders the others deflated types; she is a saving remnant from the past who accepts an objective reality that surely would be a source of dissatisfaction to her relatives: "My sacks are empty, the fluid in my eyeballs is all caked on the inside edges, my spine is made of sugar candy, I breathe ice; but you don't hear me complain. Nobody hears old people complain because people think that's all old people do. And *that's* because old people are gnarled and sagged and twisted into the shape of a complaint (*Signs off*)" (1: 117). Albee counterbalances Grandma's acceptance of the self and humanity with Mommy and Daddy's rejection of their first child. After buying the baby twenty years ago through Mrs. Barker's agency, Mommy and Daddy watched in disbelief as their boy failed to grow into their own version of the American Dream.

Albee intensifies the absurdist dialogue by juxtaposing the appalling account of the dismemberment of their child with Grandma's matter-of-fact recollection:

> GRANDMA: But that was only the beginning. Then it turned out it only had eyes for its Daddy.
> MRS. BARKER: For its Daddy! Why, any self-respecting woman would have gouged those eyes right out of its head.
> GRANDMA: Well, she did. That's exactly what she did. [...] But *then*, it began to develop an interest in its you-know-what.
> MRS. BARKER: In its you-know-what! Well! I hope they cut its hand off at the wrists!
> GRANDMA: Well, yes, they did that eventually. But first, they cut off its you-know-what.
> MRS. BARKER: A much better idea!
> GRANDMA: That's what they thought. But after they cut off its you-know-what, it *still* put its hands under the covers, *looking* for its you-know-what. So, finally, they *had* to cut off its hands at the wrists.
> MRS. BARKER: Naturally!
> GRANDMA: And it was such a resentful bumble. Why, one day it called its Mommy a dirty name.
> MRS. BARKER: Well, I hope they cut its tongue out!
> GRANDMA: Of course. And then, as it got bigger, they found out all sorts of terrible things about it, like: it didn't have a head on its shoulders, it had no guts, it was spineless, its feet were made of clay ... just dreadful things. (1: 127–128)

The child did not produce satisfaction, refused to conform, so within the inverted logic of an absurdist act Mommy and Daddy mutilated the boy. Albee further calls into question the myth of the American Dream when he suggests that Mommy and Daddy's motivation for the physical and spiritual dismemberment stems from their measurement of humanity and fulfillment completely in financial terms. As Grandma reports: "Well, for the last straw, it finally up and died; and you can imagine how *that* made them feel, their having paid for it, and all. So, they called up the lady who sold them the bumble in the first place and told her to come right over to their apartment. They wanted satisfaction; they wanted their money back. That's what they wanted" (1: 129).

The appearance of the Young Man allows Mommy and Daddy the chance to reinvent their American Dream myth. As she did twenty years earlier, Mrs. Barker delivers the new version of a "bumble," a handsome walking symbol epitomizing the emptiness of Mommy and Daddy's values. Like his new parents he is nameless. Their namelessness is Albee's technique for diminishing their humanity; each is a human reduced to a functional type. A vain incarnation of a sterile culture, the young man admits he will "do almost anything for money" (109). A cartoonish figure, the Young Man boasts, "[I am] almost insultingly good-looking in a typically American way. Good profile, straight nose, honest eyes, wonderful smile" (1: 133).

Curiously, the Young Man possesses some of Grandma's self-awareness, a quality that becomes evident during his reminiscence of his twin brother, a reflective moment in which he discusses a favorite Albee theme – a sense of loss, a "fall from grace," an inability to love: "I no longer have the capacity to feel anything. I have no emotions. I have been drained, torn asunder ... disembowelled ... I am incomplete ... I can feel nothing" (1: 138–139). His account, of course, would serve as a perfect description of Mommy and Daddy, although they are incapable of such self-examination. Unlike Mommy and Daddy's first child, their second will survive because he is an actor, the perfectly pliable man, one able to don any social mask precisely because he is drained of all substance and individuality. His external attractiveness and internal spinelessness make him a suitable match for the unreal demands of Mommy and Daddy. In other words, he is the one who forces the audience to reassess what this particular family might nurture. Of course, on one level the Young Man succeeds: he brings Mommy and Daddy their most tangible form of fulfillment, material satisfaction. But the quickness with which he turns from self-awareness to mindlessness confirms the overwhelming lure of surface illusions. The last opportunity for spiritual regeneration is lost when Grandma leaves and the Young Man moves in. The somewhat curious portrait of the Young Man points to Albee's keen awareness of ambivalences. The playwright is drawn to the kind of lament the Young Man voices regarding the loss of love, his fall from grace; at the same time, Albee rejects those very cultural and personal attitudes which produce such defleshed persons as the Young Man and which produce spiritual dislocations, personal vacuity, and self-annihilating myths.

If much of the play's anger is directed toward the American family, much comes from autobiographical sources as well. Albee's own childhood accounts for part of the unsparing satire, as discussed in the chapter on *The Sandbox*. Such issues as rejection, abandonment, loss of love, misplaced values, and withdrawals from human commitment dominate the early plays. Perhaps Albee's homosexuality only added to the strained relations between uncaring parents and child and, in the plays, expresses itself through the animosity between the sexes. But, as noted in the preceding chapter, Albee did love his grandmother. She shared her love, an authentic care for the young Albee; the boy in turn regarded her as the one person in the family not corrupted by wealth, the one who represented a past whose values were not tainted. "I could communicate with her," Albee recalled. "She was at the end of it and I was at the beginning. So both of us were outside the ring."[33] Again, his feelings for Grandma Cotter explain his positive treatment of Grandma in both *The Sandbox* and *The American Dream*.

The American Dream, for some, seems somewhat dated today. Audiences are now accustomed to the outrageousness of absurdist images and techniques; the political and aesthetic richness of absurdism, while still compelling, has been so incorporated into public art and mass media that its shock value has dissipated somewhat. Historically, however, the play exerted a tremendous influence on American theater following its January 24, 1961 premiere at the York Playhouse in New York City, giving inspiration and added significance to Off-Broadway. The play was also an important work dramaturgically for a maturing playwright struggling to forge craft into art. Still, when well staged, *The American Dream* sparkles in the twenty-first century.

This play very much reflects the *zeitgeist* of its 1960 original production. Relationships are subordinated to social categories, and often these categories are used as psychological screens behind which the characters lose all sense of original thought or ethical purpose. The characters become mere extensions of the play's set design: they are objects, types living in a sterile apartment filled with gaudy furniture. But the ultimate force of the play lies not so much in its social critique as in its presentation of the enervated individual. If the characters in the play appear beyond redemption – and there is no epiphanic moment, no coming to consciousness that might pave the way for even the possibility of salvation – it is because Albee would like to alter the audience's perceptions about the self, the other, and the cultural milieu. *The American Dream* succeeds in presenting its universal theme, "a personal, private yowl" that "has something to do with the anguish of us all."[34] Albee continued in his next play, *Who's Afraid of Virginia Woolf?*, to explore the personal experience that precipitates a fundamental anguish within us, but with a success that surely exceeded his dramatic expectations.

Chapter 5

Challenging Broadway

Who's Afraid of Virginia Woolf?

> Love had a thousand shapes. There might be lovers whose gift it was
> to choose out the elements of things and place them together and so,
> giving them a wholeness not theirs in life, make some scene, or meeting
> of people (all now gone and separate), one of those globed compacted
> things over which thoughts linger, and love plays.
>
> – Virginia Woolf, To the Lighthouse

> Before they slept, they must fight; after they had fought, they would
> embrace. From that embrace, another life might be born. But first they
> must fight, as the dog fights with the vixen, in the heart of darkness, in
> fields of night.
>
> – Virginia Woolf, Between the Acts

Who's Afraid of Virginia Woolf? is Albee's most affirmative play. Given the
accusatorial narrative animating the play, calling this his most affirmative
work may seem a bit curious. After all, George and Martha, and Nick and
Honey, are characters who take delight in attacking others, in belittling those
whose self-interests differ from their own, and in betraying those whose conception of reality differs from their own. Irony and sarcasm are borne from
characters who increasingly obey compulsions they seek to resist. And those
compulsions have become so suffused within their language and action that
these characters have devolved, in the Beckettian sense, into habit, their routines anesthetizing their responses to the self, the other, and the culture they
inhabit. Moreover, after some three-and-a-half hours of bloodletting, many
in the audience point to the verbal and psychological assaults as evidence
that this is a drama whose negativity and ambiguity confirm the playwright's
essentially pessimistic stance. By the end of so many Albee plays, and especially *Who's Afraid of Virginia Woolf?*, these critics argue, a kind of nihilism
infiltrates the stage. Indeed, for many, an ungovernable Darwinism pushes
George and Martha as well as Nick and Honey onward, their shared lack of

clear purpose in their respective lives the only discernible certainty in a play filled with uncertainty.

On the surface, such a reading is understandable. George, a less than successful associate professor of History at a small New England college, and Martha, his wife, "seem to be having *some* sort of a ..." marital meltdown (1: 175). The daughter of the college's president, Martha is an angry, frustrated – and remarkably strong woman. George, a humanist whose private life and professional career have foundered, has become so preoccupied with history that he has, in effect, abrogated claims to self-reliance and has withdrawn from any real commitment to the self and the other. After a faculty party, Martha has invited Nick and Honey over for a night cap. Nick, a young biologist new to the college, emerges as a smug opportunist, a patronizing scientist who married, we discover, for money, not love. Honey, his wife, on the one hand, is a comedic airhead who provides much humor, and who also appears subjugated by her husband and endures his trivializing remarks throughout the evening. On the other hand, Honey, like Martha, harbors much frustration and, beyond that, is plagued by a sense of dread and terror. What first seems to be merely an obligatory brief, late-night visit turns into an all-night party in which George and Martha, and, in their own way, Nick and Honey, come to terms with their own troubled lives. And coming to terms, in this play, involves verbal insults, physical attacks, and, finally, a series of epiphanic moments in which their own fundamental conditions are laid bare. So it is not surprising that many regard this play as a quintessentially negative work.

Such a bleak assessment, however, does not really capture the spirit and resolutions that ultimately reveal themselves in *Who's Afraid of Virginia Woolf?*. Such spirit and resolutions may be best located in the final moments of the play. For here Albee shifts the texture of the action in the drama's denouement. After the intense exorcism scene in Act 3, and after Nick and Honey make their final exit, Albee fills the last four pages of the script with thirteen brief questions ("Martha: It was ...? You had to? George: (*Pause*) Yes." [1: 310]). The questions are first tactical, then personal, and finally metaphysical. Unmasked by their own actions, shorn of the fictional and dramatic world they have constructed this evening, George and Martha, and perhaps Nick and Honey, have just experienced a cathartic, purging moment – what Albee calls "the cleansing consciousness of death"[1] – and now recognize the importance of facing their lives without illusions. Faced with the alternative – abandonment, aloneness, loss, rejection, anger, and so on – George and Martha reformulate their own minimal but important society amongst themselves. The fragility of their sanity, of their marriage, of their very existences acknowledged, this couple reunites. Forgiveness is brokered. Mixing self-disclosure with self-awareness,

George and Martha recognize their sins of the past and are, perhaps, ready to live their lives without the illusions that have deformed their world for the past two decades. They will, Albee implies, work within their own freshly understood emotional speed limits to restore order, loyalty, and perhaps even love to their world. In brief, their language at play's end, I believe, privileges a grammar of new beginnings, however uncertain such new beginnings may prove to be.

Who's Afraid of Virginia Woolf? also signaled a new beginning for its author. Until this point Albee had staged his work abroad, in Germany, and in small Off-Broadway venues in New York City. However, Albee, Alan Schneider, the director, and Richard Barr and Clinton Wilder, the producers, decided to stage the play at Broadway's Billy Rose Theatre. Starring Arthur Hill and Uta Hagen as George and Martha, and George Grizzard and Melinda Dillon as Nick and Honey, the play, which premiered October 13, 1962, became an instant hit, bringing the still relatively underappreciated Albee from the margins to the very epicenter of the American stage. The play ran for some 664 shows before packed houses. Whether in praise or scorn, theatregoers responded. It was, many hoped, a play that demonstrated that Broadway – ever on the verge of financial collapse and increasingly becoming a showcase theater – could still be an initiating theater, where daring, fresh work could be staged before mainstream audiences. What was true, the critics felt, for O'Neill, Williams, and Miller, might be true for this new, iconoclastic playwright. Although Broadway, it turned out, would never return to the glory days of the earlier twentieth century – when it was the site for staging the best in new American drama – Albee succeeded with *Who's Afraid of Virginia Woolf?* in rekindling an excitement about the American theater. Suddenly the theater mattered again. When Albee published a slightly irreverent piece in the *New York Times* nine months before *Who's Afraid of Virginia Woolf?* premiered in which he called Broadway the true theater of the absurd because of its cultural production of and its preference for superficial work; when Albee found himself on the cover of *Newseek* magazine (then one of the more influential magazines in the United States) and traveling at the height of the Cold War to the Soviet Union with John Steinbeck and others; when the play was denied the Pulitzer Prize it so clearly deserved; and when he championed such unknown playwrights as Sam Shepard and Adrienne Kennedy, Albee was seen as the new anger artist, one whose moral seriousness and acerbic wit made him the one who surely would help revive the American stage.

And to a degree *Who's Afraid of Virginia Woolf?* did just that. It went on to win numerous awards and was widely taught at universities throughout the country. When the play was subsequently staged in various cities here and abroad, it was sometimes censored or even banned. Some psychologists used the play as a perfect "case study" for their patients undergoing marriage counseling. The movie version, starring Elizabeth Taylor and Richard Burton, became one of the most lucrative films of 1966 for Warner Brothers and garnered thirteen Oscar nominations that year. The play remains enormously popular, and if cultural tastes have shifted since its 1962 premiere so that its once-shocking language no longer seems nearly so, it still is regarded as one of the key works in American dramatic history. Albee's language opened the Broadway stage to a riposte that was as refreshing to 1962 audiences as was Williams's lyrical dialogues in *The Glass Menagerie* seventeen years earlier and as Mamet's street-wise dialogues were in *American Buffalo* thirteen years after. It is hardly surprising that some of the contemporary era's most talented actors and actresses – Richard Burton, Paul Eddington, Uta Hagen, Diana Rigg, Colleen Dewhurst, and Billie Whitelaw, to name a few – have poured themselves into *Who's Afraid of Virginia Woolf?*

With *Who's Afraid of Virginia Woolf?* Albee altered the aesthetic battleground of defining nationhood with a dissenting voice of genuine theatrical and cultural power. So beyond the clever naming of his characters – George and Martha supposedly being named after George and Martha Washington, the country's first First Family, and Nick being named after Nikita Khrushchev – lies a politicized cultural critique of a country that, for Albee, was in moral decline. It was, Albee also felt in 1962, a decline fueled in part by a refusal of a large number of Americans to look beyond the surface platitudes of the day and who fostered the banalization of national ideals and of Western civilization itself. And this is why, when reflecting on the script, it is important to consider George's telling "marrow" allusion.

Near play's end, George explains to a baffled Honey, "When you get down to bone, you haven't got all the way, yet. There's something inside the bone … the marrow … and that's what you gotta get at" (1: 292). The marrow allusion is significant, for it provides a key moment in the action, a controlled emotional high point for George, a revelatory emotional still point for the audience. Here George finally realizes what is necessary to save, not his marriage, but his and Martha's very existence: the son-myth deforming their world must be confronted and, against unfavorable odds, purged from their psyche. The marrow allusion signifies George's awareness that stripping away the illusion governing their lives is essential for their very being in the world. Such knowledge prepares the audience for the ambivalent resolutions established after three long acts. Beneath the play's playfully devastating gamesmanship and animosity lies the animating principle of genuine love which – sometimes unspeakably, sometimes ironically, always paradoxically – unites George and Martha.

George realizes that to excise the incubi haunting their psyches he must first emotionally prepare Martha for "total war" (1: 261) by externalizing the child-myth, which symbolically places us in the "marrow" or the essence of their relationship. Catharsis precedes spiritual regeneration. As Walter A. Davis perceptively observes, "Existentially and psychoanalytically, nothing can any longer be held in reserve. The self-conceptions and illusions that have protected each from the threat of psychic dissolution must be engaged."[2]

The very exorcizing process that liberates George and Martha prompts many critics to fault the play. Too sentimental, too indeterminate, the play's resolution for many produces hollow resonances. The exorcizing of the son-myth is hardly believable psychologically, and the tenuous reunion of George and Martha seems unearned. The emotional tension Albee constructs, other critics feel, collapses miserably from its own weight: the killing of the child and the denouement simply do not account for all the evening's dizzying events. "Coming after two acts of cascading turbulence," writes one reviewer, "this plot resolution is woefully inadequate and incongruous, rather like tracing the source of Niagara to a water pistol."[3] Shorn of their private fantasy, George and Martha emerge more as two infantile adults recovering from an evening of self-generated hysteria than as caring or conscious individuals. They survive, for Harold Bloom, "only to endure the endless repetition of drowning their breaths, in this harsh world, in order to go on telling their story." Bloom consigns George and Martha to shallow caricature figures whose histrionics reduce the play to little more than "a drama of impaling, of love gone rancid because of a metaphysical lack." After the exorcism, Bloom argues, George and Martha reduce themselves to near-nothingness. "George talks, ineffectually; Martha brays, ineffectually; that is their initial reality, when we come upon them. Martha barely talks, or is silent. George is almost equally monosyllabic, when we leave them. A silent or monosyllabic ineffectuality has replaced chattering and braying, both ineffectual. Nothing has happened, because nothing has changed, and so this couple will be rubbed down to rubbish in the end."[4]

However, the ending of *Who's Afraid of Virginia Woolf?* appears convincing in both performance and text when we see that it stages the re-visioning process Albee implies is necessary for his characters' spiritual aliveness. The tensions and asymmetries between George and Martha give way to rapprochement, rapprochement to relationship, and relationship to love. The threat of anomie yields to the hope of authentic engagement. The rhetorical gallantries and linguistic attacks are nowhere in evidence. These two connoisseurs of verbal dueling now communicate simply, directly, with no wasted emotion. Once so ennobled by their lexical inventiveness, by the very performativity of their performance, conferring upon an illusion the status of objective reality, George and Martha are brought to earth, not merely by sacrificing their son, but also by sacrificing the kind of language that so animates this evening's actions. The game-playing, for now, is over. In place of embellished repartee we hear a disjointed, splintered exchange, a duologue whose tonal quality emphasizes their re-entry into the here and now – and into the Real. Just as Virginia Woolf, in the third section of *To the Lighthouse* (1927), presents Lily asking a series of necessary questions, so Albee, in the third act, presents Martha asking vital questions, questions that hint at images of unity and resolution, however tentative they may be. The halting speech patterns, voiced with tenderness and love, confirm George and Martha's willingness to face their inadequacies honestly.

At the very end of the play, Albee presents a revelatory minimalist scene. After the tensions of the exorcism ease, Albee deploys a different kind of language. Structurally, the scene parallels the opening moments of the play with Martha's repeated question-asking. Whereas the opening questions were laced with sarcasm, gamesmanship, and anger, however, the closing inquiries are free from such nervous tensions. Earlier George and Martha reveled in questions that maimed. They are now more willing to ask difficult questions tenderly, questions geared toward restoring order and marriage. Anxiety and fear remain; but relationship replaces hatred, love overrides indifference. The very tone and language of their closing exchanges suggest their willingness, not to return to sanity or happiness, but to begin the complex process of confronting their essential selves honestly. The scene signifies the end of their shared fantasy, the compression of words underscoring their newfound perception. Before, they were pathologically obsessed with elevating an illusion constructed and sustained by words to the status of objective reality. Now the very nature of those words is markedly different: where once the vacant spaces were masked with a marvelously devastating language-war, now those vacancies are granted their presence, as insecurities are no longer concealed within linguistic ambushes. Personal inadequacies are now as accepted as they were once denied and then later exposed.

The play's closure affirms what Jerry in *The Zoo Story* discovered: "sometimes a person has to go a very long distance out of his way to come back a short distance correctly" (1: 21). The ending of *Who's Afraid of Virginia Woolf?* heralds in muted tones the first steps in living, in Jerry's words, "correctly." Albee resists over-sentimentalizing the ending by providing no guarantee of order, comprehension, or survival. Ambivalence prevails. And this is precisely why the play's resolution succeeds in theatrical terms: Albee concedes that the ever-real presence of human fallibility, mutability, the potency of self-annihilating myths lurk as destructive temptations. This explains, in part, the playwright's comment on O'Neill. *Who's Afraid of Virginia Woolf?*, Albee has said for nearly a half a century, stands as a response to *The Iceman Cometh* (1946), a response acknowledging that the abrogation of the self, of the will to being, is but a drink or fiction away. For O'Neill's heroes, illusions help. For Albee's, they destroy. Within *Who's Afraid of Virginia Woolf?*, as repressed desires give way to honest admissions, so denial gives way to acceptance.

An important feature of the play's ending, then, concerns the resilience of George and Martha's collective imagination to reconstruct reality by subordinating illusion to truth. Theirs is a recognition of the regenerative powers implicit in facing existence without what Henrik Ibsen in *The Wild Duck* calls "vital lies." Albee enjoys referring to the affirmative textures of his play, a play that challenges the sorts of illusions paralyzing the figures in *The Iceman Cometh*. "It's about going against the 'pipe-dreams.' After all, *Who's Afraid of Virginia Woolf?* just says have your pipe-dreams if you want to but realize you are kidding yourself."[5]

Before reaching any such insight, however, Albee leads his characters through a three-act structure that chronicles George and Martha's slow realization that their pipe-dream, their imaginary son, is "kidding" as well as killing them. Such recognition, though, comes only after two decades of fabricating and nurturing their child-illusion. Private mythology turns to public issue, however, early in Act 1, Martha's off-stage remarks to Honey about her son signaling an ominous shift in the marriage relationship and the psychodynamics of the games they play. The impact of Martha's revelation is immediately apparent not only in the dialogue but in the non-verbal language as well:

> HONEY: (*To George, brightly*) I didn't know until just a minute ago that you had a *son*.
> GEORGE: (*Wheeling, as if struck from behind*) WHAT? (1: 182–183)

Private game now jars with public façade, for this revelation, whether deliberately or inadvertently delivered by Martha, violates the rules of the game established a lifetime ago by this couple: to keep their son-myth discreet, private. Their secret history thus exposed, the "Fun and Games" of Act 1 turn more threatening, confusing, and problematic.

Albee decenters the audience. He deliberately leads them into a series of unknowns. What are we to make of George's Bergin Story? Is George the real subject of his (non?)fiction novel that Martha's father censors? Do George and Martha have a child? Indeed, he particularly generates a sense of mystery regarding the son, for George and Martha allude to him throughout the performance, obliquely at first, with greater specificity later, and often with a nervous tension. Not until the exorcism will the audience, with Nick and Honey, realize that the son is a fiction, a lie of the mind. What originally began as mere game playing, the lovers' fanciful construction of a symbolic child to substitute for a real child that they, for reasons never articulated in the play, could never have, has grown into a bizarre relationship on the verge of imploding from its own neuroses. When Martha confides to Honey, unwittingly perhaps, that they have a child, she breaks the unwritten codes of the game, forcing a confrontation regarding their grasp on objective reality. More than a social embarrassment – after all, what's so unusual about mentioning one's child? – Martha's announcing their son's existence signals, George realizes, that their private life has disintegrated into an unreal make-believe world. Distinctions between truth and illusion, and that relatively narrow space between the real and the imaginary, become blurred, not by the continual drinking, but by a psychotic reliance on – when it's convenient at least – fiction as truth. George's haunting monody about truth and illusion is more than a witty, sarcastic, or even ironic comment.

His many truth and illusion references shape some of the deeper epistemological dimensions of the play. The truth and illusion refrain also testifies to George's awareness of and commitment to sorting through the real and the imaginary (even though George, himself, cannot always do so clearly), and places his verbal attacks in a broader context. George confirms the point when the comic outburst shifts into a more tragic insight in a key passage that appears in the original production but which Albee, somewhat disappointingly, deleted when he revised the text for the well-received 2005 Broadway revival: "But you've taken a new tack, Martha, over the past couple of centuries … I don't mind your dirty underthings in public … well, I *do* mind … but you've moved bag and baggage into your own fantasy world now, and you've started playing variations on your own distortions, and, as a result …"[6] This moment crystallizes the dangers of their games and is as revealing to George as it is vital to Martha. As if coming out of a years-long drunken stupor, George gradually realizes, as booze, compromise, and passivity give way to sober insight, thought, and action, that he must shock Martha into some definitive awareness of her (and his) deteriorating state. George, like Albee himself, must become the anger artist. The implication is clear: Martha and George will descend deeper into their own form of madness if they do not relinquish their dependency on such illusions. So while it is helpful to view *Who's Afraid of Virginia Woolf?* through the truth and illusion binary, perhaps it is even more accurate to acknowledge the fluidity of the truth–illusion matrix; or, as Stephen J. Bottoms suggests, this is a play that "does not so much invert O'Neill's dichotomy [between truth and illusion] as dissolve it."[7]

Such fluidity, in part, comes from Albee's ongoing interest in presenting characters who are "imbalance[d]," who are "out of kilter." He feels his task as a playwright is to "represent what those imbalances are."[8] Hence Jerry raves throughout *The Zoo Story* (1959), Julian confesses that he was once institutionalized in *Tiny Alice* (1964), and Agnes in *A Delicate Balance* (1966) openly worries about being possessed by demons. Imbalances, even forms of madness, reveal themselves in selected later plays as well: the disturbed young woman in *Listening* (1976) slits her wrists, Himself in *The Man Who Had Three Arms* (1987) appears nearly insane throughout the play, and the "imbalances" infiltrate the action of *The Play About the Baby* (1998) and, in surprising ways, in *The Goat or, Who Is Sylvia?* (2002).

Albee inscribes the imbalances within the ostensible realism of the play's action and language, resulting in a gradual stripping away of structures of order, the façade of rationality. By Act 2 we have a sense of the characters' anger; but only in Act 3 do we comprehend the extent of George and Martha's psychic dislocations and share in the shock of recognition. What originally seems closer to anger and frustration shifts into a broader, more disarming range of human emotions. On one level their madness preserves their supposed sense of coherence and lucidity. Madness, for George and Martha, sanctions the birth and growth of the child, and provides the appropriate rationalizations needed to sustain the myth. Indeed, for years the child has fulfilled the couple. "He walked evenly between us," Martha says, "a hand out to each of us for what we could offer by way of support, affection, teaching, even love" (1: 297–298). Illusions, denials, and self-betrayals are the things used to reconstitute their previously arid world. However, the severity of their "imbalances" intensifies. Each act reflects the shift, the play's structure mirroring a disconcerting intensity: the "Fun and Games" of Act 1 build to the "Walpurgisnacht" of Act 2, and reaches a crescendo and coda in the "Exorcism" of Act 3. As the pressure of their myth reaches its critical mass, as rational analysis sparks additional marital skirmishes, George knows that they are at a crux moment in which the past, recollected in hostility, forces a calling of the question. George and Martha are not only at a turning point but a breaking point. They begin to realize the collusion, the disintegration of the self, the abrogation of responsibility, and the surrender of the spirit have pushed them too far.

George, at least, recognizes that, as he moves closer to self-awareness, another set of possibilities reveal themselves. He is not only a player-in-the-games but the author of the very rules of those games. Viewed as a metatheatrical character, George moves simultaneously from the consummate player of roles to the scripter of such roles, the director of the action, the producer of spectacle. He calls attention to the theatricality of his own theater: the parasol as gun scene; the games he orchestrates ("Hump the Hostess," "Get the Guests," and "Bringing Up Baby").

Above all, George *performs*. He first appears as the external observer of Martha's condition and then suddenly becomes an internal participant, a co-conspirator with Martha in their shared fantasies. *Who's Afraid of Virginia Woolf?* thus can be viewed as a Pirandellian work, a play whose words, gestures, absurdist moments, and epistemological questions transform much of the action – despite its surface realism – into an essentially metatheatrical experience. Like Pirandello, Genet, and Beckett before him, Albee embellishes selected scenes with a deliberate self-consciousness. At times the play calls attention to its own artificiality, deliberately making the spectator aware of the sheer theatricality of the play. George and Martha know that they are, at times, entertaining, acting, even using their guests for their own theatrical purposes. To paraphrase Martha, they rise to the occasion. At times the play calls attention to its own language while at the same time exposing the pure gamesmanship of that language. George and Martha know that they are performers performing before an audience within an audience – Nick and Honey as well as the actual theatergoer and reader. Part of the sheer playfulness of the play comes from the notion that, in certain scenes, the characters almost become different people.

Albee's Pirandellian textures function on at least two important levels. First, such textures invite the audience to question the nature of the Real. By calling attention to the very nature of theatricality, Albee experiments with the illusion of dramatic mimesis, challenging traditional responses to the theater. This is a play that suggests that, with his first foray into Broadway, Albee was eager to take aesthetic risks, to bedevil more conservative audiences with a bold language and experimentalism whose textures and models were more European than American. Soon after the play opened, Albee charged that "Broadway audiences are such placid cows," although his play succeeded in arousing even the more conservative members of the audience.[9] Second, like Pirandello's *Six Characters in Search of an Author* (1922), *Who's Afraid of Virginia Woolf?* invites the audience to break down, or at least minimize, the barrier between itself and the actors, thus creating a more intimate, and dangerous, theater experience. As Albee observed, "What really happened in *Virginia Woolf?* All the action took place in the *spectator*."[12] Despite the proscenium arch, and despite what emerges as the play's blatant theatricalism, Albee's voracious and clever script, and the play's claustrophobic set, generate an uneasy intimacy between actor and spectator. This is a play about those seeing and those seen. Albee scripts an aggressive text, testing the emotional limits of the actors and actresses, and expanding the boundaries of theater as collective, communal spectacle.

This is also the playwright's way of emotionally involving the audience as active participants. With its relentless verbal dueling, *Who's Afraid of Virginia*

Woolf? draws blood, directly immersing the spectator in its calculated violence. Albee subverts the authority of his script by casting the seers (the audience) into what is being seen (the performance). In rejecting the spectator's traditional role as voyeur, he succeeds in engaging the audience as concretely and as emotionally as possible. In this regard, Albee may be regarded as a leading proponent of using cruelty as a method of purging oneself of demons, of effecting a sense of catharsis, factors which seem germane to Artuad's "theatre of cruelty."

From early in Act 1 onward, most of George's social, psychological, and linguistic strategies center on one goal: exorcizing the son-illusion distorting their lives. Within this context George and Martha's brutalizing language, which escalates with each act, becomes a necessary dynamic as they negotiate and interrogate the highly contested interstices between truth and illusion, between performance and being. The final expiation of the illusion is made possible, then, by externalizing the lies governing their, and Nick and Honey's, relationship through the games – especially "Bringing Up Baby" – they play. In this house of games, however, conflict precedes resolution.

Who's Afraid of Virginia Woolf? stages a battle between the sexes, but Albee's real interest lies in presenting love as a unifying presence. Albee supplants the lack of compassion in *The Death of Bessie Smith* and the apathy in *The American Dream* with George and Martha's care and love. Love's opposite – indifference – is nowhere in evidence in *Who's Afraid of Virginia Woolf?* His dialogue mixes kindness and cruelty, what Jerry in *The Zoo Story* calls the "teaching emotion," making George and Martha's verbal clashes, for better and for worse, a felt element of their relationship. Thus George can describe his wife as a spoiled, self-indulgent, liquor-ridden woman, and Martha may counter with the fact that, "You see, George didn't have much … push … he wasn't particularly… aggressive. In fact he was sort of a … (*Spits the word at George's back*) … A FLOP! A great … big … fat … FLOP!" (1: 210). They are duelists who thrive off of individual and collective wizardry, shrewdness, and cleverness. Their wittily devastating repartee is borne out of a deep love for the other, a point they lose sight of but regain in Act 3. Hate precedes the restoration of love.

The last act, "The Exorcism," is to Albee's play what the final section, "The Lighthouse," is to Virginia Woolf's *To the Lighthouse*: the turning point as well as an overall image of resolution and unity. The ending of Woolf's novel focuses on Lily's coming to terms with her past as she embarks on a new life in her present world, a world that, despite death, reflects for Lily harmony and a wholeness. It is also fitting that *To the Lighthouse* was, for Woolf, an exorcism, a way for her to reckon with the anxieties she experienced in her personal dealings with her parents. It also seems fitting that Albee prepares both Martha and the audience for the kinds of questions on which Lily dwells near the end of *To the Lighthouse*. "Was there no safety? No learning by heart the ways of the world? No guide, no shelter, but all was miracle, and leaping from the pinnacle of a tower into the air? Could it be, even for elderly people, that this was life? – startling, unexpected, unknown?"[10] These are the kinds of questions Martha will ask herself, the kinds of inquiries borne of an awareness Albee would like to instill within the spectator as well. George and Martha will learn that there is no "safety," but in their journey to their own lighthouse, they will learn, as Lily did, to accept their lives without the past deforming their present.

The very title of Albee's drama is richly symbolic. Invoking the name of one the exemplary modernists of the twentieth century invites all sort of speculations, although Albee downplays the significance of her presence. Originally entitled *The Exorcism*, the play became *Who's Afraid of Virginia Woolf?* when, as Albee was working on a draft of the play months before its premiere, he remembered seeing, in the earlier 1950s, in a bar in the Village, some graffiti scrawled on the mirror, "Who's Afraid of Virginia Woolf?" He liked it and had his new title. However, beyond the supposed randomness of selecting his play's title looms the specter of Virginia Woolf. In her diaries, essays, and novels, as in her personal life, Woolf explored the gulf between the ideal and the real, and the attendant anxieties inscribed with the long shadow between. Albee did not compose his play with Virginia Woolf per se on his mind, and yet there is that conspicuous title. To dismiss the Virginia Woolf allusion is to risk not appreciating some of the deeper symbolic resonances within the play. Beyond the nursery rhyme tune of the "Mulberry Bush," whose words Albee replaces with the title of the play, remains Virginia Woolf. For Albee's is a play about those reckoning with a lifelong struggle against one's inner demons. It is equally a play about a Martha who can finally answer the question posed by the play's title by admitting, "I ... am ... George ... I am ..." (1: 311). Like her own fictionalized child, Martha fears being alone, abandoned, and, indeed, fears life itself to such an extent that she has constructed, with her husband, a complicated set of false illusions. Perhaps this is why the playwright has said, "And, of course, who's Afraid of Virginia Woolf means who's afraid of the *big bad wolf* ... who's afraid of living life without false illusions[?]."[11] The differences between Albee's and Woolf's works – in terms of language, subtlety, genre, identity politics, and psychology, are vast, yet certain links reveal themselves.

What is seen and how the real is knowable, the impending decline of civilization, the intermingling of lucidity and forms of madness, the fusion of new imaginative inventions, death and sexuality – these are just some of the issues to which both writers seem drawn. Perhaps the most compelling link between Woolf and Albee concerns their preoccupation with fear. Woolf's public art mirrored her private anxieties, and in *To the Lighthouse*, as elsewhere, she drew on such tensions while sculpting her narratives. As a child, she was fearful that the fire in her nursery might flame high enough to touch the walls in her room; in *To the Lighthouse* Cam fears the dancing shadows on the nursery wall; in *Who's Afraid of Virginia Woolf?* the fictional son as a child kept a toy bow and arrow under his bed, we are told, out of fear. In her autobiographical work, *Moments of Being*, Woolf reported that, to allay her child's fears at night, her mother would tell Woolf to think of beautiful distractions to get her mind off of the fire; in *To the Lighthouse* Mrs. Ramsey, the mother, does the same thing for Cam, the child. In *Who's Afraid of Virginia Woolf?*, Martha recalls how she comforted her boy from similar types of fear. Fear of the unknown, of psychic dark spaces, of living without psychological crutches – these fears paralyze George and Martha, although their ultimate awareness of such ubiquitous fear enables them to rise above its coercive influence.

Albee's awareness of and sensitivity to fear informs the exorcism of the play. Whether in praise or scorn, the exorcism that brings the play to a climax has been the source of much debate. It is also the source of the play's theatrical largeness. Throughout the play Albee challenges the audience's sense of logic and the nature of the Real. This subversion of audience perception reaches its apogee through the exorcism of the son-myth. Although after seeing the play the audience realizes that Albee has worked carefully to orchestrate what turns out to be the murdering of the son-myth, the audience has little or no clue that the child is anything but real. While seeing the play unwind, live, the audience finds itself caught, with Nick and Honey, in the crossfire, and the furthest thing from our minds is the notion that the child does not live. Until Nick's epiphanic moment of comprehension minutes before the play ends – "JESUS CHRIST I THINK I UNDERSTAND THIS!" (1: 307) – we are led to believe the son lives. Although there is undoubtedly something ambiguous about the status of the son throughout the play, he is mentioned moments into the play and will be referred to with growing frequency as each act develops. In the midst of the exorcism, Albee draws upon that very illusion to highlight the mixture of appearances and realities, and to keep the audience's sense of what is verifiable ambiguous, even mysterious. If the audience harbors doubts about the son's existence, such misgivings seemingly are laid to rest in Act 3. The meticulous recall of the child confirms his very being-in-the-world. Even a reluctant George concedes that "the one thing in this whole sinking world" that he is sure of is his "chromosomological partnership in the ... creation of our ... blond-eyed, blue-haired ... son" (1: 202). While surely some in the audience begin to suspect that the son cannot be real, others believe that the frequency with which George and Martha refer to their child reinforce the perception that the child lives. In effect Albee sets us up: he prepares us for an even greater emotional shock by emphasizing the presence of the illusion that, through the unexpected reversal and subsequent recognition, will explode before our gaze. Since the play is now so well-known, today many in the audience know going into the theater that the kid is but an illusion in much the way they know, now, that Godot will never come when seeing *Waiting for Godot*. However, in October 1962, when theatergoers were experiencing the play for the first time, there was, for many, a surprise when discovering that the child is but a lie of the mind. It's not unlike the surprise felt when one first realizes that the three women inhabiting the stage simultaneously in *Three Tall Women* are really one woman at three differing times of her life.

In Act 3 Albee explores the interstice generated by the truth and illusion matrix. Here the fictive son assumes a most real place within Martha's consciousness during the exorcism. She has a pathological obsession with her child, a fantasy conceived out of her fearful need twenty-one years before to fill a void in her marriage and her own existence. Psychologically dependent on her fantasy, she crosses a threshold, for her child does not merely occupy her thoughts – he possesses her, like some demon spirit. George knows this and, especially in the final act, sets his sights on banishing the son-myth.

George precipitates a ritualized form of expiation through the exorcism performance. Albee mediates much of the third act with a stylized process of expunging what at one time was an innocuous game that has now mutated into a pathological obsession. For Albee wishes the audience to associate the exorcism with the mythological history of past rites of cleansing demon spirits inhabiting individuals. Mythologically, an exorcism is a ceremony that attempts to dispel or frighten away demonic forces. Structurally, then, Act 3 plays counterpoint to the Walpurgisnacht of Act 2. In old German lore, St. Walburga, a British missionary, worked in an eighth-century convent that became one of the centers of civilization in Germany. She gave her name to Walpurgisnacht, the May Day festival in which witches reveled in an orgiastic, ritualized Sabbath on Brocken, the tallest peak in the Harz Mountains. These are rugged mountains that in St. Walburga's day were thickly forested. During "Walburga's Night," the witches' Sabbath, demon spirits are exorcized from villages and villagers by a rite in which a cacophony of loud noises, incense, and holy water are used to achieve purgation. The mysteriousness of all the religious and cultural connotations we bring to our understanding of the exorcism myth and ritual becomes an invisible force, part of the iconography of Albee's play. By invoking the rite of exorcism, Albee broadens the scope of his domestic drama: the sacredness of the unknown, the inscrutability of an existential terror become the mystical stage upon which George and Martha enact their fears. In Act 3 demon spirits are first confronted, then externalized through "Bringing Up Baby," and are finally frightened away by the exorcism itself.

In his influential study of myth and ritual, René Girard theorizes that sacrifice is essential if community order and harmony are to be restored. "Violence," Girard writes in *Violence and the Sacred*, "is the heart and the secret soul of the sacred."[12] Sacred violence in the form of a ritual sacrifice, suggests Girard, ultimately cleanses the community of violence. Girard develops a fascinating account concerning the relatedness of anthropology, classical tragedy, and Freud; and his ideas about the roles of violence, sacrifice, and the ways in which these forces influence community and spiritual vitality place the violence and exorcism we see in *Who's Afraid of Virginia Woolf?* in a positive context. George, by the third act, must come to terms with the sacred violence that he must unleash. Thus, as conductor of the exorcism, George first must provoke his wife, a point that critics often take as proof of the couple's viciousness and hatred for the other. But just the opposite is the case. To orchestrate the exorcism, George necessarily begins with an invocation to the inner demons released in Walpurgisnacht by enraging Martha to a psychological breaking point. He thereby can bring up the demons for an essentially religious reckoning. Hence his declaration of total war. The viciousness of their arguments is a key ingredient, as Girard might suggest, a method of exteriorizing the unconscious fear, the demons lurking within Martha's psyche.

George constructs a set of fictions to reorder reality. Confiding to Honey news that his son is dead, he initiates the exorcizing process. He discusses the need to "peel labels" (1: 291), a reference to stripping away the emotional attachments blocking Martha from accepting the death of their son. While he seems unsure of his exact procedure, he knows how far the peeling process must go: through the skin, bones, and to "the marrow" (1: 292). As George probes from the skin toward the marrow, so, Albee suggests, the aware individual must explore the various levels of perception, from the surface to the deeper levels of consciousness and experience. As part of the exorcism, George involves Nick and Honey in this performance within the performance, and throughout Albee balances the heaviness of the occasion with humorous moments, his method of blending wit and witchcraft, of defamiliarizing the gazing spectator. So it is that a mystified Honey, while in the throes of her own awakening and who may know more about what is transpiring this evening than she lets on, can back up George's outrageous story about his son's death: Yes, she lies, George devoured the Western Union telegram "crazy Billy" delivered, which bore the terrible news (1: 303). The directing force of the whole exorcism is a passionate involvement in the process itself: to get at the marrow means to bring up the baby, demystify the child, excise the illusion, and, perhaps, restore spiritual health. Playing the game by his rules, George guides Martha through the ritual, providing the objective corrective when needed, the loving assurance when necessary. The dramatic focus is on the depth and power of Martha's attachment to their myth, a child whose presence counterbalanced the absence within their marriage, whose very being was created out of a fear of unfulfillment, an existentialist experience of nothingness.

As George recites the Mass of the Dead, its polyphonic quality fills the theater. The contrapuntal structure of Martha's English side by side with George's Latin give the performance a musical texture. This stands as the emotional highpoint of the play, all of the verbal assaults leading to this moment of expiation, a cleansing intensified by George's religious plea for mercy evoked by his *Dies irae* allusion, the portion of the Requiem Mass that describes the judgment and is a prayer to Jesus for divine mercy. Apocalyptic in nature, at once a mixture of a penitential rite and secular plea, the exorcism ushers forth a host of mythical-religious associations. No wonder that, within the exorcism scenes, Albee's stage direction reads that there is a *"hint of communion"* in George and Martha's tender exchanges at play's end (1: 308). Albee, at least, feels that the exorcism is a cleansing, positive way to end his drama: "George and Martha end the play having exorcized some self-created demons and cut a way through all nonsense to try to make a relationship based on absolute reality. Strikes me as being a fairly affirmative conclusion to apply."[13]

The denouement of *Who's Afraid of Virginia Woolf?* suggests that the son-myth, for now, is nowhere in evidence. The *"hint of communion"* (1: 308) underpinning George and Martha's verbal and nonverbal communication implies the start of a loving armistice, a definitive change in their relationship to the self and the other. Albee's ending implies more than the reconciliation of husband and wife. It also implies that they can accept life, its ambiguity and flux included, without illusion. It signifies the vital shift from performance to being. In their resolution, they, and perhaps Nick and Honey, acknowledge the value of living authentically. The inconclusiveness of the play's closure, then, minimizes sentimentality while outlining some of Albee's larger concerns: the playwright provides no promise that their marriage will be redeemed, that the illusion is inexorably purged from their world. Uncertainties linger. Questions remain. Self-doubt continues. It remains to be seen if Nick will grow to be something other than a selfish opportunist who married for money and who patronizes his wife. It remains to be seen if Honey, who finally acknowledges her fear of childbirth, will be able to mature into a more independent woman. There seems to be more hope for George and Martha, as Albee presents the possibility for a truthful, loving renaissance for his heroes. Their new-tempered union will be measured in terms of their willingness to keep at bay their illusions.

There is in Albee's characters' often irreverent and hostile debates a fractured poetry, there is a nervous energy and a passion to the lives of those whose demons he stages. There is, toward the end of the drama, an intensity, a resonance, and a power which lift at least George and Martha (and, perhaps, Nick and Honey) above their illusions that have wreaked havoc in their personal lives. George and Martha are consummate performers, accomplished storytellers, masters of deceit who implicitly challenge the nature of the Real and hence the elaborate structures erected upon it. George and Martha clearly do not always agree with each other within the alienated environment which they inhabit, but they make important contact with the self and the other within the fictions which they deploy with such evident relish during this evening as if these constituted the real drama. Ultimately their over play-acting, their performances within performances, yield to an acceptance of the Real. Despite their intense fighting, George and Martha forgive, and in forgiving create the possibility for a sense of love to reassert itself.

In *Who's Afraid of Virginia Woolf?*, Albee allows his characters to confront their lives shorn of the bizarre fictions that inhabited their lives for so long. They face a problematic reality. Such realities, however, allow George and Martha to accept and, with acceptance, to love and, with love, to repair the ruins of their past. Through their long night's journey into day, they have come a very long distance out of their way to come back a short distance correctly. Again, they progress from performance to being. This is why Albee is a mythmaker who deconstructs myths, a storyteller aware of the coercive power of story. He is, like Tennessee Williams before him and Sam Shepard after, a poet of the theater who himself discovers poetry in the broken lives which are the subjects of his plays, and in the broken society which they inhabit. This is also why *Who's Afraid of Virginia Woolf?* is Albee's valediction forbidding mourning.

Tiny Alice

Having achieved an epochal Broadway debut with *Who's Afraid of Virginia Woolf?* and after a well-received adaptation of Carson McCullers's *The Ballad of the Sad Café* (1963), Albee demonstrated with *Tiny Alice* a refusal to compromise artistic instinct for box office revenue, an eagerness to take aesthetic risks, a delight in challenging an orthodox Broadway sensibility. With Alan Schneider directing Irene Worth and Sir John Gielgud in the lead roles, the play drew eager crowds. William Ritman's set – an ornate library in a mansion, complete with a replica of the castle, 38-foot-high walls, giant 17-by-7-foot doors, a 6-foot candelabra, and a phrenological head placed on a huge reading table – impressed audiences as they took their seats. Most felt that the excellent cast and set covered for a less than satisfying play, however. Not surprisingly, the reviews were as mixed as the play was mysterious.

Indeed, the play remains one of Albee's more baffling productions. By now, each new Albee work spawned divided loyalties, the Albeephobe's attack matched by the Albeephile's defense. *Tiny Alice*, which opened December 29, 1964 at New York City's Billy Rose Theatre, only intensified the critical debates. They play was so confusing that many asked Albee to explain the "obscure points in the play" in an author's note for the published text version. "I have decided against creating such a guide," responded Albee, "because I find – after reading the play over – that I share the view of even more people: that the play is quite clear" (1: 421).

However, in his opening remarks for a press conference Albee clearly and rather fully explained some of the mysteries of what he called a "metaphysical dream play":

> *Tiny Alice* is a fairly simple play, and not at all unclear, once you approach it on its own terms. The story is simply this:
>
> A lay brother, a man who would have become a priest except that he could not reconcile his idea of God with the God which men create in their own image, is sent by his superior to tie up loose ends of a business matter between the church and a wealthy woman. The lay brother becomes enmeshed in an environment which, at its core and shifting surface, contains all the elements which have confused and bothered him throughout his life: the relationship between sexual hysteria and religious ecstasy; the conflict between selflessness of service and the conspicuous splendor of martyrdom. The lay brother is brought to the point, finally, of having to accept what he had insisted he wanted … union with the abstraction, rather than [a] man-made image of it, its substitution. He is left with pure abstraction – whatever it be called: God, or Alice – and in the end, according to your faith, one of two things happens: either the abstraction personifies itself, is proved real, or the dying man, in the last necessary effort of self-delusion creates and believes in what he knows does not exist.
>
> It is, you see, a perfectly straightforward story, dealt with in terms of reality and illusion, symbol and actuality. It is the very simplicity of the play, I think, that has confused so many.[14]

Albee's remarks, while undoubtedly helpful, do not (nor should they) fully account for the events unfolding before the theatergoer.

Tiny Alice is a provocative, if not fully successful, examination of the role of truth and illusion, and the way in which truth and illusion influence the individual's religious convictions. The play concerns Julian, a lay brother who, upon his cardinal's orders, tries to finalize a multimillion-dollar donation to the church, which will be given by Miss Alice. She is beautiful – and happens to be the wealthiest woman on earth. He enters her house, a castle, only to find himself the object of a conspiracy: Lawyer, Butler, Miss Alice, even Cardinal, succeed in destroying Julian's faith in God. They convince him that he worships a denatured abstraction of God, not God himself. Julian's quest for meaning and his fear of the unknown leave him completely vulnerable to his antagonists' scheme, which culminates in Julian's marriage to Tiny Alice (not, as he thinks, to Miss Alice), yet another abstraction, a false deity who lives in the model of the castle. When Julian protests and threatens to thwart his enemies, the Lawyer shoots him. As he lies bleeding to death, he finally confronts an appalling reality: that he cannot rely on metaphysical abstractions; that he has been betrayed by his own faith; and that consciousness is pain.

The play's obscurity and mystery, its homosexual textures, and its indictment of the church sparked the critical jousting, as John Clum reminds us.[15] And the ruthlessness of the Lawyer and Butler, the seductiveness of Miss Alice, and the complicity of the Cardinal, forming an unholy assault on Julian only added to Albee's reputation as a social protester. However, once again Albee's real interest centers not so much on public crimes of business and of church as on private crimes of the heart. He raises broader epistemic issues than in the earlier plays, as staged through Julian's various struggles: the ambiguous tensions created through truth and illusion, abstract and concrete knowledge, the relationship between sexual ecstasy and religious celebration, and, of course, humankind's idea of God versus the reality of God. Even the model of the castle, an exact replica of the stage set, functions to objectify the complexity and mystery of the universe in which ambivalences are the norm.

On one level Julian seems an honorable man, one whose selfless devotion to God earns the audience's admiration; he performs all tasks dutifully, faithfully. Serving his fellowman and God fulfills Julian, as his directing force in life evolves around self-effacing gestures. Julian is an innocent, benevolent servant of God. He refuses to compromise his search for God, and is unwilling to embrace a false deity, even though he cannot fully certify his own faith. In certain respects Julian is – like Jerry in *The Zoo Story* and George in *Who's Afraid of Virginia Woolf?* – a truth seeker. This is why Mary E. Campbell sees Julian as one possessing "far fewer frailties than most of us mortals. Albee has formed him with marked success, for he is able to stand up to the considerable dramatic competition of his antagonists, and is personally a thoroughly admirable kind of man, courageous and good, sensitive and scrupulous both spiritually and intellectually."[16] Hence the image of Julian the kindhearted, one victimized by an evil conspiracy, an Everyman brutalized by the business-assacrament world of Miss Alice and cohorts.

On another level, however, Julian appears as an immature, naive fifty-year-old. He has withdrawn, Albee suggests, from the complex responsibilities that go with being an aware adult. Hiding behind the mask of the ministry becomes an unconscious social stratagem, a convenient method of evading reality, of avoiding confrontations with a secularized world in which people worship a representative of God more often than God himself. Sexually repressed and spiritually confused, Julian appears as a cosmic waif, befuddled by his belief in a God who is at once tangible and real, but who also seems unfathomable unless externalized in abstract, and therefore denatured, form. His adult life consists of a series of tactful evasions designed to confirm Christian mythology despite some disturbing possibilities: that such faith is verifiable only through corrupt secular agents and abstractions; that serving humanity is meaningless; that greed and money subvert the Cardinal and the church; that scorn undercuts humility; that the ultimate mysteries of the universe are better left mysteries; and that his own blood will ultimately "lubricate" the "great machinery" powering the Lawyer's schemes (1: 521). Julian's attitudes seem conspicuous when the viewer realizes that his words and deeds are largely cover-ups for a terribly insecure man transferring to the church all responsibility that goes with being a mature adult. Albee deleted the following telling line in *The Collected Plays of Edward Albee* edition used here, but I cite them now from the 1965 first edition of the play; ironically enough, Julian appears "dedicated to the reality of things, rather than their appearance"[17] but succumbs to the very symbols which he professes to renounce. Unable to reconcile himself "to the chasm between the nature of God and the use to which men put ... God," realizing he should worship "God the creator, not the God created by man" (1: 452), Julian retreats from living itself, using the church to absorb outside pressures and conveniently absolve him of responsibility. Thus he abrogates any individual power: "(*Quivering with intensity*) I WISH TO SERVE AND ... BE FORGOTTEN" (1: 504).

Julian leads a death-in-life existence. Like Charlie in *Seascape*, Julian chooses the path of lesser resistance regarding social encounters, shrugging off duty in the guise of decorum. "I will not ... I will not concern myself with ... all this" (1: 449) becomes one of his life's characteristic responses. But the Lawyer's verbal punch serves as a pitiful reminder of Julian's powerlessness: "You're quite right: bow your head, stop up your ears and do what you're told" (1: 450). More a mannequin subjugated to evil forces than a human being fighting with a sense of purpose, Julian is the indecisive man, conscious enough to discern the importance of one's capacity to distinguish clearly between truth and illusion but confused and frightened by sexual engagement and the ontological status of God. Julian lacks the moral courage to act definitively, to sort through the experiential thicket embodied within an outer world filled with duplicity and choice. Julian's greatest sin, we discover, concerns his withdrawal into an unreal world, an election to sequester himself within the confines of passive nonexperience. Living as if he were not present to the external world, he becomes a doll-like figure, suitable for imprisonment in the "*doll's-house*" (1: 437), Albee's description of the model of the castle. Innocence in Julian must be understood, then, not so much as naivety or freedom from evil corruption but as a betrayal of self, a collapse into unforgivable ignorance. "Innocence in a fifty year old man," Anita Marie Stenz correctly asserts, "can only be described as grotesque."[18]

Clearly Julian is no match for his adversaries. Lawyer and Butler view him as a mere object for their manipulation. They both know that Julian "is walking on the edge of an abyss" and "can be pushed ... over, back to the asylums" or "over ... to the Truth" (1: 494). Moreover, Lawyer and Butler display an awareness of human frailty and doubt, a point confirmed throughout *Tiny Alice* by their self-conscious playacting in which they often discuss man's self-fabricated "Gingerbread God with the raisin eyes" (1: 495). Shrewd and calculating, and probably realistic, Lawyer and Butler understand that for people like Julian, God becomes real when perceived as a prop or symbol, even though such emblematic reconstruction is an inadequate formulation of Him. This is why Lawyer argues: "The mouse. Believe it. Don't personify the abstraction, Julian, limit it, demean it. Only the mouse, the toy. And that does not exist ... but is all that can be worshipped... Cut off from it, Julian, ease yourself, ease off. No trouble now; accept it" (1: 495).

Unable to impose divine order on the messiness of human desire, Julian falls from grace. Lawyer and cohorts, supreme manufacturers of sin, accept the necessity of the scar; Julian cannot. Julian resists initiation into a noncloistered world because such a reality embodies modes of experience – temptation, free will, sexual intercourse, choice – which he cannot resolve and which he has sidestepped for years. As Lawyer bluntly explains:

> (*Sarcasm is gone; all is gone, save fact*) Dear Julian; we all serve, do we
> not? Each of us his own priesthood; publicly, some, others ... within
> only; but we all do – what's-his-name's special trumpet, or clear lonely
> bell. Predestination, fate, the will of God, accident ... All swirled up in

it, no matter what the name. And being man, we have invented choice, and have, indeed, gone further, and have catalogued the underpinnings of choice. But we do not know. Anything. End prologue. (1: 530)

Miss Alice appears as an evil conspirator, a sophistic temptress hastening Julian's fall. After all, she deceives and seduces the lay brother and is an accomplice to his murder. And yet she provides him with what Jerry in *The Zoo Story* calls "the teaching emotion." As she understands the mercurial nature of reality, so she accepts (and contributes to) its flaws. When Julian suggests that "we ... simplify our life ... as we grow older," she interjects the vital distinction: "But from understanding and acceptance; not from ... emptying ourselves" (1: 500). Within Albee's presentation Miss Alice counters Julian's habitual emptying patterns of withdrawal. He pontificates. She provides, Albee implies, a healthy dose of skepticism: "The history of the Church shows half its saints were martyrs, martyred either for the Church, or by it. The chronology is jammed with death-seekers and hysterics: the bloodbath to immortality, Julian. Joan was only one of the suicides" (1: 504).

Her seduction of Julian is part deception, part realism, the lovemaking symbolic of his reentry into truth, the "teaching emotion" concretized through the release of repressed sexual desires:

> Oh no, my little Julian, there are no games played here; this is for keeps, and in dead earnest. There *are* cruelties, for the insulation breeds a strange kind of voyeurism; and there is impatience, too, over the need to accomplish what should not be explained; and, at the end of it, a madness of sorts ... but a triumph. (1: 506)

Thus, on one hand Miss Alice performs her role as trickster. She deceives Julian into marrying, not herself – Miss Alice – but Alice, "the mouse in the model," the abstraction "that can be understood" (1: 495). On the other hand, she exerts a positive influence on Julian. Transforming religious celebration into sexual ecstasy through lovemaking, Julian – for the first time in years – participates in a *real* experience. Through Miss Alice he begins regenerating his spirit. Through Miss Alice he experiences the ontological difference between abstract and concrete knowledge. And after marriage, Julian *"is like a bubbling little boy"* (1: 516). The ambiguity of concrete truth paralyzes him. He enters into the most profound relationship of his life, only to discover that he has wedded a replica dwelling within the model of the castle, Tiny Alice. Since the model of the castle functions as a microcosm of Miss Alice's castle and, by extension, of the outer world, Tiny Alice becomes as real as anything else within the inverted logic of the play. Miss Alice is a surrogate, an agent consummating Julian's marriage to Tiny Alice. In the midst of kind of epistemological vertigo,

Julian short-circuits his rational faculties to fit the demands of external reality: as people accept their faith in God as reality, so Julian must accept as reality his faith in Tiny Alice. The constant role-playing of Lawyer, Butler, and Miss Alice reinforces the point, undermining Julian's ability to identify what is morally defensible, what seems empirically conclusive. Even the Cardinal playacts, assuring Julian that the marriage to Tiny Alice is the real thing, which he must accept on faith since, as Julian protests, "THERE IS NOTHING THERE!" (1: 532). Pressed into the conspiracy, the Cardinal stutters, this is all "an act of faith" (1: 533).

By Act 3 Julian experiences an existentialist sense of absurdity and isolation. He rebels against the Nothingness, refuses "to be MOCKED" (1: 533). Albee again combines kindness and cruelty as the teaching emotion, as Julian's coming to consciousness is realized through death. Victimized by the unholy tricksters, Julian finally leaves his past life of dull waste and confronts his own being with clearer resolution. He passes from ignorance to awareness, incurring the penalty of perception: "Consciousness, then, is pain" (1: 542). Julian now comprehends, Albee implies, Camus's philosophy – "For everything begins with consciousness and nothing is worth anything except through it"[19] – although his newfound perception is born out of the negative epiphany.

Spiritually bereft and mortally wounded, Julian internalizes the concept of nonbeing. With finality the abstraction of death turns into a concrete presence. His closest death experience, he recalls in a stream-of-consciousness outpouring, occurred when he ripped his leg open on a piece of jagged iron. Now, bleeding from the Lawyer's gunshot, there will be no one to save him, no God to redeem him. With the light in the model fading and audible breathing and heartbeats filling the theater, Julian succumbs to his new secular faith. As an act of faith, a way to confirm the presence of a God, as a last pathetic gesture to believe in some divine presence, Julian accepts Tiny Alice as God: "I accept thee, Alice, for thou art come to me. God, Alice ... I accept thy will" (1: 548).

Tiny Alice is a dreamplay. Albee objectifies the ethical dilemmas and contradictions within Julian's subconscious. Albee stages the inner conflicts of Julian's psyche, dramatizing, as Thomas P. Adler suggests, "man's need for concretizing the abstract, for anthropomorphizing the Unknown."[20] Julian tries, without success, to establish his humanity by making the abstract concrete. His acceptance of Alice suggests he "believes in what he knows does not exist," as Albee explained.[21] Indeed, Albee suggests that the substitution of illusory props between the individual and the concreteness of human intercourse creates, like Robert Frost's walls, divisions between human beings. "What man needs," according to Sartre, "is to find himself again and to understand that nothing can save himself, not even valid proof of the existence of God."[22] *Tiny Alice*, first staged during the Holiday season, is Albee's image of what Saul Bellow calls "the spiritual profile of the U.S.A."[23] The final irony in *Tiny Alice* concerns Julian's finding himself again, but only within a universe whose mysteries define the inscrutability of God and the reality of death.

A Delicate Balance

In 1996, Albee remarked that *A Delicate Balance* concerns "the rigidity and ultimate paralysis which afflicts those who settle in too easily, waking up one day to discover all the choices they have avoided no longer give them any freedom of choice, and that what choices they do have left are beside the point" (2: 13–14). Thus many regard *A Delicate Balance* as Albee's most blatant staging of the existential predicament. He does not chart cataclysmic changes. Rather, he intimates the subtle shifts in human relationships, shifts from engagement to habit, from commitment to estrangement, from love to indifference. They play concerns the way in which "we submerge our truths and have our sunsets on untroubled waters" (2: 75), a pattern by now assuming a preeminent position within Albee's aesthetic. The plot's lack of action perfectly captures the spiritual inertia that has gradually ossified this family. Consciousness comes too late, it seems, for by the play's closure Agnes and Tobias's awareness reveals a Nothingness, a void, nil. Agnes acknowledges this sense of wasted opportunity: "Everything becomes ... too late, finally. You know it's going on ... up on the hill; you can see the dust, and hear the cries, and the steel ... but you wait; and time happens. When you *do* go, sword, shield ... finally ... there's nothing there ... save rust; bones; and the wind" (2: 118). Indeed, Albee discussed with me the sense of wasted opportunities within *A Delicate Balance*:

> Agnes says it in their third act of *A Delicate Balance* with the metaphor of the battle going on up the hill; that you wait and when you do go it's all over. People find out about their lives, too. What could be worse than ending your life with regret about what you haven't done and end up your entire life realizing that you haven't participated? What could be worse?[24]

A Delicate Balance, first performed at the Martin Beck Theatre, New York City, September 12, 1966, signaled Albee's return to critical favor after his disastrous adaptation of James Purdy's *Malcolm* in January of 1966. *A Delicate Balance* went on to capture a Pulitzer Prize, Albee's first (of three). The play concerns Agnes and Tobias, a couple nearing their sixties whose comfortable suburban life seems as well ordered as it is fulfilled. But Claire, Agnes's alcoholic sister who lives with the couple, Julia, their often-divorced daughter, and Harry and Edna, the family's best friends who move in because of their "terror," upset the complacent home. The unexpected and largely unwanted intrusions of these characters force Agnes and Tobias to reassess the nature of their love, their values, indeed their very existence. However, as the play closes, Albee ironically suggests that Agnes and Tobias willingly accept the failure of their own individual nerve; accept what essentially has developed into a death-in-life manner of living. Thus, *A Delicate Balance* presents a sense of aloneness in the midst of company, dread in the common, terror in the real. Moreover, the characters fail to salvage their lives in qualitative terms; at best Agnes and Tobias realize their condition too late. As Albee remarked, "But by the time Tobias is able to take a stand and make a choice and say 'yes, and come live with us,' the opportunity, the options have been removed from him. He can't do it ... and so the terror in the play is about waste, yes, waste."[25] The play largely concerns forms of waste, then: wasted marriages, familial relations, whole existences.

Each character struggles with some form of terror, a sense of dread repressed until Harry and Edna upset the delicate balance by admitting their fear:

> HARRY (*Looks at Edna*): I ... I don't know quite what happened then; we ... we were ... it was all very quiet, and we were all alone ... (*Edna begins to weep, quietly; Agnes notices, the others do not; Agnes does nothing*) ... and then ... nothing happened, but ... (*Edna is crying more openly now*) ... nothing at all happened, but
> EDNA (*Open weeping; loud*): WE GOT ... FRIGHTENED. (*Open sobbing; no one moves*)
> HARRY (*Quiet wonder, confusion*): We got scared.
> EDNA: (*Through her sobbing*): WE WERE ... FRIGHTENED.
> HARRY: There was nothing ... but we were very scared. (*Agnes comforts Edna, who is in free sobbing anguish. Claire lies slowly back on the floor*).
> EDNA: We ... were ... terrified.
> HARRY: We were scared. (*Silence; Agnes comforting Edna. Harry stock still. Quite innocent, almost childlike*). It was like being lost: very young again, with the dark, and lost. There was no ... thing ... to be ... frightened of, but ...
> EDNA: (*Tears; quiet hysteria*): WE WERE FRIGHTENED ... AND THERE WAS NOTHING. (2: 46)

The authenticity of Harry and Edna's confession seems vague yet felt, vague because they cannot concretize their uneasiness, felt because they are frightened about their very being in the world. William Barrett, in *What Is Existentialism?*, discusses Martin Heidegger's *Angst*, which correlates precisely with Harry and Edna's condition as well with Albee's overall thematic concerns in the play:

> Anxiety (*Angst*) is the fundamental feeling precisely because it is directed toward the world more plainly than any other feeling. Anxiety is indefinite: it is not about this or that object, we are simply anxious and we do not know about what; and when it is over, we have to say that "it was about nothing." This is what the psychoanalysts call free-floating anxiety; anxiety without any discoverable object ... What we are anxious about in such states, Heidegger tells us, is our very Being-in-the-world as such. That is why anxiety is more fundamental to human existence than fear. Fear is always definite; about this or that object in the world; but anxiety is directed toward our Being-in-the-world itself, with which every definite object, or thing, within the world is involved. Thus anxiety, more than any other feeling, discovers to us the world: i.e., brings us face to face with a world, to which we now sense ourselves to be in precarious relation.[26]

Harry and Edna's uninvited anxiety disturbs the characters' sense of well-being, forcing them to sense the precariousness of their being in the world. Harry and Edna's intrusion forces Tobias, for one, to question his Daddy-like apathy. As Barrett argues, "but in ordinary life we usually evade the condition: we try to transform this indefinite anxiety into a definite fear or worry about this or that particular object. Thus authentic anxiety disappears, in our banal existence ... a state in which man perpetually busies himself with diversions and distractions from himself and his own existence."[27] Barrett describes the banality of those – as T. S. Eliot writes in *Four Quartets* – "Distracted from distraction by distraction."[28] But Harry and Edna's terror undermines the flaccidity of Agnes and Tobias's family. "Anxiety," writes Barrett, "thus gives us the first clue to an authentic existence possible for the human person."[29] Their surprise invasion, like Elizabeth and Oscar's unexpected arrival in Sam and Jo's home in *The Lady from Dubuque*, triggers a consciousness that comes too late for Agnes and Tobias.

The anxiety and wasted potential embodied in *A Delicate Balance* surface through the self-government of the players. Claire seems the most honest, and perhaps the most perspicacious, character, despite her alcoholism. Her account of the horrors of her addiction, moreover, testifies to an honest awareness of her personal form of terror. Her vivid speech matches the intensity of Jerry's stories in *The Zoo Story*:

> Pretend you're very sick, Tobias, like you were with the stomach business, but pretend you feel your insides are all green, and stink, and mixed up, and your eyes hurt and you're half deaf and your brain keeps

turning off, and you've got peripheral neuritis and you can hardly walk and you hate. You hate with the same stinking sickness you feel your bowels have turned into ... yourself, and *everybody*. Hate, and, oh, God!! You want love, l-o-v-e, so badly – comfort and snuggling is what you really mean, of course – but you hate, and you notice – with a sort of detachment that amuses you, you think – That you're more like an animal every day ... you snarl, and *grab* for things, and hide things and forget where you hide them like not-very-bright dogs, and you wash less, prefer to *be* washed, and once or twice you've actually soiled your bed and laid in it because you can't get up ... pretend all that. No, you don't like that, Tobias? (2: 31)

Although Claire is an alcoholic, her often-accurate appraisals provide a healthy contrast to Tobias's wafflings, Harry and Edna's vagueness, Julia's childishness, and Agnes's orderliness.

Claire is direct. She can identify the most conspicuous absence in the family – the lack of love. Eloquently blunt, she gains the audience's attention, and perhaps admiration, by slicing through the irritating rhetorical gallantries of Agnes and the banal cackle of Tobias. Despite her frivolity and humor – the swimsuit story, her hamming with the accordion, the flippant one-liners – Claire seems disarmingly honest. Because "we live with our truths in the grassy bottom," Claire explains "we better develop gills" (2: 75). Her reference to gills suggests a way of adapting to and surviving a confusing reality. Though she will never sustain a meaningful relationship, Claire values engagement. But her awareness finally merely accentuates her own sense of loss; she is intelligent enough to pinpoint personal anxieties but lacks the wherewithal to change.

Her lack, an inability to use adaptive "gills," so pervades her life that she emerges as impotent as Julia or Tobias. Drinking neutralizes her impulse to live. She may be the least susceptible to the Hemingway-like dread, but what she gains through her purported resilience seems lost through the half-life she lives: she is one of "the walking wounded" (2: 110). Desiring love and companionship, she never enters into meaningful relationships, so, as Jerry from *The Zoo Story* laments, "What is gained is loss." Commitment to anything beyond a drink seems unmanageable. On one level her detachment from the others helps. "Sidelines! Good seats, right on the fifty-yard line, objective observer" (2: 61). Her role as objective observer gives her sufficient emotional distance from familial tensions. Seen from a different angle, however, her role also functions as a social buffer neatly preventing involvement in vital familial relationships. Claire exhibits no genuine pledge of commitment. Claire is the watcher watching the watchers watch. She seldom benefits from her disinterested interest, thus failing in the pragmatics of human communication, her insightful comment one moment negated by her subterfuge or by her lack of resolve the next.

While Claire is the uninvolved adult, Julia remains the thirty-six-year-old confused child. She is old enough to have ventured in and out of three (and probably four) marriages, yet young enough to demand, or need, parental pampering. Like Martha in *Who's Afraid of Virginia Woolf?*, Julia's troubled past emotionally cripples her present world. Seeking shelter in her childhood home, she returns to find that Harry and Edna have usurped her room, and their occupation is a mark of rejection to her. Throughout much of the play she appears in "*controlled hysteria*" (2: 50). In *A Delicate Balance*, a room of one's own will not soothe her psychic scars. Julia's old home, Anne Paolucci observes, becomes "a mirage, a long-lost dream, the dead past, and in choosing to return to it, Julia is merely aggravating her already serious emotional difficulties."[30] Her failed marriages only increase her emotional dependency on her parents. An inability to order her life forces the homecoming, an ill-fated effort to locate her identity.

Parental rejection exacerbates Julia's sense of abandonment. In her youth she felt neglected after the birth of Teddy, her brother. Immediately following Teddy's death she sensed an opportunity to regain her parents' recognition: she would come home, her skinned and bloodied knees a deliberate attempt to win back her parents' love. As a teenager, she continued the disturbing pattern. Exiled to boarding school, she skinned her knees in a different way, deliberately failing courses as a way to return to what she hoped would be a loving home. Now that she is an adult, the pattern remains. She dissolves her marriages, surely in part because of incompatibility, but also, perhaps because she still yearns subconsciously for her parents' love. While her tantrums are socially immature, her outbursts become more understandable once we realize their psychological underpinnings. She "strikes out at Tobias as the author of the soap opera her life has become," as M. Gilbert Porter writes,[31] because she has lost psychic balance through the years of feeling abandoned.

The familial tensions stretch Julia's already unstable condition to its limits. She endures Claire's snide remarks, stumbles at her parents' judgments, and breaks when Harry and Edna usurp her room:

> EDNA (*Calm*): You may lie down in *our* room, if you prefer.
> JULIA (*A trapped woman, surrounded*): *Your* room! (*To Agnes*): *Your* room? MINE!! (*Looks from one to another, sees only waiting faces*) MINE!! (2: 79)

Julia's room stands as a last symbolic connection with some vestige of security. The strangers occupying the room overwhelm her; the tonal quality of her language – she begins talking as a child would, calling for "Daddy" – is indicative of her psychic vertigo, her collapse of nerve. Home for emotional succor and replenishment, she discovers only additional rejection. At one point she appears trapped in the throes of a nervous breakdown:

> (*Julia appears in the archway, unseen by the others; her hair is wild, her face is tear-streaked; she carries Tobias' pistol, but not pointed; awkwardly and facing down*) Julia (*Solemnly and tearfully*): Get them out of here, Daddy, getthemoutofheregetthemoutofheregetthemoutof heregetthemoutofheregetthemoutofhere. (2: 87)

Her collapse only begets further wrath: Agnes wants her whipped because her daughter is an embarrassment to her family. She frightens Edna and Harry. Godmother Edna supplies the *coup de grâce* by slapping her. Reduced to a confused child, her terrifying fear of abandonment reconfirmed, Julia exits, shattered.

Agnes is the delicate balancer. She emerges as the one capable of pinpointing articulately the loss of will, the non-love, and takes on the responsibility of imposing some coherence within her family. Her strength of being stems from her ability to deal with raising and counseling Julia; with rescuing Claire from binges; with the death of her second child; with Tobias's capitulation to death-in-life existence. She concedes certain hubristic faults, although such flaws are products of leadership qualities:

> If I am a stickler on points of manners, timing tact – the graces, I almost
> blush to call them – it is simply that I am the one member of this ...
> reasonably happy family blessed and burdened with the ability to
> view a situation objectively while I am in it. [...] There *is* balance to
> be maintained, after all, though the rest of you teeter, unconcerned, or
> uncaring, *assuming* you're on level ground ... by divine right, I gather,
> though that is hardly so. And if I must be the fulcrum ... (2: 67)

She valiantly tries facing the facts of their all-too-human conditions. Rising above the indifference or perverse anger of the others, Agnes struggles to maintain the dynamics of her family. Her self-appointed generalship and inner strength stand out.

However, Agnes's effort to keep her family together ironically promotes the family's spiritual inertia. Maintaining a delicate balance within this play means sustaining an entropic present. Even the preciosity of her speech patterns – the highly mannered cadences – suggests not merely her method of preserving sanity by articulate sheer will but also her way of gaining the upper hand with others. Language, for Agnes, becomes a manipulative more than communicative vehicle. Virginia I. Perry points out that Agnes's language also correlates to the illusion of her well-being: "Verbal dexterity is Agnes' weapon against what she cannot understand, articulateness her mooring in the world."[32] Thus her social strategy evolves into a corrosive force as devastating as the withdrawals of Peter in *The Zoo Story* or Julian in *Tiny Alice* or the Son in *All Over*. Her maintenance generates stasis. Her attitudes and assumptions neatly preserve what Eliot in *Four Quartets* calls "the mental emptiness" paralyzing her family. Albee heightens the sense of waste in that Agnes seems intelligent enough to discern fundamental public issues and private tensions – but does nothing about them. Rather, Albee implies, she sells out to a cushioned bourgeois existence: "There are no mountains in my life ... nor chasms. It is a rolling, pleasant land ... verdant, my darling, thank you" (2: 23). She perceives terror, which ushers forth a moment of crux in her life, only to revert – through language – to the comfortable holding pattern characterizing her world. As Albee observes, "Agnes and Tobias in *A Delicate Balance* realize they can't handle the precipice."[33]

The exhilarating language of Albee's plays before *A Delicate Balance* often reflected a liberating force, a means by which the individual communicated meaning directly with another person. From *A Delicate Balance* onward, however, language tends to conceal rather than reveal, the splits between words, meanings, and deeds becoming noticeably larger. Thematically the language his characters invent not only defines but confines their very place within the world. Language entraps as much as it explains.

Albee demonstrates the extent to which language entraps through Tobias. Apparently, Tobias's material comforts blunt ambition, the luxury of servants and country clubs filling the vacant spaces created by his unwillingness to communicate with a sense of urgency or purpose. But he is not Albee's latest version of an emasculated Daddy figure, in part because the author develops his character more completely, but also because Tobias himself elects consciously to withdraw from the complex business of living. Like Charlie in *Seascape*, he is a victim of his self-imposed exile from commitment. Inertia, not strength of will, carries Tobias into his sixties. He wants his well-ordered world untroubled so he can better nurture the calm civility of his home, the illusion of his love.

Two important events psychically jolted Tobias: the deaths of the cat and of Teddy, his son. In the story of the cat, Tobias recalls his intense relationship with the animal and her lack of love. Somewhat like the narrator in Poe's "The Black Cat" (1843), Tobias became "*fixed* on" the animal, thus sealing her doom: "I had her *killed*!" (2: 39–40). And, like Poe's narrator, Tobias feels haunted by the cat's death. Symbolically, the story of the cat correlates to the lack of love in Tobias's world, for just as the cat responded indifferently to him, so Tobias responded indifferently to Agnes and Julia. Just as Julia tried winning her father's affection, so Tobias tried earning his cat's attention, unsuccessfully. In brief, he felt *"betrayed"* (2: 39) by the cat. The trauma of his relationship with the cat and her murder began his emotional withdrawal from human encounters.

If his marriage and prosperity helped Tobias's recovery, the death of Teddy soon after birth irrevocably plunged him into psychic imprisonment. His self-ordered celibacy for some thirty years signifies much more than sexual disinterest; it's the outward form of complete internal retreat from any risk taking, from any kind of significant human engagement. An affair with Claire immediately following his son's death does not fill the void; Julia obviously cannot replace Teddy; even Agnes cannot restore his physical or spiritual vitality. Rather than risk another loss he becomes remote, detached, a man whose "mind is conscious of nothing," to borrow Eliot's phrase.[34] A generation later Agnes recalls his descent into indifference:

> I think it was a year, when you spilled yourself on my belly, sir? "Please? Please, Tobias?" No, you wouldn't even say it out. I don't want another child, another loss. "Please? Please, Tobias?" And guiding you, *trying* to hold you in?
>
> TOBIAS (*Tortured*): Oh, Agnes! Please!
> AGNES: "Don't leave me then, like that. Not again, Tobias. Please? I can take care of it: we *won't* have another child, but please don't ... leave me like that." Such ... silent ... sad, disgusted ... love. (2: 101)

Unable to face another possible loss, Tobias enamels his emotions. Tobias contributes to the family's illusion of equilibrium simply by not being there; he fails in what Heidegger meant by *Dasein*, or the state of being fully present to one's place within the world. He is a total stranger, even to his own wife.

Harry and Edna ignite his awakening. Uncharacteristically vocal, Tobias accepts the terror his guests bring: "YOU BRING YOUR PLAGUE! YOU STAY WITH US! I DON'T WANT YOU HERE! I DON'T LOVE YOU! BUT BY GOD ... YOU STAY!! (2: 117). Such an awakening, however, does not lead to a definitive change. With Agnes, he realizes their lives have been wasted, and his climatic ravings near the play's end merely serve as a painful reminder of the wasted opportunities, of the emptiness of his life. When I worked with the legendary actor and writer, Joseph Chaikin, who directed *A Delicate Balance* at Seven Stages Theater in Atlanta in 2002, we worked carefully with the actors in rehearsal to capture precisely this sense of waste and emptiness. As Thomas P. Adler notes, " 'Too late' ... has been a recurrent refrain in" in the play.[35]

A positive reading of Agnes's closing speech might suggest the possibility of regeneration. Maybe Tobias and Agnes will, like George and Martha before them, live more honestly "when daylight comes again" (2: 122). A bleaker reading of the end, however, seems more in accord with Albee's world view. Both Agnes and Tobias have the chance to confront the illusions governing their world, Tobias's epiphanic litany at the end signaling a qualitative shift from an anesthetized stance to a state of aliveness. But they consciously choose to maintain the delicate balance which tragically preserves their vital lies.

Box and *Quotations from Chairman Mao Tse-Tung*

Box and *Quotations from Chairman Mao Tse-Tung*, a pair of companion plays "enmeshed," are still regarded as Albee's most experimental works. They emerge as pieces of verbal music, a partita, and invite audiences visually and aurally to enjoy, as Albee writes in the Introduction to the plays, "the dramatic experience without a preconception of what the nature of the dramatic experience should be" (2: 261). Preconceptions set aside, the audience, Albee hopes, will let the plays "wash over" people; the audience in turn works hard watching and listening this spectacle, for there is no plot, no communication or significant interaction between the characters, and any sense of realism or standard theatrical conventions are nowhere in evidence. The plays challenge precisely because Albee attempts to use musical forms to stage theater. In his "General Comments" prefatory section to the plays, Albee suggests that these works have a "musical structure – form and counterpoint." Always the grammarian, Albee also advises that through his precise use of "commas, periods, semicolons, colons, dashes and dots (as well as parenthetical stage directions)," we can better understand "the speech rhythms" (2: 270).[36]

Albee explains what he had in mind in staging *Box* and *Quotations from Chairman Mao Tse-Tung*. He discusses how important it is in his plays to have a "tragic sense of being alive" and how "All of my plays concern consciousness; people participating in their own lives; denial, refusal to do so. But I think each of my plays is about that central issue [consciousness]. Regarding *Quotations from Chairman Mao Tse-Tung*, he further explains:

> *Quotations from* is a fairly straight-forward play. It's about not listening. Nobody talks to anybody else in that play. The Long-Winded Lady talks to the minister who doesn't say anything and falls asleep while she's talking. Nobody hears what anybody says. She goes on at some length and decides that nobody's hearing, nobody's listening, they're not even on the same stage. Chairman Mao is not on that boat. The old lady is not on that boat. They're all there – but they're not "there." There's absolutely no communication going on between the people. That's

one of the points of the play. It's very interesting – you stop listening to Chairman Mao, to what he says. I was Interested in contrast in that play; and in the particular kind of rhetoric of Chairman Mao; and the complexity of the language. The virtue of the acting edition of the play is that printed in the back is the Long-Winded Lady's speech entirely, all by itself. This helps in one's understanding of the play.

Albee then discusses his experiment, the opening and closing companion play, *Box*:

> *Box* is an experiment in isolation; making each person in the audience an Individual rather than part of the mass group. Reverse theater thrust, because theater is a community experience. At a movie, despite the crowd, you're always with yourself; at a play you're always with other people and are aware that you're part of the mass. I tried to reverse that procedure with *Box*. I didn't know I was doing it at the time, but I've since become aware of this.[37]

Theatergoers immediately experience the experiment in isolation, for after taking their seats at the Studio Arena Theatre in Buffalo, New York, on March 6, 1968, they saw only an open-ended cube constructed slightly incongruously. The same visually intriguing set was also deployed during the plays' New York City September 30, 1968 premiere at the same Broadway theater in which *Who's Afraid of Virginia Woolf?* was staged – the Billy Rose Theatre. The audience gazes into the cube, a cube that is perhaps Albee's allusion to the cubes serving a separated hotel rooms in Tennessee Williams's *The Night of the Iguana* (1961), whose characters are more isolated than they realize. A characterless play, *Box* commences with a woman's Voice from the back or side of the theater, very near the spectators. This is, Albee's opening stage direction announces, the Voice "*of a woman; not young, but not ancient, either: fiftyish. Neither a sharp, crone's voice, but not refined. A Middle Western farm woman's voice would be best*" (2: 263). Her five-page-long opening monologue, filled with moments of silence between her observations, varies from the banal – how well the cube is built and its ample size – to the more politically and poetically meaningful – the ways in which art is being downgraded and, later in the case of Chairman Mao, how art is used merely in the service of propaganda. Voice also alludes to the death of some 700 million babies, and the relationship between art and cultural order. Albee creates a powerful dialectic with the "tension and the tonic" (2: 265; 291), which contains more than a hint of T. S. Eliot's *The Hollow Men* (1925), whose figures are ineluctably caught "Between the idea/ And the reality." Voice laments corruption – the rupturing of art and culture in this post-apocalypse drama – and reflects that the individual must "cry from loss" (2: 265; 266; 298). Once again Albee limns allusions to animals, in this case, millions of birds flying just above the ocean's waves against the *"sound of bell bouys and sea gulls"* (2: 267; 299). If Albee alludes to Eliot, there is also more than a hint of O'Neill's *Long Day's Journey into Night* (1956) when he refers to the "sea-fog" (2: 266; 299). Voice utters several times in what becomes a haunting monody and one of the central subjects Albee explores, "When art begins to hurt, it's time to look around" (2: 265; 298).

As *Box* melds into *Quotations from Chairman Mao Tse-Tung,* the outline of the cube remains but now four characters appear on what Albee wants us to imagine is the deck of an ocean liner, bathed in bright sunlight. Present are two minor characters, the white-haired Minister, who stays in his deck chair, occasionally dozes off, and utters not a signal word during the entire show; and the Old Woman, whose lines are the recitation of a twenty-one-stanza poem by Will Carleton entitled "Over the Hill to the Poor-House" (1872). Of course standing is Chairman Mao Tse-Tung, who at the time of the play's premiere was the leader of communist China and who, in the play, drones on reading from his *Little Red Book* (1964), a volume widely distributed throughout China during the Cultural Revolution. Finally, if there is a protagonist to this play, it may be the Long-Winded Lady, sixty years old, who mainly stays in her deck chair.

Quotations from Chairman Mao Tse-Tung is a kind of anti-play. As Albee noted earlier, there is no meaningful communication between the characters, who often ignore each other – and whose self-absorption subverts traditional dramatic action. Interestingly, the Old Woman speaks only to the audience. Albee describes her as being shabby and quite poor. She has in her possession some fruit, some canned beans and meat, utensils, and she occasionally pulls an item out of her bag to eat. Although she recites the poem, it is clear that "Over the Hill to the Poor-House" provides a metanarrative of the Old Woman's life. The poem itself, while sentimental and largely forgotten in the twenty-first century, nonetheless garnered national attention for Will Carleton in the 1870s. The poem struck an albeit minor nerve with the public, as it captured something about selected public issues of a nation as reflected through the private anxieties of the individual – precisely the dialectic that Albee captures in *Box* and *Quotations from Chairman Mao Tse-Tung.* For Carleton's poem chronicles the plight of the elderly and those with alienated family members who abandon their kin. None of the Old Lady's six children take her into their homes. She remains as homeless as the speaker of the poem. The poem, then, has its corollary in such plays as *The Sand Box, The American Dream,* and so many other Albee dramas.

The Minister's role is minor. When not sleeping, he serves as a sounding board, Albee says, for the Long-Winded Lady. If she is a kind of confessor, then the Minister plays his role – not particularly well – within this confessional. The seventy-year-old Minister, we see, mainly busies himself with his matches, a pipe and pouch, his silence standing as perhaps a symbolic gesture of the church's ineffectual presence in a world with 700 million babies dead and a China that succeeds in pushing genuine art to margins of cultural *energia*.

Mao Tse-Tung, a polarizing figure in twentieth-century world history, appears reasonable, speaking to the audience in measured tones. "*He is not given to histrionics,*" Albee writes in the opening stage direction (2: 269). It is a curious demeanor for a communist leader who, many historians claim, is responsible for killing millions of people. As Baotong Gu, who was born and raised in China, observes, "the exact figure of the people who died in the Great Leap Forward alone is a matter of controversy, but researchers put that figure somewhere between 30–50 million."[38] For others, to be sure, he was responsible for ushering China into the modern era, but that march to modernity, others believe, also led to his killing of genuine art and culture. At first his lines engage but soon they become monotonous. As Albee mentioned earlier in this chapter, the audience soon tunes him out. His pronouncements are necessarily highly politicized: "In the final analysis, national struggle is a matter of class struggle. Among the whites in the United States it is only the reactionary ruling circles who oppress the black people" (2: 278). His attacks on imperialism and capitalism are as predictable as they are, in this play, flat and decidedly untheatrical. Still, to audiences seeing the premiere of these plays in 1968, Mao Tse-Tung was a loaded cultural figure to put on stage. After all, the Cold War was on, as was the Vietnam War, and it was to be another eight years before the communist leader died. The fear of communism was also at its height in the United States, even while in 1968 – the very year *Box* and *Quotations from Mao Tse-Tung* were staged – The Beatles' "Revolution" rocked with the lyrics, "But if you go carrying pictures of Chairman Mao, you ain't going to make it with anyone anyhow," John Lennon's voice bringing the leader into popular culture itself.

The Long-Winded Lady lines appear as fragments interjected throughout the action while Mao Tse-Tung continues discussing the socialist system, Marxism, and class struggle. Her "name" foreshadows the number of passages Albee gives her, for she goes on and on about her past and her own losses. As she bellows at one point, "ME! WHAT ABOUT ME!" (2: 287). At times she addresses the Minister; at other times she seems to be ruminating about her past to herself only. Isolation, lack of interaction dominate the action. Moreover, death and dying – especially in reference to her husband – are her main preoccupations. Recalling when she cupped her "hands around his lovely scrotum" while discussing the nearness of dying, she recounts her husband's "cruel" death by cancer (2: 287). Earlier she recounts a terrible car crash – the "carnage! Dead people and the wounded" (2: 276). We learn that she is estranged from her daughter. She also recalls falling overboard from an ocean liner, which may or may not have been a suicide attempt. Albee's writing the Long-Winded Lady's account of falling into the ocean is notable for its evocative power and attention to detail.

Throughout the plays, Voice periodically interjects telling commentary, such as "Nothing belongs" (2: 295) and, in the Reprise, brings these inventive works to a close by repeating "When arts begins to hurt," and a few moments later adding, "Then the corruption is complete" (2: 298–299). With millions of birds skimming over the ocean, with bell buoys and sea gulls all around, and with the sea-fog allusions returning, the lights slowly fade to black as the plays end. There certainly is no single way to interpret the ending, as the plays' multivalent conclusion invites the audience to participate emotionally in the dramatic experience in any variety of subjective ways. There is a sense, however, despite the overwhelming emphasis on "*loss*" (2: 298), that primordial Nature will endure and, with it, perhaps, art will be restored to its proper place within civilization.

If *Box* and *Quotations from Mao Tse-Tung* are performed infrequently today, they remain important plays within the Albee canon. Albee had just turned forty years old and continued to burnish his image as an iconoclastic dramatic innovator, one willing to explore the very ontological status of the theater itself in these interrelated plays. Commercial success was less important to him than making "some statement about the condition of 'man'" and making "some statement about the nature of the art form with which he is working. In both instances he must attempt change." Moreover, Albee writes in his Introduction to the plays, "the playwright must try to alter his society," and "since art must move, or wither – the playwright must try to alter the forms within which his precursors have had to work" (2: 261–262). Within such a context, these "enmeshed" plays work beautifully. Finally, these plays were also very much a product of the 1960s, where the daring, the experimental, the anti-establishment voices were defining part of the *zeitgeist* of that era. In *Box* and *Quotations from Mao Tse-Tung*, Albee was once again regarded as being on the cutting-edge of American drama, staging plays whose musicality and daring images animated the stage.

With these two plays to his credit, Albee closed out his impressive work of the 1960s. These plays were as robust as they were exciting. By the end of the 1960s, Albee was a force of nature, enhancing both his reputation and the American stage. However, as his career matured in the 1970s and 1980s, the public grew less satisfied with his dramas. The critics were increasingly hostile, some theatergoers actually fell asleep during some performances, and Albee, he admitted later, was drinking too much. Undaunted, Albee continued to experiment, to challenge, in what were to be, to paraphrase William Faulkner, some of his greater failures.

Chapter 6

"The greatest sin in living is doing it badly – stupidly, or as if you weren't really alive"

All Over

After *Breakfast at Tiffany's* (1966), a musical based on Truman Capote's book, *Everything in the Garden* (1968), an adaptation of Giles Cooper's play, and the inventive companion plays, *Box* and *Quotations from Chairman Mao Tse-Tsung* (1968), Albee staged *All Over*, a play whose subject matter revolves around death, the essential event, and whose critical reception was, to put it charitably, decidedly mixed. The reality of death forms the shaping principle of the drama, which was first staged at the Martin Beck Theatre, New York City, on March 27, 1971. Albee's working title for the play was simply *Death*.[1] His real concern is not death, however, but the kinds of pressures death exerts on those still living. Albee reconnoiters a psychic terrain, as tempered by the dying man, of those remaining. Or as the playwright puts it, "*All Over* examines the dregs of a family during the deathwatch of its most important member" (2: 8). Thus *All Over* extends the author's absorption with individual and social responses toward death and dying. As the Long-Winded Lady put it in *Quotations from Chairman Mao Tse-Tung*, "Death is nothing; there … there *is* no death. There is only life and dying" (2: 286). Or to paraphrase Blanche DuBois from *A Streetcar Named Desire* (1947), death is easy; dying is the hard part.

In terms of story and plot, not much happens. All the characters congregate around a famous man who is dying, forming a socially awkward death watch. Social awkwardnesses stem from the various characters' psychohistories. Each character's past forms a subtle but important part of a larger whole; the play's real subject matter, it turns out, deals with the petty deceits and minor betrayals which, over the course of a lifetime, have grown into nothing less than a death-in-life pattern of existence. The play ends with the famous man's death, but Albee implies that it has been "all over" for the living characters for too long.

Elisabeth Kübler-Ross's theories influenced Albee while composing *All Over*. Her research on familial and cultural reactions to death, published two years before *All Over*, centers on the unique stresses both the living and the dying experience psychologically during the various stages of the dying process. Among her complex findings she voices a simple observation that could well serve, in dramatic terms, as Albee's point of departure: "The dying patient's problems come to an end, but the family's problems go on."[2] Albee's interest lies well beyond the dying man, for what strikes us most forcibly about the play is the other characters' problems and their responses, not so much toward the dying man, but toward themselves. Albee's concern, furthermore, is not with what happens, but why.

The "why" is revealed through the play's structure, set, and narrative. The action occurs in the dying man's paneled bed-sitting room in the foreground, and with a huge canopied bed in the back. The dying man, the most influential figure in the family, lies behind a hospital screen. His visual absence, paradoxically, defines his vital presence in the play, although he never utters a single word. Albee accentuates the reality of death by describing the dying man as if he were an octopus-like machine: "the body of the beast, the tentacles, electrical controls, recorders, modulators, breath and heart and brain waves, and the tubes!, in either arm and in the nostrils" (2: 308). Within this set Albee structures the dialogue so that each character's past history, always in relation to the dying man, is brought into relief, producing a composite image of mostly failed or frustrated relationships. This is a family united through the dying man, their gathering by necessity a civic as well as personal ritual of mourning and reminiscing, a cultural and private way to gain collective energy during the death vigil. But what emerges during the man's last two hours seems anything but unifying, for Albee presents familial schisms, disassociations, dissonances. Any mythic or regenerative powers implicit in such a family reunion become lost, the artificiality and tensions of the occasion rivaling the reality of death. Issues of adultery, rejections, and withdrawals surface as the individual existences of the characters intersect. Despite the tremendous influence the dying man apparently exerted throughout his life on those within his orbit, each character ultimately seems unwilling or incapable of celebrating anything external to the self. Their selfishness overshadows the dying man's predicament. Throughout *All Over*, Albee presents the tension of the situation, the strained psychodynamics between the characters, and, perhaps most importantly, the way in which each individual interprets reality only as it applies to his or her own personal opportunities. "It is a play about the excluding self," Christopher Bigsby points out, "about that rigorous egotism which Albee sees as lying at the heart of human interaction."[3]

Within *All Over* the egocentric interests of the characters so infiltrate their motives and language that such human values as love and compassion fade, become distant social forces. A special kind of death replaces such humanistic values: not the physical disintegration of body but the metaphysical dissolution of the individual spirit. The death-in-life motif, so prevalent in the early plays, continues in *All Over*, and the subsequent plays. Albee accentuates the deadness of the characters by denying them names; their namelessness, juxtaposed with their formidable egos, contributes to the audience's perception that each family member is alienated from the others.

The Son and the Daughter embody all the wasted potential Albee seems fixed on dramatizing. The Son, a Tobias-like figure, views his job as a convenient distraction, although he admits his uselessness within the firm and merely goes through the motions as "a way of getting through from ten to six, and avoiding all I know I'd be doing if I didn't have it ... (*Smiles a bit*) those demons of mine" (2: 336). Perhaps his father's dying evokes genuine grieving or honest reflection, but the Son's awareness of loss, like Agnes's in *A Delicate Balance*, comes too late. A variation of the emasculated Daddy-figure, the Son willingly accepts his anesthetizing routines. The Daughter complements her brother, as she appears similarly entrapped in her version of a death-in-life world. She differs from her brother in her pent-up rage and is closer in temperament to Julia of *A Delicate Balance*. The Daughter is the rejected, confused child venting her personal setbacks by verbally attacking, by projecting her inner anxieties on her mother – "You make me as sick as I make you" (2: 350) – and the Mistress. At the end of Act 1, after the Wife and the Mistress join forces in their berating of the Daughter, she screams repeatedly, "*You fucking bitches!*" (2: 331). This explains why one of her principal cares, as she admits to her brother, concerns how much guilt she can generate within those involved in this death watch. Embodiments of inertia and anger, the Son and the Daughter, the inheritors of the famous man's legacy, are fitting symbols of the play's death motif.

The Nurse, the Doctor, and the Best Friend, despite their well-meaning intentions, cannot counterbalance the egotism pervading *All Over*. For example, the Best Friend appears as impotent as the Son and as ineffectual as the Daughter, especially in light of the lurid events of his past – the affair with the Wife, how he contributed to his own wife's insanity – events signaling the start of his own forty-year pattern of calculated indifference. Clearly, then, a central theme of *All Over* concerns various kinds of loss, particularly the loss of love. The Mistress, throughout the drama, defines the differing ways in which loves loses its potency. On an obvious level she experienced physical losses of love: both her husbands died unexpectedly – one from a heart attack, the other from an automobile accident. The Mistress can also locate an equally devastating form of death, the symbolic passing away of love between two individuals, a betrayal prompting a willful enameling of the self from the other:

> It's when it happens calmly and in full command: the tiniest betrayal –
> nothing so calamitous as a lie held on to in the face of fact, or so
> niggling as a fantasy during the act of love, but in between – and it
> can be anything, or nearly nothing, except that it moves you back into
> yourself a little, the knowledge that all your sharing has been .... (2: 312)

To the Daughter, the Mistress is an opportunist, the conspiring temptress who has loved for greed and money. And surely Albee's naming her the Mistress conjures images of a sly seductress (at least when she was in her early thirties, the age she would have been when she first met her famous suitor). But her thirty-year liaison with the famous man is grounded on more than money or sexual fulfillment, as the Daughter and perhaps the Wife would have it. Rather, Albee presents the Mistress as a woman who, like the speaker in John Donne's seventeenth-century poem "Break of Day," values honest commitment and genuine love – even at the risk of social awkwardness. A wealthy woman long before meeting the famous man, she enters into a relationship out of desire, not need. She provides a corrective to the Daughter's unfounded reasons for their lifelong affair: "And I told your father I wanted nothing beyond his company ... *and* love. He agreed with me, you'll be distressed to know, said *you needed it*. So. I am not your platinum blonde with the chewing gum and the sequined dress" (2: 343). After seventy-one years of living, the Mistress has developed a sensibility that allows her to rise, with some grace, above the Daughter's derisive attacks. Despite her outward composure, however, the Mistress agonizes throughout the play, for the dying process of her lifemate, unlike the sudden death of her past husbands, forces her to confront and accept her greatest loss. She will carry on but fears her future will lack clarity; outer experience will lack focus, she concedes.

The Wife confirms the extent of loss permeating *All Over*. She, more than the others, experiences the lack of love. Reviewing her seven decades of living, she recalls the past when she and her husband connected "with talk and presence" (2: 314). The death watch, of course, reminds her of isolation, aloneness, the products of what has been essentially her non-marriage. Like Agnes in *A Delicate Balance*, she maintain the status quo – at the cost of living itself: "I've settled in to a life which is comfortable, interesting, and useful, and I contemplate no change" (2: 361). The spoils of practicing widowhood render the Wife incapable of changing the dismal patterns of her solitary world.

At the close of *All Over*, the Wife addresses both the incompleteness and complexity of her life and marriage. Moments before the famous man dies, the Mistress tries bolstering the Wife emotionally: "Shhhhhhhhh; be a rock" (2: 364). Whatever positive, strength-giving associations her reference to the rock provides pale in the face of the overwhelming reality of death, the finality of which certifies the Wife's loss of love. "*You* be; *you* be the rock," she firmly replies to her rival. "I've *been* one, for all the years; steady. It's profitless!" (2: 364). The image of the rock thus turns into a telling emblem for the Wife. The rock gives off merely the illusion of strength and rootedness; but, as the Wife now admits, the rock image refers to the rigidity and stasis of her existence. Realizing her whole life has been as static and deadened as a rock, she ends the play with an outpouring of years of frustration. With a felt sense of loss, she denies loving any of the others. Estranged from her husband for a generation, she confesses her care for the one on whom she has remained fixed: "I LOVE MY HUSBAND!!" (2: 365). Albee plainly dramatizes the intensity of her purging release of emotion and misery:

> (*It explodes from her, finally, all that has been pent up for thirty years. It is loud, broken by sobs and gulps of air; it is self-pitying and self-loathing; pain, and relief*) Because ... I'm ... unhappy. (*Pause*) Because ... I'm ... unhappy. (*Pause*) BECAUSE ... I'M ... UNHAPPY! (*A silence, as she regains control. Then she says it once more, almost conversational, but empty, flat*) Because I'm unhappy. (2: 366)

Until this outburst the Wife seems curiously accepting of those around her, her composure and rapprochement with the Mistress masking her terror. Her confession shatters the forced, artificial coherence cementing her world. More than defining personal vacancies, the Wife highlights the degree to which the family has certified their own losses through their self-serving interests:

> All we've done ... is think about ourselves. (*Pause*) There's no help for the dying. I suppose, Oh my; the burden. (*Pause*) What will become of *me* ... and *me* ... and *me*. (*Pause*) Well, we're the ones have got to go on. (*Pause*) Selfless love? I don't think so; we love to *be* loved, and when it's taken away ... then why *not* rage ... or pule. (*Pause*) All we've *done* is think about ourselves. Ultimately. (2: 365–366)

Perhaps the Wife's account of her aunt best captures the source of such egocentrism. Her aunt lived until the age of sixty-two, but "died when she was twenty-six – died in the heart, that is, or whatever portion of the brain controls the spirit" (2: 333). This is the surrender of the will, the deadening capitulation of one's vitality, a kind of spiritual malaise afflicting each character, in some cases for decades, in *All Over*.

Like Bessie in *The Death of Bessie Smith*, who is never seen in the play, the dying man never appears on stage in *All Over*. Yet like Bessie Smith, he asserts his presence throughout the play. His dying, ironically enough, gives definition to the others' lack of aliveness. Albee deliberately hides the famous man behind a screen, the symbolic separator of the dying patient from the living family members. The screen represents, for Albee as for Kübler-Ross, a disturbing cultural distancing response, a way to deny an unpleasant reality. The screen also reinforces the separation of man and wife, parent and child. Not once, for instance, do the Best Friend, the Son, the Daughter, the Wife, or the Mistress actually visit the dying man. Clearly the death watch ritual in this play never embodies authentic meaning for the characters; none gains any communal or individual energy or soothing. Each character has withdrawn from graspable human relationships and entered a dream world.

Albee reinforces the inactive spirit of the characters by having them exist as if they were partially anesthetized, living in a dream world. In text as in performance they often converse *"languorously"* (3) in Act 1; by Act 2 they are *"dozing,"* and *"exhaustion has overwhelmed them; even awake they seem to be in a dream state. What one says is not picked up at once by another"* (2: 335). Albee refers, in symbolic and dramatic terms, to a kind of dream world, a form of moral sleep which so appalled Thoreau and, closer to our time, Camus and Bellow. Such a relinquishment of the spirit is, for Albee, unacceptable. The playwright will rethink some of the broader thematic issues raised in *All Over* – the interplay of death, dying, and the manner of living – in his next and more optimistic work, *Seascape*.

Seascape

Albee's theater challenges those who, as the playwright has said, "turn off" to the complex business of living, who "don't stay fully awake" in relationships, who for various reasons choose not to immerse themselves in an "absolutely full, dangerous participation" in experience.[4] *Seascape* once again reflects those cultural and personal concerns to which Albee continually gravitates. In *Seascape* he explores three interwoven forces: animal nature, as imaged by the sea lizards Sarah and Leslie; human nature, as reflected by Nancy and Charlie; and the kind of existentialist imperative forged by the curious intermixing of the animal world with the human world. Originally titled *Life*, the play reconfirms Albee's ongoing battle to stage the various kinds of ethical problems with which his heroes struggle, whether they know it or not – or even care to know.

The design of *Seascape* seems simple enough. Nancy and Charlie are vacationing at the beach, where they have finished a picnic. They are relaxing, reminiscing, figuring out what they will do with their lives now that their children are grown and their own years are numbered. They give voice to different selves and motivations, but during their encounter with the sea lizards their purposes ultimately unite, fixing on a shared consciousness concerning, to go back to Jerry's words in *The Zoo Story*, "the way people exist with animals, and the way animals exist with each other, and with people too" (1: 34).

Charlie contends that they have "earned a little" rest from the hectic business of living (2: 375). Nancy, however, rejects this notion. In spite of their successful marriage, Charlie and Nancy, currently on the threshold of retirement, disagree on the way in which they will live out their remaining years. As in so many of his earlier plays, Albee again joins opposites as a method of producing dramatic tension. Charlie is passive and inert, Nancy active and alive. Charlie withdraws, Nancy engages. He resists, she persists. She acts as a kind of benevolent instructress, he the indifferent student. Charlie is tired of living, seems bereft of emotion, while Nancy is eager to investigate new terrain, willingly embracing change. Both clearly want to relax, but their interpretations of relaxation clash. Nancy craves to use their new free time by traveling along the world's shoreline as "seaside nomads" (2: 372), exploring the wondrous sights of the earth. For Nancy life becomes meaningful when one *lives* it. She may have, in her older age, slight physical handicaps, but she does not suffer from the disabling psychological wounds that paralyze so many Albee protagonists. Albee shows her exuberance, enthusiasm, and spiritual vitality: "I love the water, and I love the air, and the sand and the dunes and the beach grass, and the sunshine on all of it and the white clouds way off, and the sunsets and the noise that shells make in the waves and, oh, I love every bit of it, Charlie" (2: 372).

The first act presents Nancy's optimistic stance toward living, as the tonal quality of her language suggests. Unlike the tonal quality of language in, say, *Counting the Ways* and *Listening*, which seems so mannered that the act of viewing or reading often becomes difficult, the language in *Seascape* emanates (in selected scenes) a lighthearted, humorous quality. Nancy voices this quality. For example, as her rapture with travel dreams continues, she exclaims to her lethargic husband, "My God, Charlie: See Everything Twice!" (2: 375). Albee's point centers on portraying a wife concerned with her husband, with loving attempts to revitalize his spirit.

Charlie resists. He has to be pushed into adventure because, as he informs Nancy, "I don't want to travel from beach to beach, cliff to sand dune, see the races, count the flies" (2: 374). Retirement for Charlie means he can rest – and do nothing. He seems in many ways reminiscent of Peter in *The Zoo Story*, Daddy in *The American Dream*, Tobias in *A Delicate Balance*, and the Son in *All Over*, for Charlie also elects to withdraw from authentic engagement: "I'm happy ... doing ... nothing" (2: 374). More than retiring from work, Albee suggests, Charlie is retiring from life itself, his spiritual laziness a willful surrendering of self-freedom.

Charlie defends his position. Claiming that Nancy's adventurous spirit would lead to some illusion, he believes that there is comfort in nothing. After all, Charlie argues that he has been a good husband, and this is apparently true. He courted and loved Nancy, and fathered her children, just as she desired. By all accounts he has been faithful and forthright, the dependable provider and parent. From his point of view, Charlie has earned the right to do nothing. For him, the choice to withdraw suggests that the whole affair of traveling, of being alive like Nancy, is too bothersome. This is, we come to understand, his choice.

His attitude disturbs Nancy. They have not earned a little rest but, counters Nancy, "We've earned a little *life*, if you ask *me*" (2: 391). She appears determined to begin anew, in qualitative terms, their life together. Nancy advocates what for the author is an important tenet when voicing her desire to experience life as fully as possible. Specifically, she is aware of the finiteness of their existences: "We are *not* going to be around forever, Charlie, and you may *not* do nothing" (2: 374). Nancy's zest for living, her impulse to respond, may remind the audience of Henry James's Lambert Strether, who, in *The Ambassadors* (1903), confides to Bilham: "Live all you can; it's a mistake not to. It doesn't so much matter what you do in particular, so long as you have your life. If you haven't had that what *have* you had?"[5] Like Strether, Nancy feels her old age on a physical level but refuses to capitulate on a spiritual level; she too wishes to "live all you can." Because of her insight Nancy appears objectively open toward experience, and will try anything, as long as they remain engaged with the world. Her zest for living takes on a larger, more compelling dimension because her stance is not a product of philosophic intellection but emerges from her conviction to experience fully her surroundings. Even years ago when, just married, Charlie slipped into a period of psychological withdrawal from both Nancy and life itself, Nancy felt a driving impulse to live. As she said, "The deeper your inertia went, the more *I* felt alive" (2: 381).

Albee dramatizes Nancy's passion for life throughout the play. This is comically as well as seriously presented when Nancy catches Charlie speaking of their relationship in the past tense. Nancy ardently believes that they are having "a good life," not that, as Charlie sometimes states, they have "had a good life" (2: 389). For Nancy and Albee alike, it is more than semantic nitpicking. Rather, it points to a whole way of being. Charlie rationalizes, perhaps convincingly, that "it's a way of speaking!" but Nancy objects: "No! It's a way of thinking!" (2: 389). Nancy exclaims that they now have "two things!" left, namely, "ourselves and some time" (2: 390). Aware of the significance and precariousness of these two precious elements – the self and time – Nancy squares her hopes on experiencing qualitatively the world external to her self. She appears innately opposed to the Tobias-like acquiescence that can neutralize the individual's impulse to live.

In the midst of their conversation during the waning moments of Act 1, Nancy and Charlie encounter the two anthropomorphic, green-scaled sea lizards, Sarah and Leslie. At this point Albee begins accentuating Nancy's and Charlie's differing attitudes toward experience. He spotlights this difference by the couple's initial reaction to the sea lizards. Charlie panics, Nancy beckons. While he issues a call to arms – and brandishes a feeble stick – she gazes at the two creatures in celebratory awe. As the two imposing, curious sea lizards approach, Nancy takes peaceful command, assuming a submissive pose. Finally, Charlie takes heed, holding his fright in check.

What follows, as in so many Albee plays, is the interacting of two distinct yet clearly related worlds – here represented by the human world and the animal world. The reader or viewer has witnessed this technique of joining two contrasting worlds before in the encounter of Peter and Jerry in *The Zoo Story*; in the contrast of Grandma's earlier values versus the newer values of Mommy and Daddy in *The Sandbox* and *The American Dream*; and in the meeting of the secular and the religious in *Tiny Alice*. In *Seascape* the yoking together of the human world and the sea lizard world provides a clear definition of Albee's cultural interest: that love, sharing, and awareness are all necessary forces, forces to be integrated into one's inner reality if one is to live life honestly. But unlike some of Albee's earlier works, especially *All Over*, *Seascape* emphasizes the presence of love, sharing, and awareness. In *Seascape* the bringing together of opposites – humans and sea lizards – does not produce illusions, deceit, or hatred. And it does not produce a Pyrrhic victory in which consciousness is gained, but with such terrible losses – alienation, suicide, murder, death – that the value seems dubious. Rather, the joining of Nancy and Charlie's world with that of Sarah and Leslie's generates understanding, education, sharing, and love, perhaps at the cost of merely two bruised male egos.

Act 2 embodies the education of the characters. It starts simply enough, with Leslie and Sarah asking a barrage of questions ranging from the banal to the profound. As Charlie's fear and Nancy's confusion wear away, as Leslie's skepticism and Sarah's apprehension subside, the characters establish communication. As the difficulty of the questions increases, Nancy and Charlie fumble with imprecise explanations regarding birth and children, as when Nancy notes that humans keep their offspring for eighteen or twenty years because of familial love. Pressed to explain what love signifies, Nancy discusses human emotions to an impatient Leslie. The two humans struggle to elaborate and to educate their companions about human life, as their reliance on abstract concepts suggests. But abstractions do not adequately account for the richness and complexity of actual experience. A frustrated Charlie turns the tables on the sea lizards by asking them about their past. What follows ostensibly concerns the sea lizards' account of their courtship. Through their honest and humorous tale of courtship, however, Sarah and Leslie reveal very humanlike emotions: love, hate, anger, hurt, jealousy. Leslie fought to win Sarah's affection and this show of commitment forever united them. This memory emerges as a point of illumination. For now Leslie provides a graspable illustration of the emotions and the way in which they function. He succeeds in making the abstract concrete.

Of all their discussions, from prejudice and bigotry to aerodynamics and photography, one topic appears crucial to the play. Nancy and Charlie have been discussing tools, art, mortality, those qualities and things which separate man "from the brute beast" (2: 442), and again the concept of emotions, particularly love, surfaces. Charlie, miffed at Leslie's presence but wanting to show him the concrete reality of love, turns to Sarah. He pointedly asks what she would do if she lost Leslie. Her response:

> I'd … cry; I'd … I'd cry! I'd … I'd cry my eyes out! Oh … Leslie!
>
> LESLIE (*Trying to comfort Sarah*): It's all right, Sarah!
> SARAH: I want to go back; I don't want to stay here any more. (*Wailing*) I want to go *back*! (*Trying to break away*) I want to go *back*! (2: 444)

Here is Sarah's sudden experience of terror, her sense of aloneness, her understanding of the possibility of profound loss. The precariousness of her life with Leslie suddenly made real, Sarah is, for the first time, experiencing an awakening. Sarah's dread brings forth Leslie's emotions, and in the only violent scene in the play he attacks Charlie, the instinctive response to terror:

> LESLIE: You made her cry! (*Hit*)
> CHARLIE: STOP IT!
> LESLIE: I ought to tear you apart!
> CHARLIE: Oh my God! (*Leslie begins to choke Charlie, standing behind Charlie, his arms around Charlie's throat. It has a look of slow, massive inevitability, not fight and panic*). (2: 445)

While communicating (and fighting), the characters reveal one of Albee's basic concerns in *Seascape*, namely, the importance and process of evolution. For the playwright is clearly rendering what occurs, in part at least, when the species evolves into a higher form of life. "Like Arthur Miller's somewhat similar allegory, *The Creation of the World and Other Business*," observes

Christopher Bigsby, "*Seascape* is best regarded as a consciously naïve attempt to trace human imperfection to its source by unwinding the process of history and myth."[6] Sarah explains that their evolutionary process was caused by a sense of alienation. As with most complex growth patterns, Albee suggests, their evolution did not occur in an epiphanic moment but developed over a longer period of time, reflecting a gradual coming to consciousness. In Sarah's words, "It was a growing thing, nothing abrupt" (2: 436). This is not to suggest, however, that *Seascape* celebrates a naturalistic evolution, that it is simply a Darwinian piece dramatizing the advancement of the saurians. Rather, the impact of Sarah and Leslie's realization of their estrangement from their familiar environment radically altered their perceptions not only of place, but of themselves within their natural place. Although she finds it difficult to articulate, Sarah still persists in her efforts to define their "sense of not belonging," even over Leslie's objections:

> ... all of a sudden, everything ... down there ... was terribly ... interesting, I suppose; but what did it have to do with *us* any more?
>
> LESLIE: Don't Sarah.
> SARAH: And it wasn't ... comfortable any more. I mean, after all, you make your nest, and accept a whole ... array ... of things ... and ... we didn't feel we *belonged* there any more. And ... what were we going to do?! (2: 436–437)

Leslie and Sarah have experienced the divorce between man and his environment that Albert Camus described as the "feeling of absurdity."[7] They have been experientially forced to question the whole of their existence. Further, the passage illustrates Albee's deft interweaving of a serious subject within a lighthearted context. In spite of the humor permeating much of the play, the scene presents the characters as quite earnest because Albee stages the effects of alienation. But whereas in the earlier plays alienation typically begot more estrangement, even death, here it gives way to a sense of belonging, a sense of community. Even a stubborn Charlie begins lowering his defenses, becoming shy one moment, enthusiastic the next, all in an effort to understand the sea lizards' process of evolution.

The theme of evolution continues with Nancy and Charlie's explanations. Charlie, for example, reflects on the origins of humankind, linking the sea lizards' home with his own environment: "What do they call it ... the primordial soup? the glop? That heartbreaking second when it all got together, the sugars and the acids and the ultraviolets, and the next thing you knew there were tangerines and string quartets" (2: 437). Besides suggesting a mere biological interpretation of humankind's development, Charlie and Nancy also connect human evolution with the sea lizard's animal evolution: "Listen to this – there was a time when we *all* were down there, crawling around, and swimming and carrying on – remember how we read about it, Nancy?" (2: 438). The comments transcend a report of biological history, for they also operate on an archetypal level, unifying the animal world with the human world. As Charlie figuratively sums up to a skeptical Leslie and a fascinated Sarah, "It means that once upon a time you and I lived down there" (2: 438). Nancy carries on the discussion, saying that the primitive creatures of long ago necessarily evolved to a higher plane of existence because they were dissatisfied with their lives, just as Sarah and Leslie were not comfortable any more with theirs.

The reader or viewer, of course, sees the parallels between the worlds of the two couples. As Sarah voices her displeasure with their lizard life undersea, so Nancy voices her dissatisfaction with their human life on land. As the women are open and enthusiastic, the men are closed, skeptical. Both couples throughout the drama are upset by the loud jets that fly over the dunes. The two couples come to recognize and appreciate the similarities between their worlds, and through their questioning and answering they learn about much more than the biological origins and evolution of the species. In Albee's presentation they also learn about the evolution of the spirit.

The evolution of the spirit draws the two couples intimately together. Nancy and Charlie, and Sarah and Leslie not only play counterpoint to each other but also mirror each other. Sarah's confession that they "considered the pros and the cons. Making do down there or trying something else" (2: 437) directly mirrors Nancy's admission that her life with Charlie needs reevaluation too. If Leslie exemplifies brute bestiality, Charlie's actions at times reflect precisely such animalistic behavior. Like their sea lizard counterparts, the humans must try "something else" if their lives are to avoid the potential stagnation inherent in "resting" too much. What this means, Albee implies, is that they should immerse themselves in the shape and energy of experience itself.

In *A Delicate Balance*, Claire mentions the value of developing gills as a way of adapting to and surviving life. But for Claire and most others in *A Delicate Balance*, such evolutionary capability functions as a means of coping with a confusing, puckish reality. The subterfuges in *A Delicate Balance* are not present in *Seascape*. Here humankind's ability to evolve, to use "gills" when needed, becomes necessary if the individual is to grow. Charlie argues this very point when discussing the value of one's capacity to evolve:

> Mutate or perish. Let your tail drop off, change your spots, or maybe just your point of view. The dinosaurs knew a thing or two, but that was

about it ... great, enormous creatures, big as a diesel engine – (*To Leslie*) whatever that may be – leviathans! ... with a brain the size of a lichee nut; couldn't cope, couldn't figure it all out; went down. (2: 441)

One need not be a devout follower of Animal Studies to see Albee accentuate the connectedness of the humans and sea lizards when Charlie describes his boyhood immersions in the sea. Nancy even asks if he developed a fish-like form: "Gills, too?" (13). In one passage in the play Charlie lapses into a pleasurable recollection:

And I would go into the water, take two stones, as large as I could manage, swim out a bit, tread, look up one final time at the sky ... relax ... begin to go down. Oh, twenty feet, fifteen, soft landing without a sound, the white sand clouding up where your feet touch, and all around you ferns ... and lichen. You can stay down there so long! You can build it up, and last ... so long, enough for the sand to settle and the fish come back. And they do – come back – all sizes, some slowly, eyeing past; some streak, and you think for a moment they're larger than they are, sharks maybe, but they never are, and one stops being an intruder, finally – just one more object come to the bottom, or living thing, part of the undulation and the silence. It was very good. (2: 379)

As Sarah and Leslie explore the solid earth, so Charlie, years ago, explored the sea. In both contexts sea creatures and humans are "eyeing past" each other. Thematically, Charlie's recollection of his submersion into the water directly correlates to the obvious archetypal patterns embodied in *Seascape*.

Returning to the sea, archetypalists tell us, is one way for humankind to reestablish a rapport with the natural cycle. It also symbolizes our attempt to reestablish contact with our own psyche. As Carl Jung writes, "Water is no figure of speech, but a living symbol of the dark psyche."[8] Although as a boy Charlie could not intellectualize about his water experience, his account suggests that the immersion concretely placed him within his own dark psyche. In Charlie's account living on the surface was equated with "breakers" and "a storm, or a high wind" – chaotic forces which affected his external world. But "to go way down" to the cove's bottom, living underneath the surface, was equated with solitude and calming silence. Seeking adventure and a comforting refuge, Charlie established an intuitive, sympathetic correspondence with his self and the underworld. Jung discusses the influence of this kind of immersion:

The unconscious is the psyche that reaches down from the daylight of mentality and morally lucid consciousness into the nervous system that for ages has been known as the "sympathetic." This … maintains the balance of life and, through the mysterious pathways of sympathetic excitation, not only gives us knowledge of the innermost life of other beings but also has an inner effect upon them.[9]

In his underwater experience, Charlie was privy to just this form of unique "knowledge of the innermost life." Thus, on an archetypal level, Charlie's submersion allowed him to be present to his inner self, his hidden self, as well as to the world external to himself – the ocean world. Charlie's archetypal water experience serves as a rite of passage, a form of initiation into a primordial setting that precedes any capacity to evolve. In Jung's words, "The descent into the depths always seems to precede the ascent."[10]

But where is Charlie's "ascent"? Apparently his psychic ascent came long after his physical surfacing. As a teenager, he came in touch with his inner psyche, but integrating the meaning of this experience is only achieved a lifetime later. In his unique encounter on the dunes, Charlie rekindles contact with the natural cycle and with his self. Leslie and Sarah, of course, represent that vital contact. They represent what Charlie and Nancy were eons ago. Thus, the random encounter of the two couples on the dunes symbolically reveals the connectedness of animal nature and human nature, the biological as well as spiritual kinship which exists, at least in this play, between beast and human.

The intermingling of the animal and human world in *Seascape*, finally, precipitates an existentialist imperative which has become a familiar trademark of any Albee play: the need to communicate authentically with the other. Through mutual communication the characters of *Seascape* evolve into what Jung calls a "higher consciousness."[11] In a state of higher consciousness, Nancy voices one of Albee's central concerns in the play, saying, "And I'm aware of my own mortality" (2: 442). Passing middle age, Nancy feels the nearness of death. For Charlie the nearness of death remains, like his childhood experience, distant. Only when Leslie nearly strangles him do Nancy's attitudes become tangible to Charlie. Through their collective experience the characters begin to understand and live with, in Albee's words, "the cleansing consciousness of death."[12] That is, the characters gain an acute awareness of the proximity of extinction, of the finiteness of their existence, which in turn creates the possibility for living life fully, as Nancy advocates throughout.

In spite of the evolving spirits of the characters, the mythical uniting of brute beast with civilized person, Albee does not formulate a purely fairy-tale ending: there is no guarantee that their lives will be substantially changed. Sarah, for example, shyly voices her concern surrounding evolution: "Is it … is it for the better?" and Charlie can only reply honestly: "I don't *know*" (2: 441). The tentativeness evident in Charlie's response, like George's "maybe" to Martha's questions at the close of *Who's Afraid of Virginia Woolf?* captures something of the precariousness of their newfound knowledge. But they discover that, with each other's compassion, they can help each other. As Leslie says in his play-closing line, "All right. Begin" (2: 448).

If the couples learn anything during the play, Albee suggests that it involves the recognition of and the need for involvement, engagement, and love at a consciously aware level. Through their explanations of their respective roles on earth, the couples come to view themselves in a larger context. If the seas lizards have much to learn about life on the surface, so, too, do the humans. Their shared struggles only highlights the fusing of the animal and human worlds. Nancy and Charlie realize that they are not better but are perhaps "more interesting" than animals (2: 442); that they are but a more-developed link on the physical and spiritual evolutionary chain. Albee implies that through the sweep and play of evolutionary patterns, humankind has transcended noble savagery and the instinctive response to nature, to become beings whose mentor increasingly is reason. Surely the power of reason, Albee would say, is useful, necessary; still, in *Seascape* the dominance of rational faculties poses a threat. The danger is that, with rationality triumphing over the instinctive, the primordial life-giving passions will dissipate, and, for Charlie at least, there will be no other source of vitality to replace them. Unless reason and the emotions exist in equipoise, more will be lost in the wonders of evolution than gained. Albee implies that evolved humanity will cease to feel deeply, or, continuing to feel at all, the individual may care only for the wrong things. Perhaps this is why Albee has called *Seascape* "triste."[13]

Seascape, which opened on January 26, 1975, at the Sam S. Shubert Theatre, New York City, and which won Albee his second Pulitzer Prize, represents Albee's persistent concern with dramatizing what may occur if the human spirit withers. Here Albee is not writing merely about the naturalistic evolution of the human species, but about growth patterns of humankind, about combining the visceral and the intellectual into a new whole – the consciously aware person.

Listening

In Ken Kesey's *One Flew Over the Cuckoo's Nest* (1962), Chief Bromden says of the narrative to come, "But it's the truth even if it didn't happen,"[14] an observation that could equally apply to Albee's *Listening*. For audiences listening to this radio play seek the truth within this drama in which events past and present may or may have not happened. Truth is an elusive force. We listen but are never fully sure of what precisely we are hearing. The radio play, with Albee himself speaking as the Voice, first aired on March 28, 1976, on BBC Radio Three in London. The play featured Irene Worth as The Woman, James Ray as The Man, and Maureen Anderman as The Girl. Albee directed the first staged version of the play at the Hartford Stage Company, Hartford, Connecticut, on January 28, 1977, starring Angela Lansbury as The Woman, William Prince as The Man, and Maureen Anderman as The Girl. Albee also directed the play in San Francisco in 1978 and at the Kennedy Center in Washington, D.C., in 1979. The play finally had its New York City premiere at the Signature Theatre on November 5, 1993. *Listening*, while receiving some positive reviews, drew mainly negative responses from the critics. In any event, the *One Flew Over the Cuckoo's Nest* allusion seems fitting, as this play, as Albee biographer Mel Gussow puts it, "is a mysterious, abstract colloquy among a cook, a therapist, and a catatonic young woman, who encounter one another at a fountain in the garden of an insane asylum."[15]

Listening emerges as a kind of dream scape. The drama, which Albee subtitles *A Chamber Play*, charts a brief encounter in twenty scenes (each announced by a taped Voice) between The Man, who seems to be a fifty-year-old cook at the asylum. The Woman, also fifty, who Albee calls the Nurse, is in charge of overseeing mentally disturbed and suicidal The Girl, who is about twenty-five years old. Albee constructs a fascinating stage, for there is a large fountain just above "*A great, semicircular wall.*" There is, too, "*a monster head in half relief, the spigot of the fountain emerging from the mouth,*" and two benches (2: 452). Given the title of the play, what strikes the audience or reader is how often the characters do not listen, do not pay attention, and are often more interested in their own versions of reality.

The Girl, especially, begs to be listened to, to be understood. Oscillating between a stupor and being hyper-alert, The Girl, we gradually learn, has been traumatized in the past: her family – grandmother, mother and father, sister, family dog, a possible boyfriend – came to visit her at the asylum, but she "sent them all packing" (2: 509). Albee implies the family has never returned. Further, her parents died; her husband abandoned her; and she murdered her own baby: "Took it by its ankles and bashed its head against the wall" (2: 494). Thus it is scarcely surprising that she is presently living in her own cuckoo's nest. She is sixty minutes from taking her own life. The Woman, her nurse, berates her in the present, calling her time and time again a "praying mantis" (2: 508). The Girl obsesses over some blue cardboard she has created, even getting into a fight with another woman who she thinks was trying to steal her cardboard but who was merely examining it. But there is not another woman. Albee told me nearly four decades ago that the other woman is actually The

Girl. This is The Girl, after all, who is savagely divided against herself. Hence when The Woman recalls the other woman, she is really recalling The Girl, who before being committed to the asylum, said, " 'Reality is too *little* for me' " (2: 492). Interestingly, Maureen Anderman, who played The Girl in the first two original productions of the play, asked Albee during rehearsals why The Girl fixates so much on the color blue. Albee told her she should dress in blue for the show, and when she asked why, the playwright responded "that blue represented the sky and freedom," the very things largely absent in The Girl's current life.[16] Living in a world of attenuated possibilities, The Girl insists it is best to "mistrust laughter" (2: 502); her response is understandable because in those rare moments when there is laughter in the play, it is more often than not of a nervous or sarcastic or even sinister kind. Further complicating matters, Albee continually subverts the authority of The Girl's – and The Man's and The Woman's – version of the Real. There are, in this play, multiple versions of actual experience, competing narratives whose authenticity Albee always calls into doubt. Hence The Girl's adamantine insistence that others need to pay attention to her emotional needs. They need to *listen*. The audience certainly listens, but we can never be sure of whose version of reality can be trusted, a predicament Albee will return to four years later in *The Lady from Dubuque.*

The Man appears as the kindest of the three characters. We eventually learn that a lifetime ago he and The Woman were lovers but that their relationship was "not destined to be one of the great romances" (2: 501), a point that has bothered the cook for much of his life. He still remembers, after performing oral sex on The Woman, that she rejected his further entreaties, a rejection he still remembers vividly – a notable point in a play where memory, desire, communication, and love are increasingly nowhere in evidence:

> I rose from the hot moist suffocating center of your etcetera ...
> I rose – to be exact – I rose my *face* from the hot moist etcetera of your whatchamacallit, and and I brought my face to your face – my hot and moist face – and I opened my mouth to say to you, but you must have thought I was going to kiss you, my mouth from your cunt become a cunt, a cunt descending on your mouth, *yours* on your mouth, you must have thought I was going to kiss you ... for you turned your face away. *(Long silence).* (2: 501)

And, Albee suggests, she turned away from the entire relationship with The Man. Albee eases the tension, however, as The Man and The Woman soon roar with laughter, which prompts The Girl to scream her "mistrust laughter!" lines (2: 502). We do not really learn much more about The Man, whose lines decrease as the play nears its end. A thinly sketched figure, The Man is more of a man – a minor character who mainly helps the others speak.

The Woman, while hardly Kesey's Nurse Ratched, emerges as a mean-spirited, selfish, and uncaring Nurse. Sometimes she is clearly play-acting. Other times she is reflective. But she is equally comfortable in controlling those who near her, often snapping her fingers at The Girl, who suddenly comes out of her stupor. Still, she has some of the philosophically most important lines in the play, observations that clearly outline Albee's central subjects in the play. While recalling her grandmother's suicide and her grandfather's disappearance (also another suicide?), The Woman remembers her grandmother telling her, " 'We don't have to live, you know, unless we wish to; the greatest sin, no matter what they *tell* you, the greatest sin in living is doing it badly – stupidly, or as if you weren't really alive ...' (2: 489). This is Albee's call to become an engaged and engaging citizen, to be aware of the force of consciousness. The Woman's lines once again spotlight, more broadly, a dimension of Albee's world view. The Woman near the end laments that she "cried" at key moments throughout her life – when her parents died, when her cats died, when someone first lied to her, when she experienced her first orgasm. An overwhelming sense of loss pervades her life. Hence "I cried when *I* ... died" (2: 513).

Albee brings this brief play to a startling close. In the fountain, The Girl slits her wrists. Her hands filled with blood, she commits suicide. The blood reinforces what The Man had said minutes before: "Blood is the color of pain!" (2: 514). Interestingly, The Woman – a nurse – does not try to save The Girl. Rather, she tells her in a gentle voice that her suicide is "Done beautifully. There *was* something, then" (2: 517). When I asked Albee to clarify the ending, he referred to The Woman's grandmother's words discussed earlier, "the greatest sin in living is doing badly, stupidly, or as if you weren't really alive" (2: 489), noting:

> One of the things that the Woman is trying to do here in the course
> of the play is to suggest and gently urge the Girl toward suicide which
> she finally makes; to suggest it to her. But she is also making a larger
> comment there, which is that there is absolutely no point in taking up
> space unless one is going to be completely alive while one is alive. As in
> most things, it's double.

When I asked why does The Girl slit her wrists, Albee's explanation helps us better understand the nature of the dramatic action in *Listening*:

> She wanted to. But she probably wanted permission to die for a very
> long time. I'm sure she's suicidal. I'm sure she has tried a number
> of other ways ... She does say at one time that reality is too little for

me, doesn't she? I think that her mental condition is such that she could never, never make an adjustment. And I think that the Nurse is probably doing to decide that her condition is such that she'd be better off if she would take her own life and make a positive statement by doing it and enjoying the experience. When the Nurse is talking about herself, it's really instructions to us.[17]

The suicide scene, according to Mel Gussow,

> is directly from Albee's life. Once, at a dinner party at Albee's foundation in Montauk, a young playwright suddenly brought his hands up from under the table, showing that he had just slit his wrists. Albee said, "Oh, that's the wrong way to do it. Let's go upstairs and fix that." He led the playwright from the room, stanched the bleeding, and calmed him down. Then they returned to the table, one of several occasions when Albee responded quickly to an emergency.[18]

Listening is, in brief, a beautifully composed drama, a dream scape that functions in a highly experimental and non-realistic mode. There are also echoes of T. S. Eliot in this play, a drama in which "death had undone so many."[19] It's not for nothing that the fountain in Albee's play is dry. There is once again a sense of loss that underpins a play that reminds us yet again about the importance of truly listening to the Self and the Other.

Counting the Ways: A Vaudeville

In another one of his explorations of marriage, Albee's *Counting the Ways* dramatizes He and She, a couple cast in a vaudevillian short play. Indeed, the piece is subtitled *A Vaudeville* – and the idea was for the play to run for about forty-five minutes in twenty-one brief scenes. Signs *"in the old vaudeville manner"* (2: 520) periodically appear very briefly, including numerous blackouts. "I think that it is sort of a vaudeville as a play," Albee once noted:

> There's a certain frippery, a certain openness, and it is a series of set turns. And the black outs in the play are used to end scenes. They begin other ones and they force the actor to instantly change time, to change age, and they are meant to jar the audience into a new awareness ... They change age, the characters change from scene to scene. Time is not sequential. It doesn't matter that the actors choose what age they want to be.[20]

Interestingly, Albee's grandfather, E. F. Albee, made a fortune thorough his co-ownership of one of the largest vaudeville theater chains in the United States, as Linda Ben-Zvi notes.[21]

The clear narratives of Albee's earlier works are not manifest in this vaudeville. There is no discernible plot. Albee has said that the ages of He and She may even change from scene to scene, yet there are no stage directions or lines to mark a shift in chronology. Albee explores the theme of love but in such a way that He's and She's dialogues are more of a series of mannered debates rather than emotionally engaged exchanges filled with confrontation, climax, and expiation. We barely know anything about He's and She's real selves, their inner realities. Passion is nowhere in evidence. Such dramatic structure, it must be said, is testimony to Albee's willingness to experiment, to take dramatic risks in form, structure, indeed, meaning itself. These characters may try to count the ways of loving, but in their personal equation, the number of ways is very small, veering dangerously, perhaps, toward the number zero.

The play may be staged as a vaudeville, but this is hardly a comedy. Albee invokes a key image from *Who's Afraid of Virginia Woolf?*, having his characters repeat "Bone marrow" three times throughout the play. In the former play, getting to the marrow signified George and Martha ultimately getting to the essence, the very core of their marriage, ultimately without the debilitating illusions that were killing (Albee's word) their relationship. In *Counting the Ways*, He and She attempt to get to the marrow, only to discover that their marriage has ossified to the point where any vibrancy has long been drained, leeched from their very bones, indeed, metaphorically, from their marrow. As He reflects, "If you can get *away*, if you can *watch* your emotions, you know that pain is a misunderstanding; it's really *loss; loss* is what it's *really* about" (2: 538). For Albee, increasingly, loss is the norm: the loss of Self, the Other, and what She near play's end more broadly calls the loss of "the veneer of civilization" (2: 546).

Counting the Ways premiered on December 6, 1976, at the Olivier Theatre within the National Theatre in London, and had its American debut on January 28, 1977, at the Hartford Stage Company in Connecticut. Three years after the first American production, I asked Albee about He's *loss, loss* lines noted above. His response illuminates:

> Well, I think what I meant there is that loss is what it's [the play] really about. The after-effect of the immediate thing is probably far more important. After all, if you survive pain you are left with the thing afterwards – which is loss, and dealing with it. You remember in one of my plays, I think it's in *All Over*, the Mistress and the Wife are talking about "He has only his dying; I will have his dying; I will have his death as well." Yes, it's in the first act of *All Over*. "And *I* will be left with the lack. He will merely have the pain of his death. I will share that, and

I will also have to go on with this thing afterwards." I think the loss in *Counting the Ways* probably relates to this.[22]

Indeed, in this fast-paced play, the couple ponders the nature of love, the status of their relationship, and ultimately conclude that what they are confronting is the reality and inevitability of dying and death. Albee clarified his thoughts about *Counting the Ways*, thoughts that deepen our understanding of the play's central subject:

> The play concerns the loss of time, the loss of innocence, loss of opportunity, loss of freshness. Loss happens, time happens ... And during the precious time of our lives, we suffer losses, injuries, some of which are self-inflicted, others of which come from outside. We're aware of these events happening to us. We gain and we lose simultaneously. Theoretically we gain wisdom just in time to lose everything. I guess that is one of the awful ironies of the human condition.[23]

The title of the play is Albee's allusion to Elizabeth Barrett Browning's well-known "Sonnet XLIII" (1850), whose opening line reads, "How do I love thee? Let me count the ways."

He and She, probably in their middle-age years, reflect back on their lifetime together. She begins the play with the simple but telling question, "Do you *love* me? (2: 523). Albee ends the play with the couple still debating the answer, with He asking, "Do *you* love *me?*" to which she gently replies, smiling to reassure her husband, "I don't *know* ... I *think* I do" (2: 253–254).

Between the opening and closing questions, the couple discusses such subjects as the difference between love and sex, their younger years, their three grown children, flowers, and her prom night. Love, they concede, is full of misunderstandings, confusion, bitterness, bile, regrets, pain – all words to be found in the text. He thinks that "Silence is a reply" (2: 539) and fears that soon they will be sleeping in separate beds that are fit "for a corpse!" (2: 543); she suggests that they may even live in separate rooms. Moments later, after a brief blackout, a sign descends: "IDENTIFY YOURSELVES" (2: 544). They improvise biographical sketches about themselves for the audience, but it becomes increasingly clear that the question of identity, their place in the world, is suspect. As one reviewer observed, "He and She don't exactly spar, but they do jostle ... They're a well-bred, upper-middle-class Punch and Judy, wielding verbal bats, who are conducting an inquiry into the human heart almost as if neither of them had one."[24]

Sam Shepard staged a play entitled *Heartless* (2012), a title that may well apply to He and She. To be sure, they are not heartless in the cruel sense of the word; they are civil, articulate, outwardly balanced individuals. That said, they exude a certain lack of feeling. They are spiritless. Even the simple set – a table, two armless chairs, bare walls – creates a telling sense of space. As Philip C. Kolin observes, "the physical space between the scenes of the play and between the characters' lives is, of course, symbolic of the emotional emptiness of their married life. Space erupts in that life as an inevitable consequence of their escape from intimacy and their journey toward meaninglessness."[25]

Counting the Ways at times humors, saddens, and enlightens in ways that allow actors and audiences to gain insights into the human condition. And, to invoke Jerry's remarks in *The Zoo Story*, what is gained is loss. If *Counting the Ways* is a minor play within the Albee canon, it nonetheless embodies many of the central themes and moral seriousness embedded in his major plays.

Chapter 7

A Quest for Consciousness

The Lady from Dubuque

The Lady from Dubuque, first performed in New York City at the Morosco Theater on January 31, 1980, focuses on vintage Albee themes – death, dying, and failed communication among the living. What makes the play engaging is its examination of how the central couple, Jo and Sam, ultimately respond to the complex process of living and dying. While Sam and the other characters witness Jo's experience of dying, Albee suggests that, although Jo's life is physically about to cease, she radiates more life than do the physically healthy characters. Jo, in brief, is not the only character who is dying. Her companions, long before this play begins, have succumbed to a debilitating disease which now paralyzes them. Indeed, the spiritual malaise from which they suffer pervades *The Lady from Dubuque*, for throughout one finds an array of wasted relationships, wasted love, and wasted lives.

Albee chronicles such waste through the two-act structure of the play. The first act serves chiefly to introduce and define the principal characters, whose painful vacuity and self-centeredness far overshadow any claim to individuality that each might make. Because each character becomes merely a hollow variation of a wasted life, the first act also serves to weld these types into a collective, a society of beings brought together through waste and mutual weakness. Having firmly established the normative values of this insular gathering, the playwright begins the second act by challenging those values through the introduction of two "alien" characters who are not of the world of the first act. Within *The Lady from Dubuque* these outsiders, by providing Jo with the warmth and compassion that are absent in the first act, present a threat which is ironically more strongly felt than Jo's disease or the sense of mortality it may introduce into the various characters' lives.

Within the play's first act, what becomes most apparent is not only the lack of action but also the lack of interaction. Each of the characters speaks for himself but not to the others, so that the game played in the first act appears as a type of play within a play where the players adopt suitably Pirandellian roles of self-conscious characters who explain themselves directly to their supposed audience.

Fred surfaces as the clearest emblem of a wasted life. His conduct and prejudice reveal a dulled, coarsened sensibility. Foolish enough to be duped by a practical joke in which Carol staves off Sam's feigned entreaties, Fred responds in the only fashion he knows: by physically asserting this presence. When threatened, Fred, according to stage directions, characteristically readies himself "*for battle*," resorting to verbal aggression and vulgarity (2: 581). A few other telling scenes highlight Albee's portrait. Near the end of the play a bound and exasperated Sam screams, prompting Fred to arms so that he punches his friend "*hard in the stomach*" (2: 658), doubling Sam over in pain. Moments later Carol decides to have coffee, and Fred, threatened by her show of independence and reluctance to leave with him, sweeps the entire coffee service to the floor, shattering saucers, cups, and any claim to civility that he might have had (2: 659).

Fred's propensity to assert himself physically suggests that for him reality is defined solely in terms of his own self-interest and by his severely limited, bigoted perceptions. In contrast, the audience of *The Lady from Dubuque* can only recoil from Fred and his animalism. This reaction occurs because he treats those around him as objects rather than as human beings. Fred may be perceptive enough to ask, with respect to Sam and Jo's home, "Where else can you come in this cold world, week after week, as regular as patchwork, and be guaranteed ridicule and contempt?" (2: 579), but he fails to see that he is the one creating dissonance. If his treatment of Carol is any indication, it is hardly surprising that he has been divorced three times. As Carol testifies, despite whatever sexual fulfillment she finds in Fred, he clearly provides little emotional or spiritual support. From the racial slurs with which he accosts Oscar to the physical attack on his host, Fred consistently affirms his self-centeredness.

Carol emerges as a practical-minded woman. Described as young and "*ripe*," Carol considers marrying Fred, though she admits her uncertainty about Fred and matrimony. Because she remains confused about marriage, she quells her fear with simplistic reasoning. Lacking in social refinement, Carol seems well matched with Fred. A woman who dyes her naturally blond hair brunette, Carol remains a comic figure, breaking certain tense scenes with her matter-of-fact and sometimes humorous lines. As a newcomer to the group, Carol enjoys a freedom from the long-established, deadening patterns of the others. Her role as an outsider allows her to comment more honestly about their and her own responses. In certain respects she seems akin to Claire in *A Delicate Balance*: both appear outspoken, humorous, and capable of observing the others from a somewhat neutral vantage point, from the "fifty-yard line," as Claire says (2: 61). Like Claire, Carol also succumbs to her own emotional condition and seems unable ultimately to better herself.

Carol has a genuine, if limited, ability to be aware of the world around her. Unlike the others, her ego does not prevent her from experiencing the world apart from her self. Her judgment of character is surely flawed, for a relationship with Fred seems earmarked for failure. Still, Carol radiates an openness that distinguishes her from the others and gains for her the audience's sympathy. For Carol, however, waste looms because she reduces her needs to relatively simple and confining terms. She neither requests nor receives much. If she is open, sharing, and honest, she also fails to improve her predicament, succumbing as she does to Fred's demands. Her obedience to Fred's callous requests foreshadows her final acquiescence to a wasted life, a surrender confirmed when she confides to Elizabeth her reason's for marrying Fred: "He's on his way downhill; he's a barrel of laughs; he's a lush; he's a great fuck; I'm not doing anything else this week; I'm not twenty-two anymore, and I'm scared? Take your choice; they're all true" (2: 661).

For Lucinda and Edgar, the events of the evening represent part of a larger, repetitive routine. As usual, they visit Jo and Sam more out of habit than authentic concern. A former college mate of Jo, Lucinda has settled into being Edgar's housewife. Polite and quick to observe propriety, she attends to social appearances, interjecting the banal or predictable remark when appropriate. Though Edgar confesses that they have "as much ridicule and contempt as the next house" (2: 580), Lucinda objects simply because they do not communicate "with talk and presence," as the Wife in *All Over* recalls about her early life with her husband (2: 314).

Lucinda's life, in accordance with her values, has been an untroubled one. Consequently when Jo berates her, she is hardly equipped to defend her values and convictions. After being ignored and then dismissed by Jo as essentially a bore, Lucinda loses emotional control. In her opportunity to cut through the cackle and communicate honestly with her dying friend, Lucinda fails, choosing instead to exit and pout. It is her way of asserting that she, not Jo, suffers. (42).

Edgar emerges as the most fully sketched of the minor characters. Like Sam, Edgar lives in a comfortable suburb, and by all indications he has been a forthright husband. He knows that the others dislike and mock his wife, which finally prompts a defense of his relationship. But what distinguishes Edgar is the quality of his awareness regarding Jo's and Sam's predicament, an awareness extending beyond his acknowledgment that the night "was your nice, average, desperate evening" (2: 588). He emerges as the first character who addresses

Jo's illness, but he immediately evades further discussion of her condition. He broaches the subject only much later when, significantly enough, Jo is absent.

Sam and Edgar's private dialogue progresses through two distinct stages, the first of which Albee laces with a series of virulent confrontations. Initially, Edgar becomes annoyed, then angry, with Sam's sarcastic remarks. Pushed to emotional limits, Edgar suddenly explodes: "JESUS CHRIST, WHAT KIND OF HOUSE DO YOU RUN AROUND HERE?" (2: 597). Clearly both men are angry, and long-suppressed emotions surface. However, their dialogue enters into a second stage, one characterized by a series of honest remarks. Progressing from tension to tonic, the two lower their defenses in a rare moment of rapport. Edgar offers assistance while Sam declines, reasoning that "nobody can help" (2: 599).

But even here a sense of waste exists, since Edgar, in spite of his levelheadedness and sensitivity, fails to pinpoint the true source of Jo's suffering. Rather than talking with Jo about her illness and behavior, Edgar chooses to talk with Sam. Further, his remarks suggest that he is unable or unwilling to understand Jo's actions and the motives that fuel her outbursts. For a well-mannered, rational Edgar, Jo's outbursts are both embarrassing and unacceptable. His concern, it seems, is not so much with Jo as it is with her behavior, with her maintaining a civil, respectable disposition. Albee heightens the sense of waste since the audience expects more from Edgar. The quality of Edgar's perceptions, after all, appears sharper, more refined than Fred's, Carol's, or Lucinda's, and therefore the possibility for his understanding Jo's plight seems greater. Like the others, however, Edgar misunderstands the full nature of Jo's suffering. Such misunderstanding only accentuates the wasted potential for communication and love to surface during the evening's encounters.

Against this backdrop of the waste and self-centeredness of the supporting cast Albee presents the barrenness of the lives of the play's central characters. On one level the evening represents for Jo and Sam merely another social gathering of friends. But on a deeper level the events of the evening bring out the essence of Jo and Sam's relationship. Their public and private responses reveal that their lives together have largely been wasted. Jo's imminent death makes such barrenness all the more disheartening. For her it appears too late to redeem what has been a good marriage, in part because her friends offer little support, and also because physical frailty and decay are overtaking her. For Sam even his wife's dying cannot dislocate his self-serving interests; frailty and decay, on a symbolic level, are overtaking him. By the close of the drama we learn that their respective "reality needs," as Albee calls them,[1] do at times converge but more often remain at cross-purposes. Through the course of the play, Albee suggests that Jo yearns for love and understanding, desires which Sam apparently cannot fulfill. Waste for this couple stems, not from Jo's physical deterioration and inevitable death, but from a crucial breakdown in communication between man and woman, from an inability to salvage qualitatively what scant time remains for Jo.

For Jo, an attractive and perspicacious woman, the gathering of friends for an evening of games and drink seems more bothersome than soothing. Moments into the play she voices her displeasure, expressing both her boredom and disgust with their presence and games. Her friends, respecting though not really understanding her predicament, uphold social appearance, either overlooking or enduring her remarks. But their well-meaning, if awkward, responses only exacerbate Jo's condition. Throughout the first act, Albee presents Jo as one who vents her frustrations, berating longtime friends one moment, her husband the next. She displays little patience for Fred, who she calls "a reactionary, Bush-loving fag baiter" (2: 592), though she accepts Carol. (In the original manuscript, Albee called Fred a "Nixon-hating fag baiter.") The unassertive, complacent Lucinda riles Jo; she tolerates more than enjoys Edgar; and, while she loves her husband, ridicule overshadows her care for him. Frustrated by their unwillingness or inability to understand the real source of her suffering, Jo lashes out at everyone, taking comfort in aggressive verbal assaults. Albee portrays her friends, in turn, as failing to comprehend the underlying reasons for her actions, for they think that they must bear with Jo because she is, after all, ill.

Sam plays peacemaker in Act 1. In trying to placate and make amends for Jo's brusque behavior, he continually explains and clarifies, attempting to smooth over social rough spots. A handsome forty-year-old, Sam mainly concerns himself with tactfully sustaining social appearances. In his efforts to please everybody, however, Sam ends up angering his guests and, more importantly, alienating himself from Jo. Significantly, only at the end of Act 1 do Jo and Sam communicate as if they are truly married. Here, husband and wife attend to each other, talking and touching with a sense of commitment behind their deeds. In their rare moment of rapport there exists a still rarer expression, in this play, of genuine commitment. The tonal quality of the closing scene of Act 1 is reminiscent of the rare loving expressions between George and Martha in *Who's Afraid of Virginia Woolf?* Significantly, during this unique time when Sam displays authentic affection for Jo, she willingly capitulates, relishing the expression of love that has been too long repressed:

> JO: (*Instinctively, they run to each other and embrace*): Oh, my Sam, my
> Sam! I'd marry you in a minute!
> SAM (*Picks her up in his arms*): Shhh, shhh, shhh, shhh. (2: 606)

If Sam offers compassionate assistance, then Jo gladly receives it. Moreover, at this juncture Sam is presented as one still in control; it is still his house and Jo remains within his influence.

And yet and yet. The closing moments of Act 1 also anticipate Sam's ultimately wasteful stance toward living. For example, he reasons that, as Jo dies, he must respond to the loss by holding "on to the object we're losing" (2: 600). Reflecting on the meaning of her death, Sam seems unable to accept the reality of nonbeing. He clings selfishly to Jo "the object" to the extent that she becomes spiritually manacled. Importantly enough, the period in which Jo is most free in the play occurs when Sam is physically bound with a rope. The sense of waste becomes accentuated by his inability to distinguish between different forms of bondage – the kind Jo experiences versus the kind he endures. And the psychological damage caused by Sam's refusal to allow Jo or himself, in Albee's words, to "exhibit too much 'relatable' pain, psychologically"[2] fosters a profound sense of estrangement. In this light Sam does as much damage to the relationship as does Jo's physical disease. Like so many Albee characters, Sam avoids confronting painful truths.

Jo and especially Sam are in many ways a suitable nucleus for the society which has gathered around them, reflecting as they do so many of its values. However, as has already been noted, Act 2 disrupts the social order which Albee so carefully established in the first part of the play. In what might loosely be called a borrowing of the Romance device of the outsider whose entrance serves as a simultaneous threat to order and a call to adventure, Albee shatters the self-congratulation and complacency of the first act through the introduction of the outsiders, Elizabeth and Oscar. Functioning much like the White Rabbit who disrupts the well-established order of Alice's Victorian environs, the two strangers in *The Lady from Dubuque* lead a disbelieving Sam into a wonderland where the laws of time and space and logic established in the first part of the play are no longer in force, a world in which Elizabeth from New Jersey can be Jo's mother from Dubuque.

As denizens of the world beyond the tightly circumscribed realm of Sam and Jo's living room, Elizabeth and Oscar are markedly different from the regular habitués of the house. Elizabeth is a stylish, elegant woman, and much of her stunning presence emerges from two contrasts. First, she looks markedly different from the other characters – patrician, eloquent, and a world traveler, radiating an air of mystery and sophistication. Her deportment acts as a counterpoint to the more common and at times raucous behavior of the other characters. Second, Elizabeth subverts the audience's as well as the other characters' expectations regarding her actual identity. That is, throughout the first act Jo's mother is described as a small, thin woman. With stylish hat and fur cloak, Elizabeth hardly resembles Sam's description of his mother-in-law and emerges as anything but the less-cultured woman that her hometown title/name suggested to the New York critics. Coupled with Oscar, her black confidant, who is as debonair and composed as she is urbane and commanding, Elizabeth is set to usurp Sam's authority.

That usurpation is achieved by the making over of Sam's world into an abstract looking-glass world where everything is made over or reversed. Thus just as Act 1 opens with a series of questions, Albee again uses this technique at the outset of the second act. Sam is quite serious in his exchange with the intruders, and this question-and-answer scene clearly mirrors the game of Twenty Questions which Sam delighted in playing the night before, much to his discomfort now. Fixed on Elizabeth and Oscar, Sam relentlessly probes, as his friends had regarding his identity in the game of Twenty Questions. By insistently pursuing his own rights, Sam spoils their last hours together.

Jo instinctively knows this. The intensity of her sarcasm in Act 1 is a measure of her loss. Her responses stem from an awareness of the impending loss of her own life as well as from the realization that her relationship with Sam has deteriorated into a non-marriage. With the support of Elizabeth, the outsider, Jo is able to confirm and accept her husband's beliefs, beliefs which are emotionally understandable in context but which also preserve their non-marriage. Thus, Elizabeth and Oscar allow Jo and force Sam to redefine their reality. And to redefine their relationship in authentic terms is to unmask the lack of love between them. Jo detects and is attracted to the truth and comfort afforded by Elizabeth and Oscar.

But Jo is dying. Her rational faculties, clouded by pain-dampening drugs and her body's decay, give way to emotional needs, needs that Elizabeth and Oscar satisfy. Albee's imagery gives shape to Jo's present state of being. In contrast to her remarks in Act 1, her responses in Act 2 are described as being timid, dreamy, vague, and faint, words which, in context, evoke deathlike images. As Jo nears death, her movements become hesitant, her utterances feeble. Like Sam, she is clothed in a sleeping gown as she begins her descent toward the living room and her dying room.

Elisabeth Kübler-Ross explains that as one approaches death, one experiences an increasing need for sleep "very similar to that of the newborn child."[3] Jo not only lapses into longer periods of sleep, but the quality of her voice actually shifts into a childlike tone when Elizabeth cuddles her. Lured by the protection offered by the lady from Dubuque, Jo converses as *"a little girl,"* giving herself over as a child to a mother. Albee's stage direction is emphatic: *"Finally, with tears and a great helpless smile, Jo rushes into Elizabeth's arms; their embrace is almost a tableau, so involved is it with pressing together"* (2: 639).

In direct contrast to Jo's letting go of the world she has known, Sam tries to maintain the status quo by claiming rights to his dearest possessions: Jo and home. In the hour of Jo's need, Sam appears unable to help because of his stubborn belief in "rights." He mistakenly thinks that he can lay claim to, and have control over, Jo's emotions. Like Peter's claim to the park bench in *The Zoo Story*, Sam's claim to his possessions reduces him to a pathetic figure, one who perceives Jo and home as bits of "property" (145). Sam contributes to his own fall by perceiving the world around him solely from his own point of view. Sam interprets Jo's acceptance of Elizabeth and Oscar as a mark of rejection and loss of control. For now he must abdicate his power, his possessions, his "rights."

Here, then, lies the irony of the drama. As in *All Over*, death is a ubiquitous force, encompassing not only Jo's literal death but also including figuratively the death of her friends and husband. All the physically healthy characters, with the exception of Elizabeth and Oscar, conduct themselves as if they were anesthetized to both their inner and outer worlds. Even the gray-colored interior of the setting appropriately captures the bleakness of the characters' inner existences. Finally, the presence of death gives Sam a chance to confront his real self and allows him the opportunity to participate in life honestly and compassionately. That Sam and the others apparently do not accept this kind of immersion into daily encounters confirms the wastefulness of their lives. If there is hope for a redemptive force, perhaps it lies with the audience, whose perceptions may be altered by the spectacle. As Albee has implied throughout his theater, that it is too late for his characters to change does not lessen the importance of self-awareness.

The Man Who Had Three Arms

After a controversial and unsuccessful adaptation of Vladimir Nabokov's *Lolita* (1981), Albee completed his next original work the following year, *The Man Who Had Three Arms*. In this play, he addresses what he perceives as another form of waste: the collapse of the individual's moral nerve because of a public which demands a hero, despite the utter lack of substance within that hero.

The Man Who Had Three Arms, which opened October 4, 1982 at the Goodman Theatre in Chicago (it had its New York City debut at the Lyceum in the spring of 1983), presents a hero savagely divided against his self and his world. Himself, the protagonist fixed behind the podium, emerges as one of Albee's more repulsive characters, for what strikes the viewer most forcibly about Himself is his stance toward the audience: he relentlessly lashes out at the theatergoer. Himself berates the audience in a desperate attempt to come to terms with the incubi haunting his soul: his undeserved fame and subsequent fall from undeserved stardom. After he mysteriously grew a third arm, the media and the public instantly elevated the man to celebrity status; but when the arm mysteriously disappeared, so went his fame, money, family – and a sense of self-control. Apparently the confluence of the public exposure and the private tensions within Himself explains his militant attitude toward the audience. His conspicuously aggressive attitude toward the audience only increases as he pathetically tries to come to terms with his predicament. In *The Zoo Story*, *Who's Afraid of Virginia Woolf?*, *A Delicate Balance*, and *Seascape*, Albee created a certain objective distance between the actor and the audience; in *The Lady from Dubuque*, the playwright diminished the actor/audience barrier, although the boundary remains clear. In *The Man Who Had Three Arms*, however, Albee banishes the fourth wall altogether. Himself lectures his invisible audience for two acts, presenting his own ethical conflicts directly to both an imagined and real audience. Himself launches a verbal attack, not on an unsuspecting Peter, a bewildered Nick and Honey, an anesthetized Tobias, or a retiring Charlie, but on his audience.

It is once again a Pirandellian audience, of course. That is, *The Man Who Had Three Arms* quickly establishes itself as a play whose words, gestures, character changes, repartee – its total content – transform the action into a metatheatrical experience. The play blatantly calls attention to its artificiality and deliberately makes the spectator aware of the theatricality of the theater; it is a play which calls attention to its own language while simultaneously exposing the meaninglessness of that language. Characters suddenly become different people. Himself also takes on multiple roles, but in another way: he is an actor within the play but also becomes the dramatist of the play, acting and writing his own pathetic script as he lectures the audience. The interplay of truth and illusion, the subversive influence of the text on the stage action, the banishing of the actor/audience barrier – these are the kinds of dramatic innovations Pirandello pioneered and which, in *The Man Who Had Three Arms*, Albee employs. The audience, then, is both the imaginary group of listeners attending the "Man on Man" lecture series and the actual theatergoer or reader. And this give-and-take between the actor and the spectator explains why, except for the Man and the Woman, whose repartee with Himself is minimal, the actual audience becomes central participants in the drama.

The largely negative crucial reception of the play may be understandable. In the play's anti-mimetic texture, its alleged autobiographical nature (which does not make sense; the script makes it quite clear that the play is not autobiographical), and Himself's adamantine monologue of cruelty, critics found little to praise. Further, within the play's two-act structure, not much happens, twice. But what does occur – Himself's hostile account of his sudden rise to the top of fortune's wheel and his pathetic descent to the bottom of fortune's wheel – embodies Albee's thematic concerns.

In 1984, Albee was kind enough to send me galleys of the play, soon to be published by Atheneum, so I could write what was then the first scholarly essay on the play. I sent him a copy of my essay upon publication, and one Sunday morning my phone rang. It was Albee. While he had told me he liked very much what I written about his work in the past, he did not care for my essay on *The Man Who Had Three Arms* – and let me know in a gentlemanly tone. It was a cordial, professional conversation. We agreed to disagree, and we hung up. But Albee withheld the publication of the first edition of the play. Four years later, in 1988, I asked Albee over dinner whatever happened to the play, as it still had not been published. He laughed and looked me in the eye. "I read what you wrote about *The Man Who Had Three Arms*, so I decided to re-write the third act to deliberately invalidate your argument."[4] We both laughed. Surely Albee had more serious reasons for the revision, and I am not sure to this day if he really meant what he told me, but if nothing else, it was his gentle reminder of the inadequacy of critical discourse.

Albee's Pirandellianism informs the play. The stage directions, for instance, signal the multiple roles the Man and the Woman will assume, allowing them to complement or disagree with Himself's narrative. At one point the Man and the Woman become, respectively, a physician and a nurse, aiding Himself's account of the medical world's reaction to his third appendage. Also, like Pirandello before him, Albee embellishes scenes with a deliberate self-consciousness, as evident when, for example, the Man and the Woman call attention to the rhetorical gallantries – and artificiality – of their introductory exchange:

> WOMAN: … Dear friends, we *have* been fortunate over the years, being witness, as we have, to those who have made our history and shaped our culture, men and women whose accomplishments have wreaked their order on our havoc.
> MAN: Oh! What a very nice phrase!
> WOMAN: (*Genuinely pleased*): Thank you, *thank* you! (*To her notes again*) … their order on our havoc and identified our reality by creating it for us.
> MAN: Even better! (*Begins applauding*) My goodness. (3: 145)

Albee's Pirandellian technique functions on two important levels. First, such a technique invites the audience to question its willing suspension of disbelief. By calling attention to the very nature of theatricality, Albee experiments with the illusion of dramatic mimesis, challenging traditional responses to theater. Second, like *Six Characters in Search of an Author*, *The Man Who Had Three Arms* forces the audience to break down the barrier between itself and the actors. However, in *The Man Who Had Three Arms*, Albee minimizes the barrier radically, involving the audience directly as participants throughout the action. At one point Himself talks to the audience, with the stage directions and dialogue suggesting the intimacy between the actor and spectator. Note the freedom within the script Albee provides in the exchange:

> (*To someone in the front*): Do you remember what I said? Before we broke? Remember I said that if you came upon me sobbing in a corner, not to disturb? That it was a way I had and not to worry? Do you remember? (*Note: If the person says "yes," say: "You do!" If person says "no," say: "You don't!? If person fails to respond, wing it, choosing what you like*). (3: 169)

Albee does not direct Himself to start fighting with the actual audience, as Julian Beck had members of the Living Theatre do with his audience. Still, Albee creates an overly aggressive text, expanding the boundaries of theater as collective, communal spectacle. Albee discussed this point, observing the relatedness of the actors and audience within his theory of drama:

> I don't like the audience as voyeur, the audience as passive spectator. I want the audience as participant. In that sense, I agree with Artaud: that sometimes we should literally draw blood. I am very fond of doing that because voyeurism in the theater lets people off the hook. *The Man Who Had Three Arms* is a specific attempt to do this. It is an act of aggression. It's probably the most violent play I've written.[5]

The play's fictional and actual audience, for better or worse, stands as the recipient of the violence.

Himself puts into concrete voice Albee's Artaudian dramatic theory. By drawing "blood," Himself supports the use of cruelty as a means of purging oneself of demons, of effecting a sense of catharsis, two factors which seem germane to Artaud's theater of cruelty. Moments into the play Himself chides the audience, but the sarcasm is quickly transformed into a series of opprobrious verbal assaults. Act 2 begins with a tale that escalates Himself's attack on the audience. Claiming a female journalist hounded him during intermission, Himself physically assaulted her, although Albee presents the account ambiguously enough that the viewer is never sure of its occurrence:

> "You're good," she said, "you're really good." There was a loathing to it, a condemnation that I dare be articulate, coherent. "You're really good." "So are you," I said. "You've got balls."

The energy of the hatred here, the mutual rage and revulsion was such that, had we fucked, we would have shaken the earth with our cries and thumps and snarls and curses: a crashing around of Gods – chewed nipples, bleeding streaks along the back. Had we fucked … Oh, Jesus! what issue! *But* … but the only issue was the issue of me, the … dismemberment of me. "You've got balls!" I said. And I crashed my hand into her crotch like a goosing twelve-year old. "Get your hands off me," she said. "Get your filthy hands off me." I withdrew my hand: it had hit rock. "If you'll excuse me," she said, ice, shoving past me. She *is* an impressive lady. (3: 168)

In this monologue of cruelty, then, Himself not only chronicles the growth of his third arm and its enervating effect on his world but implicates the audience for contributing to his present condition. To be sure, his sudden fame had its positive points: he hobnobbed with British royalty; earned $25,000 an hour for public appearances; visited the White House; starred in ticker-tape parades; graced the covers of *People*, *Newsweek*, and *Time*; in brief, Himself became famous the world over. But the public, people like the omnipresent journalist he (may have) attacked, the fame, the wealth conspire, according to Himself, to undermine his sense of self-balance. Unable to deal with the decadence of celebrityhood, Himself loses sight of objective reality: his marriage dissolves; his own agent hornswoggles him; and after his mysterious arm disappears, the public discards him. By the time the play begins, Himself, once a freakish cultural icon, appears as a grotesque figure groveling to reorder his world. That is why he stands as a last-minute substitute speaker in this play, his last pathetic connection with a public he both needs and abhors.

The Man Who Had Three Arms thus exposes the monstrous effects of stardom on the individual's spirit. The play addresses "contemporary America's almost ghoulish need for culture heroes."[6] Within the context the public and the sycophants accentuate Himself's internal as well as external freakishness, canonizing him one moment, abandoning him the next, even though by his own admission he has no talent, has done nothing exemplary to achieve social accolades. As the third arm dissipates, so Himself's fame diminishes, reducing him to a pathetic figure consumed with self-pity. Like the unnamed hero in Pirandello's *When One Is Somebody*, Himself becomes a prisoner completely within his (post)celebrityhood. In Albee's own assessment, the play charts "the specifically American thing called 'hype': the creation of celebrity. The play is about the creation of celebrity and the destruction of celebrityhood, because his third arm starts going away … So *The Man Who Had Three Arms* is about that particular kind of hype and celebrity:

underserved, unearned, and how we need it and how we destroy the person once we created him."[7]

Albee explores the corrupting and transitory effect of celebrityhood on the Great, the near-Great, and the pseudo-Great. On top of fortune's wheel one moment, relegated to the bottom the next moment, Himself experiences spiritual as well as financial bankruptcy. This explains why near the close of the play he specifically reflects on the loss of his self. Himself's hostility toward the audience measures the intensity of such loss. His anger, his directly involving the audience in his world, is apparently his form of expiation. Disassociated from his self and the other, the hurlyburly of his life now producing a new form of freakishness, Himself closes the play with a loving plea to stay, a hateful cry to leave, a pitiful gesture to understand. Himself thus begs: "No one leaves! I am *not* a freak. I'm just like you"(3: 193).

The ambivalence of Himself's lecture reflects Albee's broader cultural concerns in the play. Himself does not wish to banish all people and institutions who have exacerbated his freakishness. Rather, he insists, without success, that those people and institutions not dismiss the private individual beneath the public façade. Himself's aggressive assault on the audience belies his inner need for sympathetic understanding of his humanness. It is a plea to be recognized as an individual, one consigned to an ordinary existence. Himself's social devoir seems so irreverent, his angry monody so relentless, of course, that he can never gain the audience's sympathy. In terms of psychology and motivations, Himself never earns the audience's compassion. Hence, Albee's efforts to involve the audience as a way to alter its perceptions about the individual's public and private worlds undercuts itself.

Interestingly, in the early 1980s Albee gave me page proofs of the play, which was set to be published by Atheneum. In this original version, the drama ends with Himself railing at all in the auditorium. There is no hope for him. His third arm disappeared, he no longer has any special claim to draw audiences to his lectures anymore. However, just before publishing the play, Albee withheld the text for further revisions. In the final published version, Albee provides a glimmer of absurdist hope: Himself is suddenly growing another appendage that might restore his freakishness: "TOES!?" Himself says now, "Just wait, world!" (3: 194).

Himself protests against a commercialized universe that divests him of self-freedom, understanding, and love. And Albee implicates the audience for its support of a Madison Avenue mentality promoting Himself's entrapment. Himself represents the latest Albee hero who has the courage to face life without absurd illusions. As Albee remarked, "The entire structure of what happens to Himself is based totally on absurdity; and it is precisely the absurdity that he's railing against."[8]

In theory and structure, in language and theme, *The Man Who Had Three Arms* attempts to extend the conventions of the contemporary theater. The play stands as testimony to Albee's ongoing willingness to experiment with text and performance, without regard to commercial pressures. Albee certainly succeeds in fulfilling one of his central goals of drama: to involve the audience as active participants. However, the play does not sustain the dramaturgic burdens the author places on it. *The Man Who Had Three Arms* does not shock the audience into the self-awareness that we sense at the closure of *The Zoo Story*; the play does not produce the catharsis we experience at the climax of *Who's Afraid of Virginia Woolf?* *The Man Who Had Three Arms* is at its best in a thematic context, although in dramatic terms Himself's monologue of cruelty is less than satisfying. Significantly enough, however, the play, like his experimental *Finding the Sun*, once again indicates that Albee is always eager to restructure his stage according to the demands of his performance instincts.

Finding the Sun

After the largely negative New York City reviews of *The Lady from Dubuque*, *Lolita*, and *The Man Who Had Three Arms* in the early 1980s, Albee headed West for his production of *Finding the Sun*. The play had its premiere at the Frazier Theatre at the University of Northern Colorado on May 10, 1983. Albee directed. One year later, Albee directed the play at the University of California at Irving, and soon after he directed the play at the University of Houston. Signature Theatre devoted its 1993–4 season to staging Albee plays, so *Finding the Sun* finally had its New York City premiere on February 4, 1994. Originally, Albee planned on staging the play in New York in 1987 but withheld production when he discovered Tina Howe's *Coastal Disturbances* was similar in setting and spirit to his own play. The Signature Theatre's *Finding the Sun*, once again directed by the playwright, was part of a trio of earlier Albee plays – *Box* and *The Sandbox* – entitled *Sand*. His directorial efforts, as Rakesh Solomon has argued, received high praise in both the *New York Times* and the *Village Voice*.[9] When *Finding the Sun* was staged at London's Royal National Theatre in 2001, one reviewer called it "one of the best new plays ever staged at the National."[10]

Set on a sun-drenched sandy beach, the play features three married couples and a mother and son who met on a chance encounter as they relax on their chairs. As it turns out, however, we learn that they share certain past experiences and relationships. There is the elderly couple, Henden, seventy years old, who's married to Gertrude, sixty. Next are Daniel and Cordelia, age thirty-seven and twenty-eight respectively. Daniel, it turns out, is Henden's son from a previous marriage while Cordelia is Gertrude's daughter, also from a previous marriage. Then there is Benjamin, age thirty, and Abigail, age twenty-three. Complicating matters, Daniel and Benjamin used to be lovers. Rounding out the cast are Edmee, a forty-five-year-old widow whose husband broke his neck and drowned years earlier, and her sixteen-year-old son, Fergus.

Like *The Goat, Finding the Sun* is a play about the nature of human relationships and versions of love – and how transgressive that love may be for some. Daniel and Benjamin, now married to their women, admit they are still in love with each other. Their mutual attraction obvious to their wives, Daniel and Benjamin's past relationship and current amorous feelings animate much of the plot. For Abigail, they are a source of insecurity and anger, fear, and anxiety. She clings to an illusion that all is well but her intuition reminds her otherwise, which explains why Benjamin says "not a word about running into Daniel" (3: 204). Worse, the young and relatively newly married Abigail wants to believe in the chimera that her husband is no longer attracted to men: "Benjamin," she asserts without confidence, "has seen the follies of his ways, his *former* ways," hoping her beach-side acquaintance will somehow agree. But Cordelia's response is telling, as it registers more accurately and honestly the truth: "Oh, bullshit!" (3: 205). Or as she put it earlier, "A leopard doesn't change its spots," she explains to a "*Too brightly innocent*" Abigail, who will moments later fume and move away (3: 204–205). By contrast, Cordelia has accepted her husband's homosexuality (turned bisexuality): "I *know* Daniel sleeps around [...] and I suspect it's with guys. I *hope* it is: I mean, I *like* being his only woman" and, she tells Gertrude, "I think Daniel is more interested in our friendship than our marriage" (3: 225–226). Cordelia, we see, accepts the nature of her marriage for what it is and carries on.

In Scene 10, the elderly Henden rises from his beach chair and addresses the audience directly. By this time in the playwright's career, such addresses have become a stylistic feature in many Albee productions. Pirandellian in texture, existentialist in theme, Henden's brief monologue spotlights some of the play's deeper public and private concerns: loss, love, dying death, with "nothing to be done about it." He repeats the word "alone" twice, "frightened" three times (3: 215–216). This is an experienced and gentle man whose wisdom and insights play counterpoint to the younger couples' nervousness. Albee was nearly Henden's age by the New York production, and there is more than a hint of the playwright in this character's lines. Scene 16 confirms the point with this revelatory exchange:

> EDMEE (*Generally*): There's danger in consciousness, in too much awareness.
> HENDEN: We go through it only once, my dear, or so more tell me than don't – better alert … than numb, or not comprehending. (3: 231)

One could transpose Henden and Edmee's exchange to nearly every Albee play, so reflective are they of the playwright's world view. The cleansing consciousness of death, Albee insists time and time again, is a necessary corollary to living an engaged and engaging life.

Gertrude near mid-play utters, "I didn't say a word!" – an observation that points to a weakness in the play (3: 232). Most of the characters would benefit if they were fleshed out more. This is especially true of Daniel and Benjamin, but it is far more evident in Gertrude, whose relatively few lines seem mainly designed to further plot movement between the others. We do learn early on of her previous marriages. And she genuinely seems content with her current husband. No marital battles here. Perhaps her most intriguing line for Albeephiles appears minutes into the action, when she asks Edmee who Henden is, to which Gertrude replies, "Or, more to the point, who is *Sylvia*? Henden is my husband ..." (3: 203). The Sylvia allusion, of course, anticipates a new play Albee would stage several years later, *The Goat or, Who is Sylvia?*

If the sexually charged atmosphere generated by Daniel and Benjamin provides a spark for the narrative action, Edmee and Fergus emerge as the more enigmatic figures in the play. To an American ear, Edmee is a curious name. Toby Zinman speculates if she appears as Albee's surrogate as in Ed+Me.[11] It is an intriguing possibility, although Zinman acknowledges that speculation leads to "silly conclusions." Edmee is, on the surface, a caring single mother who is raising a sensitive and curious teenager. Soon, however, Albee problematizes her by interjecting less than subtle Oedipal allusions regarding her relationship with Fergus. One the one hand, Edmee appears as a benevolent protectress. Moreover, the meaning of her name is sometimes defined as "prosperous protection" or "wealthy defender," which complements her son's allusion to his "wealthy mother and all ..." (3: 224). In Scene 8, however, she feels that her son may play Oedipus to her Jocasta, for, she claims, "Fergus would bed me in a moment," though she also adds, "why on earth would I want to fuck him!?" (3: 214). Once again Albee tantalizes, as he never develops the Oedipal taboo.

Fergus delivers a monologue that seems too sophisticated for a teenager. Alluding to one of Albee's favorite plays – Thornton Wilder's *Our Town* (1938) – he reveals he has led a too-sheltered life and has been groomed to attend an Ivy League university; success awaits this white, privileged young man. He closes Scene 13 by shifting to an unexpectedly onerous subject: the high suicide rates among teenagers. Before taking a bow and exiting, he ends the scene by inviting the audience to ponder that teenage reality. This is, indeed, an innocent teenager – *he* does not mention a sexual attraction to his mother – whose conversations with the others suggest a maturity beyond his years but whose fate by play's end remains unclear.

As the fast-paced twenty-one-scene play, with its intersecting conversations, nears the final curtain, whatever comedic tones shift into darker undertones. Edmee fears that her son will not fulfill his promise in life; instead, he will "tarnish" – and wonders if he will die young (3: 233). It is as if a caring mother turns her back on her son. Further, minutes later she reveals her Tobias-like sense of Terror in the common, which enhances our perception of the complexity of her being. Meanwhile, Abigail experiences a marital meltdown while Daniel and Benjamin struggle with their yearning to be together in their self-created world that, for now, will not allow it. As Daniel says, "It's hopeless, then. What did Beckett say? I can't go on; I'll go on?" (3: 246). Scholars have long noted the Beckettian allusions in Albee's work, but this is a rare instance, perhaps the only time, he explicitly mentions Beckett by name. With clouds gathering near play's end, the presence of death inhabits the stage. Abigail's parents, we learned earlier, went to their fiery deaths when their hot air balloon crashed; at play's end, Abigail has unsuccessfully tried to commit suicide by drowning. Back on shore, Henden suddenly dies. And Edmee appears now as "*a frightened child*," as Fergus is nowhere to be found. Earlier he alluded to the high rate of teenage suicide, and Edmee, Albee suggests, fears for her son's life. In the closing moments of the play, her pleas for Fergus becomes a haunting monody as she repeats her son's name ten times within the closing minute of the drama. To be sure, Gertrude reminds us, the sun is returning, but it is unclear if Edmee's son will. Small craft warnings, we see, hover over this non-realistic drama.

Given the age ranges, and various life experiences, and the fact that this is the first Albee play to feature a two homosexuals, *Finding the Sun* emerges as a play about those involved in various phases of a quest – be it a quest for love, for marriage, for acceptance, for *finding* glimmers of light in a world fraught with questions, self-doubts, frustrations, ambiguities that metaphorically and emotionally cloud our sons, our sun, our judgments. As Anne Paolucci observes,

> this aria in eight voices carries us behind the sun, beyond the calm water. Just as music carries the emotional content of an opera, so too the suggestivity of Albee's dialogue – undercurrents, premonitions, fears – carry the emotional core of his plays. *Finding the Sun* is no exception. The casual banter, the carefully detailed setting, the space defined for the action are real to the extent that they anchor us to a time and place, from which we can then take our true bearings. Our task is finding *our* sun, *our* time, *our* place.[12]

Such an achievement, Albee has said for decades, is his way of involving the audience as active participants in the dramatic spectacle. With allusions to Beckett and Shakespeare (Gertrude, Cordelia, Sylvia), and with its open-ended and ambiguous ending, *Finding the Sun* continues Albee's lifelong project of staging provocative theater whose cultural and personal meanings audiences ponder longer after leaving the show.

Marriage Play

Sam Shepard has said that he has written plays that concern predicaments "between brothers and fathers and it's mainly the same materials I've been working on for over thirty years or something but for me it never gets old ...."[13] Much the same could be said of Albee's plays, though his predicaments often concern married well-off suburban couples rather than brothers and fathers. Play after play Albee, it seems, explores married couples who sleepwalk through their lives until they realize that their lives have been wasted, lost to anesthetizing routines. More specifically, the status of "marriage," like some of the other central subjects of Albee's – dying, death, abandonment, and the primacy of consciousness – often lies at the heart of so many of his plays, including a play with the working titles of "The Old One Two" and "News from the Front" that eventually became *Marriage Play*. By this point in Albee's career, the New York critics were so hostile to his every new play that Albee first staged the play in Vienna, Austria, at the English Theatre on May 17, 1987. Five years would pass before the play made its American premiere at the Alley Theatre in Houston, Texas, on January 8, 1992, where it was co-produced with the McCarter Theatre, of Princeton, New Jersey – and where it was staged in Princeton on February 14, 1992. Finally the play had its New York City premiere at the Signature Theatre Company on October 1, 1993. Once again, most of the critics panned the play.

Marriage Play is an absurdist-tinged one-act drama featuring two characters, Jack and Gillian (perhaps an allusion to the Jack and Jill nursery rhyme), a suburban couple in their fifties who have been married for over three decades and whose adult children have long moved on to build their own lives. In a vaudevillian opening scene, Jack returns home at 3:30 p.m. one weekday afternoon and announces several times to his disinterested, and then disbelieving, wife, "I'm leaving you" (3: 252). She wonders if he is having another affair (they both have had past dalliances). Jack isn't, and says so, so Gillian remains baffled, and later infuriated, by his announcement. While he concedes he still loves her, Jack insists that he is indeed leaving her. When he tries to leave her, however, she unleashes a physical assault and the two battle in what is the longest fight seen in the Albee canon. Jillian knees Jack in the groin, and "*they try to strangle each other, striking at each other, throwing each other around, trying to escape, trying to kill."* After the fight is over, Albee asks, *"Can there be blood from his nose, say?"* and *"Can there be blood from her mouth [?]"* (3: 282–283). Order restored, the spent couple reflects upon their past – their first date, their vacations – and even on some happy moments during their long marriage. By curtain's end, however, Jack once again announces he is abandoning their marriage.

Jack emerges as another Albee character who, like Tobias in *A Delicate Balance*, senses a disconnection between the self and the other. A sense of felt estrangement occupies his mind. As Jack puts it early on in the play,

> You look up one day from your desk; you are sitting there in your
> usual manner, doing your usual things – and they are neither boring
> nor exciting: whatever they may have been they no longer are; they are
> merely your usual things. Well, you look up from them, are amazed by
> your familiar surroundings, are startled by the stranger who has been
> your secretary for fifteen years. You realize your life is about to change …
> profoundly; either that or you are mad. (3: 254–255)

Once again it is as if Albee alludes to Albert Camus's well-known passage in *The Myth of Sisyphus* (1942), where "A world that can be explained by reasoning, however faulty, is a familiar world. But in a universe that is suddenly deprived of illusions and of light, man feels a stranger."[14] It is, for Camus as it is for Beckett and Albee, an absurd world in which authentic meaning and connection with the self and the other are increasingly nowhere in evidence. Jack finds himself inhabiting a world in which the one with whom he works, Kathleen O'Houlihan, appears more as a stranger; the one to whom he is married, Gillian, feels increasingly distant; and, finally, the one whom he supposedly knows best – himself – appears increasingly like a cosmic waif whose uncertainty is his only certainty.

Within such a context, the action unwinds. After Jack's announcement and Gillian's initial trivializing of his "Unfocused anxieties" (3: 260), we learn that she has written her own version of *The Book of Days*, a day-by-day chronical of their married life, including a "record of three thousand fucks" (3: 264). Gillian continues to mock her husband's anxieties and attempts to deal with a marriage defined more by routine and indifference than love. His efforts, she says, are a lame "attempt at troof! T-R-O-O-F. Trooth," to which Jack replies, "You mock everything, don't you?" (3: 278). Gillian is a strong, independent, and intelligent woman whose logic and reason make sense to the audience but whose actions are nonetheless born out of her resistance to her husband's crises. Albee's dialogue, at times, rivals that of some of his better regarded plays. Further, Jack and Gillian's exchanges occasionally take on Pirandellian textures. They call attention to the fact that they are, in certain scenes, playing, play-acting as if they are actors in a play within a play. Audiences or readers are struck by the very theatricality of their exchanges:

> GILLIAN: Have I gotten too old for you? Too … ripe? Are you not up to me Anymore? Do I *frighten* you? Are you suddenly taken with men? It happens. Do you lust for your sister? You did when you were ten, you told me. Are you impotent … as of the day before yesterday? Have you forgotten who you are? Who *I* am? Who you were I was? Is tomorrow Wednesday? What*ever* is the matter.
> (*Waits*)
> No? Nothing?
> (*Pause. Jack begins slow, deliberate applause. Gillian smiles, bows, spreads her arms, curtsies, spreads her arms again; hold it*)
> JACK: Brava.
> GILLIAN: Thank you, thank you.
> JACK: Quite a performance.
> GILLIAN: Thank you. (3: 279)

This is, once again, Albee's way of using language to blur the distinction between truth and illusion, between performance and reality. Toby Zinman is spot on when observing, "The self-referential theatricality of their lives occurs over and over again."[15] Such theatricality also better enables Albee to draw the audience into the action itself.

The long fight scene erupts mid-way through the play, after which Albee shifts into another register. All the verbal one-upmanship games and hostile attacks recede. With echoes of the ending of *Who's Afraid of Virginia Woolf?* present, the ending of *Marriage Play* is quiet, even gentle. Jack and Gillian listen to each other, even comfort each other. However, Albee ends the play by having Jack once again announce he is leaving Jillian, to which she replies, after long silences, "I know you are." However, action turns into inaction, movement to inertia. Albee, channeling Beckett, ends the play with a telling stage direction, "*They sit, silence; no movement*" (3: 306). Audiences thus are left reflecting upon the actionlessness of this couple's actions. Jack wants to leave but still needs the comfort of home, of routine, of his wife. There is a sense of "nothing to be done" at the end of the play. This is, after all, a play, as Albee observed in the late 1980s, about "two people who are married, and who are trying not to be married, but find it very difficult not to be married."[16] This couple senses that loss is the norm. A vacuity of being, a sense of angst pervades their world. As Jillian puts it near the end of the play, "Passion in a marriage never dies; it changes. When the passion of passion wanes there are all the others waiting to rush in – the passion of loss, of hatred, the passion of indifference; the ultimate, the finally satisfying passion of nothing. You know nothing of passion; you confuse rut with everything." To which her husband adds, "… nothing is enough" (3: 302). They fear (or at least Jack fears) the presence of death, the ineluctability of death, and they become aware of what Albee always calls the cleansing consciousness of death:

> … we come to the moment we understand that nothing has made any difference. We stare into the dark and know that nothing is enough, *has* been enough, *could* be enough, that there is *no way* not to have … wasted the light; that the failure is built into us, that the greatest awareness gives to the greatest dark. That I'm going to lose you, for example – *have* lost you – no more, no less than fingers slipping from each other, that I am going to lose *me*, *have* lost me – the light … losing the light. (3: 303)

What is gained, once again, is loss. A kind of willed inertia fills the stage at play's end. Jack murmurs as if he is a *"little boy"* while Jillian signals a *"gentle"* (3: 306) acceptance of their routines, habits, and lack of marital vibrancy. When asked if their holding hands at play's end signals that this couple is closer now, Albee replied, "No. I like the paradox. It's the first time in the play that they are touching each other. Except in violence. And it's interesting to me that they're holding hands when he repeats the fact that he's going to leave her." He then called Jack's "A terrifying decision." Finally, Albee noted that the audience will have to reflect on whether Jack will follow through and actually leave or if he lacks the courage, the will to do so. This makes the ending, for Albee, "more ambiguous. Paradox does that sometimes."[17] Perhaps this is why the playwright himself explained a year later, "*Who's Afraid of Virginia Woolf?* is about not much truth in a marriage. *Marriage Play* is about too much truth."[18] Once again Albee provides no guarantee that marital stability will return, or that love will reveal itself. Rather, audiences see an immobilized couple and are left to ponder what could have or should have been.

Chapter 8

As I Lay Dying

Three Tall Women

Albee's influence was especially felt during the 1960s, when he won esteem as *the* new playwright in whose scripts the American public might find fresh theatrical validation. After all, Eugene O'Neill was dead (1953), Arthur Miller was absent from the stage for nine years (1955–64), Tennessee Williams had entered his "stoned age" (the 1960s), and Susan Glaspell was all but forgotten (the winner of the 1931 Pulitzer Prize died in 1948). New voices were heard, with Kenneth H. Brown, Jack Gelber, Amiri Baraka, Lorraine Hansberry, Adrienne Kennedy, Megan Terry, John Guare, Terrence McNally, and Sam Shepard emerging as playwrights of genuine talent. But it was Albee's voice that resonated most loudly, it seemed, on both Broadway and Off-Broadway. He was young, fresh, and reinvigorated the American stage. However, "Edward Albee also visited the outer planets of the critical world for several decades, despite picking up a second Pulitzer Prize for *Seascape*" in 1975.[1] Indeed, Albee's dramas since in the later 1970s through the early 1990s, many theatergoers and critics felt, seemed more like unfinished experiments whose scripts fell prey to narrative inertia and the mimetic fallacy. Sparkling repartee yielded to more rarified and abstract dialogues, and Albee's work in the 1970s and 1980s – though much of the plays in retrospect emerge as solid accomplishments – did little to impress audiences.

So 1994 was an important year for Albee. This is when the New York critics, and audiences, re-embraced the playwright. Positive reviews outweighed those voicing reservations. The critical scorn of the later 1970s through the 1980s was, thankfully, a thing of the past. In the 1990s, Albee regained his voice in *Three Tall Women*. The play was a success, earning Albee his third Pulitzer Prize, and was warmly received in productions throughout the world. This is a work, to some degree, in which he draws much from familial experiences. As he writes in the Introduction to the play, "I knew my subject – my adoptive mother …."[2] Even though his adoptive mother would throw him out of the house at age eighteen after learning about her son's homosexuality and would ultimately cut him out of her will and sizeable fortune, in what seemed to be the ultimate form of rejection, Albee insists he had little interest in exacting some form of revenge by writing *Three Tall Women*. As he explains in his Introduction,

> I knew I did not want to write a revenge piece – could not honestly do so, for I felt no need for revenge. We had managed to make each other very unhappy over the years, but I was past all that, though I think she was not. I harbor no ill-will toward her; it is true I did not like her much, could not abide her prejudices, her loathings, her paranoias, but I did admire her pride, her sense of self. As she moved toward ninety, began rapidly failing both physically and mentally, I was touched by the survivor, the figure clinging to the wreckage only partly of her own making, refusing to go under. (n.p.)

In his desire to treat his adoptive mother as objectively as he could, Albee's play stands as a remarkable achievement for a dramatist who has enjoyed a remarkable career. The play signaled Albee's return to critical favor, something he had not enjoyed in decades. *Three Tall Women*, which first opened at Vienna's English Theatre, Ltd, on June 14, 1991 and, after its July 30, 1992 showing at the Rivers Arts Repertory in Woodstock, New York, had its New York City premiere on January 27, 1994 at the Vineyard Theatre, seems to be Albee's most frankly personal work. As in such earlier works as *The Zoo Story*, *The American Dream*, and *The Lady from Dubuque*, *Three Tall Women* replicates uneasy familial tensions and the playwright's lifelong preoccupation with aging, mortality, and the inevitability of death. It is equally a play, as Brenda Murphy observes, that "sheds a revealing, sympathetic light on a death where there should be love but is not."[3] The play seems to have struck a nerve, too, as an aging American population were themselves caring for dying parents – and all the financial and emotional burdens therein – in record-breaking numbers.

A Beckettian play, *Three Tall Women* opens in a well-appointed bedroom in which three women – named A, B, and C – reflect upon each others' lives. A is the eldest, a woman in her early nineties whose nearness to death animates the play. With her recollections of the past at times vivid and textured, and at other times vague and contradictory, A forms the nerve center of the drama. The playwright describes her as "*a very old woman; thin, autocratic, proud, as together as the ravages of time will allow*" (n.p.). B, age fifty-two, appears as an experienced middle-aged woman and at times acerbic confidant who dutifully tends to A. And C, who is handling legal documents for A, at age twenty-six appears as a younger, restless woman lacking in the worldly experiences and life-perspectives of the older women. The setting is as far from the hardscrabble set of, say, Suzan-Lori Parks's *Top Dog/Underdog* (2002) as one can imagine.

Albee's play unwinds "in a 'wealthy' bedroom, French in feeling," with a "*bed upstage center … Lacy pillows, a lovely spread. Nineteenth century French paintings. Two light armchairs, beautifully covered in silk*" (3: 309). In Act 2, some medical equipment is added to the bedroom, a visual reminder that soon it will be "all over" for A. And the writing, itself, is classic Albee. Characters correct each other's grammar; verbal arias reach crescendos; and there are allusions to animals throughout: Albee mentions Dalmations, Pekingese, cats, ponies, horses, jaybirds, buzzards, and penguins (within one minute of monologue, penguins are mentioned four times). Above all, reflections of the past, present, and future in context of dying and death permeate the drama.

Thus *Three Tall Women* was inspired by the memory of his domineering adoptive mother, Frances Cotter Albee, with whom he felt little connection. Her arid marriage to a wealthy, submissive, and short father, their marital battles, and the reluctant son mirror Albee's own upbringing. The play is his way of putting in perspective his adoptive mother (and father) who provided material comfort but little love; he also implies that the play is a reckoning with his own mortality. More tellingly, *Three Tall Women* embodies major philosophical issues that have long been synonymous with each Albee play. As such, the play transcends the autobiographical and the biographical. As Anne Paolucci observes,

> in spite of Albee's own admission that writing *Three Tall Women* was a kind of personal "exorcism," Marion Seldes, who has played the old woman A (as well as the caretaker B), insists that the work should not be considered autobiographical: "… am I in fact playing Edward's mother? Did he write a portrait of her? I do not think so. I think he translated his conscious thoughts and memories of her to his unconscious feelings and turned them into art."

Paolucci thus concludes, "No doubt Albee's adoptive mother is reflected in the portrait he has drawn of A; but the final product is the work of a rich and creative imagination."[4] Thus, this play emerges as something more than a play about a mother; it is, in addition, yet another of Albee's reflections on what it means to be human while enduring life's archetypal passages through various phases of one's existence. C is experiencing the beginning of her adult life, who as she ages into B has gained vital experience to better understand a malevolent universe in which private betrayals dovetail with public anxieties. By the time B ages into A, her character understands, in the Miltonic sense, the necessity of the Fall. As A reflects, "We were fallible. Once you fall – whether you get up or not – once you fall, and they see it, they know you can be pushed. Whether you're made of crockery and smash to pieces, or you're bronzed and you clang when you topple, it makes no never-mind; it's the plinth is important" (3: 377).

Throughout his career, Albee has subverted audience expectation, and *Three Tall Women* extends this pattern. In Act 2 he presents a death watch scenario, reminiscent of *All Over*, in which A, bedridden, apparently lies under an oxygen mask. B appears as a composed and dedicated caretaker, while C listens and tries to learn from the other tall women. However, things turn out to be more complicated than ABC in this play. Albee shifts away from realism to nonrealism, subverting the theatergoers' sense of objective reality early in Act 2. With the surprise entrance of a very mobile and elegantly dressed A, the audience suddenly realizes that the three women are really *one* woman. Thus A reappears, the figure lying in the bed being a mannequin, allowing the play to blend the three life-narratives of A, B, and C into one woman at three different stages of her life – A at ninety-two, B at fifty-two, and C at twenty-six years of age. This sudden realization makes for compelling theatrics. Audiences loved it. Although the three women share the same life experiences, A and B clearly have gained valuable, if painful, experiential knowledge that C has yet to acquire. Deception and betrayal form the powerful illusions, they tell C, forewarning that her life will be filled with disappointment. All of the characters, representative of various phases of a single woman's life, are haunted, we see, by sickness, denials, dying, and ultimately approaching death.

Clearly approaching her own demise, A launches into a series of verbal reflections – and some vintage Albee verbal assaults – dealing with death, dying, and the manner of living. With B and C listening respectfully during this waiting-for-death play, A recalls various moments in her life – when she learned to ride horses; when she lost her virginity; how she endured her womanizing husband of thirty-eight years, nursing him for the last six difficult years until he succumbed to cancer; and, among other things, how she has had the inner strength to carry on. She points out the inevitability of death – or, as B says, "It's downhill from sixteen on!" (3: 317) – but her conception of death extends well beyond the physical. Although A appears as a mean-spirited and bigoted old woman, she also radiates a sense of elegance forged from a life of wealth, privilege, and, it seems, perseverance. A recalls a past filled with loss, and a problematic and ultimately sterile marriage. Indeed, near the end of Act 1, A remembers when she was naked in their bedroom, her husband offered her a gift:

> And I looked and there he was, and his … pee-pee was all hard, and …
> and hanging on it was a new bracelet … And he came closer, and
> his pee-pee touched my shoulder – he was short, and I was tall, or
> something. Do you want it? he said, and he poked me with it, with his

pee-pee, and I turned, and he had a little pee-pee. Oh, I shouldn't say that; that's terrible to say, but I *know*. He had a little … *you* know … and there was a bracelet on it, and he moved closer to my face, and do you want it? I thought you might like it. And I said, No! I can't *do* that! You *know* I can't *do* that! and I couldn't; I could *never* do that, and I said, no! I can't do that!

With little subtlety and much symbolism, Albee emphasizes what had devolved into a loveless marriage when the husband goes flaccid:

And he stood there for … well, I don't know … and his pee-pee got … well, it started to go soft, and the bracelet slid off, and it feel into my lap. I was naked; deep into my lap. Keep it, he said, and he turned and he walked out of my dressing room. (*Long silence; finally she weeps, slowly, conclusively.*) (3: 347)

A, as a reinvention of Frances Cotter Albee, also recalls a son who cannot reciprocate her love. Indeed, the only other character in the play is The Boy – Edward Albee himself – whose silence throughout the play stands as a reminder of the cosmic disconnect between mother and son. The extent of that disconnection is nowhere better seen than when B accuses The Boy of abandoning the family: "And he walks out the solarium, out of the house, and out of our lives" (3: 374). Albee ironizes B's lines, of course, because it was Albee who felt abandoned by his parents. Indeed, much of Act 2 features a mother's scathing attack on her son. "I'll *never* forgive him!" (3: 371). Albee directs her to speak in various tones – venom, bewildered, bitter, scathing, wistful, sad, clenched teeth, rage, angry, humiliated, and tears are all words found in the stage directions (3: 370–371) when the mother unloads on the ever-silent Boy.

There is, in the ending the playwright has constructed, an oddly affirmative tone. Or perhaps it is the acceptance of death that audiences detect. Indeed, A accepts her fate, accepts the reality of her imminent death, affirming that the happiest moment is embracing death itself. Near play's end, to be sure, A lashes out at those who have come within her orbit over a lifetime, including her silent son, a dutiful twenty-three-year-old visiting his dying mother for the last time: "I'm *here,* and I deny you *all*; I deny every *one* of you" (3: 382). A's monologue, however, ultimately tempers the closing action of the play. She acknowledges that the earlier versions of herself, B and C, are "both such children" (3: 383) – as she shakes her head and chuckles. Now she faces the audience as well as her own past demons and inner self. Her body language is telling, for, Albee's stage directions note, she speaks "*Gently*" with her "*face forward*" (3: 384). A sense of unity and acceptance fills the stage:

I was talking about … what: coming to the end of it; yes. So. There it is. You asked, after all. That's the happiest moment. (*A looks to C and B, puts her hands out, takes theirs. Continued*) When it's all done. When we stop. When we can stop. (3: 384)

In this play Albee succeeds in presenting a tall woman who, despite her considerable flaws, moved the playwright. As mentioned, Albee "was touched by the survivor, the figure clinging to the wreckage only partly of her own making, refusing to go under" as she faced her own death.

*   *   *

Albee was to have followed up *Three Tall Women* with *The Lorca Story: Scenes from a Life* – sometimes referred to as *The Lorca Play*. The Houston International Festival Committee commissioned Albee to write the play as part of the "Centennial Celebration of Spain and the New World," and, as Barbara Lee Horn reports, Albee traveled to Spain to conduct research on the play, a point confirmed by Phyllis T. Dircks.[5] Albee, in turns out, was never comfortable with his writing on this commission, which was performed only once, under Albee's direction, at the Wortham Theatre in April 1992. He never published the play.

Fragments (A Sit Around)

The title of Albee's *Fragments (A Sit Around)* suggests its theatrical scope and emphasis: this is an experimental play presenting a series of broken apart, detached, incomplete narratives voiced by eight characters sitting on chairs in a semicircle arrangement. In some of the earliest performances, the characters sit on red boxes, or cubes, and there is much laughter amongst them. The audience, in turn, laughed in approval. The characters form an octet. Indeed, this play is perhaps best understand through its musicality, a series of arias voiced by four women and four men, whose ages span from twenty through sixty-five. Albee originally subtitled the play "A Concerto Grosso," which, as Toby Zinman observes, is "a Renaissance musical style in which each instrument takes a solo. This is one of several of Albee's attempts to make drama approach the condition of music, suggesting the vital importance of time in the performance of an Albee play and the interplay of voices as if they were instruments."[6] Their fragments and fragmented reflections, once finished, form if not a whole piece, at least a coherent narrative regarding classic Albeean themes and subjects: the struggle to find love in a malevolent universe, the need for the individual to be fully engaged in living, the purging consciousness of death, the importance of understanding the Terror in the common, and the need for nurturing a social world in which the fragile, the young, and the elderly can strive for some mutual trust. *Fragments (A Sit Around)* premiered on October 10, 1993, at the Ensemble Theatre of Cincinnati. It enjoyed its Signature Theatre Company's New York City debut on April 8, 1994, at the Kampo Cultural Center. It is also a play, like so many of the later dramas, that calls attention to its own artificiality, as characters on occasion talk directly to the audience.

Albee writes in "A Note for Directors" that

> Common sense should determine the stage movement. Let groups form and un-form, but let it be so casual we're not aware of it. I have found (in directing this piece three times) that the actors' instinct as to spatial relationships usually works fine. Do *not* be specific about "where we are" or who the characters "are"; they are who they portray, and they are where they are. Be casual, be informal; let the piece build its own tensions and overall shape. (3: 387)

So within a minimalist set characters named Woman 1, age twenty-five; Woman 2, age thirty; Woman 3, age forty; and Woman 4, age sixty-five, interact with Man 1, age twenty; Man 2, who must be African American, age thirty; Man 3, age forty-five; and Man 4, age fifty-five to sixty-five. They launch into a series of proverbs, and follow up responses to the proverbs, and then some directly engage the audience with longer monologues that slowly begin to define their individual values, conditions, and fears. There is no place for realism in this play. Albee has discussed its plotlessness and its musical affinities: "*Fragments* lacks plot in any established sense; there is no clear dilemma and resolution – no 'story.' ... The piece proceeds as a piece of music does – accumulating, accumulating, following its own logic. Its effectiveness, its coherence reside in what we have experienced from the totality of it. *Fragments* is also very simple, a straightforward piece – on its own terms, of course."[7]

While the eight characters voice a number of one-liners, occasionally these strangers present some of their personal past experiences in sometimes comic and sometimes disarming narratives of self-disclosure and self-doubt. For instance, Man 1, who Albee biographer Mel Gussow calls a man "speaking for the author," reveals a horrifying story.[8] We learn that his parents were killed in a car crash and as a young man he became intimate with an older man who was caring for him. He goes on to tell about a neighbor, a father who "lusted after" his thirteen-year-old daughter. The father decided to enlist Man 1 to rape his daughter and to recount in pornographic terms "all the juicy details ... the penetrations, the humiliations" (3: 433). However, the then teenage Man 1 decided to protect the girl. They share an innocent kiss, and it was all "wonderful" (3: 434). He ultimately tells the perverted father the truth. As he explains, "I had to tell him I'd never touched her, that I loved her, that she was the sweetest, purest most beautiful creature I'd ever seen, that I'd made up all the stories I'd told him and couldn't I go now please?" (3: 434). In response, the outraged father attacked Man 1, threatening to kill the fifteen-year-old. And the pure love he experienced was forever lost: "I never saw the lovely girl again. I mean, I never saw the *town* again, or her father – thank God – or my … the guy; but, especially, I never saw that lovely girl again. My cheek has a warmth to it, though, a glow. I still feel her fingers brushing me. Perhaps it's a wound; perhaps there is a wound there" (3: 434). This is of course a similar wound Albee would sculpt into his central subject in *The Play About the Baby*. This is the most disturbing of the characters' monologues but it is equally a good example of the various ways in which, to varying degrees, they communicate with each other. Given age and experiential differences – Man 2 is understandably upset and frustrated about the time a fellow African American actor was arrested in a park "for being black, for being in the park" (3: 437) and also voices a rich allusion to Ralph Ellison; Woman 1, the youngest in the group, appears as a well-meaning but lacking figure who frets over her cat's cremated ashes and the fact that she talks "to plants" (3: 445) – *Fragments* covers a wide emotional range. While Woman 3, age forty, talks about her personal medical condition and many of her vital organs, and she rambles on, later, about an aging movie star she met at a party, Woman 2 narrates the story of her dog's frozen burial and babbles on about a "a psychologist who has been collecting nicknames for over ten years now, nicknames of married couples and …", which prompts Man 3, who suddenly rising to leave, to respond, "I haven't got time for this" (3: 438). The older female in the group, Woman 4, reflects on the past, a time of "organ grinders, knife grinders," a time when people felt more connected with their "community" (3: 409). Man 3 interjects that he struggles with his own sense of identity when gazing into a mirror: "I look at him in the mirror and I see that he's not looking back at me … I don't dare turn … because I know I won't be there" (3: 425). His self-reflection yields little comfort. Perhaps it is Man 4, the oldest in the group, however, who gives the clearest voice to Albee's world view:

> … that there is a way to get through it – so long as you know there's doom right from the beginning; that there is a time, which is limited, and woe if you waste it; that there are no guarantees of anything – and that while we may not be responsible for everything that *does* happen to us, we certainly are for everything that *doesn't*; that since we're conscious, we have to be aware of both the awful futility of it and the amazing wonder. Participate, I suppose. (3: 456)

Moments earlier Man 4 reflected on death, dying, and loneliness, other factors informing Albee's vision of the world. When I first met Albee in 1980, he essentially said very similar words and made the exact some point Man 4 makes and that so many other characters in plays before and after *Fragments* make. It is somehow fitting that Man 4 brings the play to a close when he simply says, "Thank you. *Fragments*: The End" (3: 457).

Fragments, in sum, presents eight narratives of varied tonalities that is best listened to as a musical score, one filled with some discordant chords that, on occasion for some of the characters, lead to a momentary glimpse of a harmony that has to a large extent been absent in their own lives. Life, in the world Albee constructs, is a series of ongoing fragments, and those – the characters in the play and the audience watching this unconventional piece – who willingly engage themselves with a full and dangerous involvement in living itself may one day be in harmony with both their inner and outer worlds. That not all in the play have gained the wisdom and perspectives of the two oldest characters, Woman 4 and Man 4, reminds us that struggle to live with an authentic sense of awareness is an ongoing and ever-changing process.

The Play About the Baby

The Play About the Baby is one of Albee's more absurdist plays. This is a vaudevillian fable, an allegorized drama about a post-Edenic world. It is less a play about the baby and, we gradually come to see, more a drama about comprehending the passing of time, the inevitability of being spiritually scarred, experiencing felt loss, and the necessity of the Fall. *The Play About the Baby* had its world premiere in London, at the Almeida Theatre, on August 27, 1998, and its New York City opening at the Century Center for the Performing Arts on February 1, 2001. Brian Murray as Man and Marian Seldes as Woman drew rave reviews for their sterling performances, but the play's critical reception was decided mixed.

The drama features Boy and very pregnant Girl, whose opening line is, "I'm going to have the baby now" (3: 461). Although the audience never sees the baby, Girl gives birth and the young couple returns to center stage. Soon Man and Woman mysteriously appear, an older, worldly, and much wiser pair than the immature younger couple. And they are quite clear of purpose: they are body snatchers, we hear at the end of Act 1, here to steal the newborn child. By play's end, Man and Woman plan to steal more than a baby; they metaphorically steal Boy and Girl's security, identities, and their very perception of the Real. They even try to convince the newlyweds that their child never existed.

Ultimately, Man and Woman encourage them to embark on the age-old quest of progressing from ignorance and innocence to awareness and experience. And in their first steps toward gaining worldly knowledge, even Girl and Boy finally concede they are not yet experienced enough to raise a child. If *Who's Afraid of Virginia Woolf?* concerns an illusionary child who must be exorcized for Truth to take its rightful place within George and Martha's lives, *The Play About the Baby* concerns, in part, the necessity of maintaining illusions within a Fallen world in which paradise has long been lost. With the appearance of Man and Woman, an ominous sense of Terror begins to slowly permeate the stage.

Girl and Boy emerge as innocent, young, and very much in love with each other and their newborn child. Although this is a play about the baby, we never learn if it is a boy or a girl, never hear its name, and never see the baby. The child is defined by its absence. One of the key props in the New York production was a giant baby pacifier, a visual reminder that the parents of the newborn child are, as their names imply, but children themselves. After the birth of his child, Boy utters the cliché, "It's the miracle of life" (3: 461). At times, Boy acts like a baby himself, a point reinforced when he insists that he be breast-fed after Girl nurses the baby. The embodiment of superficiality, Boy and Girl are a well-matched, youthful, and sexually active couple. They are children raising an infant. They dash across the stage naked, "*a sweet chase, giggling*" (3: 473). Man reflects, "How innocent they are" (3: 474) and, seeing them frolic, adds, "You'd think it was Eden, wouldn't you" (3: 475). But they are hardly an Adam and Eve.

Albee subverts this supposedly idyllic world in a few early telling scenes. Boy recounts seeing a group of young men trying to sneak into a "Hopeless Mothers gig" (3: 463) a few years earlier, so in his role as ticket collector, he called the security guards on the group. That group vowed to get revenge on Boy, the "motherfucker" (3: 464). Moments later they attacked him, deliberately breaking his arm. Another unzipped his pants, perhaps to urinate on Boy or, the ellipses implies, perhaps to force himself on Boy, who to this day is not sure of one of his attacker's intentions. Luckily the group decides to just leave Boy on his knees and depart. This was, for Boy, a trauma that still haunts. He has, it turns out, been living in a post-Edenic world all along.

Indeed, Albee problematizes the very genesis of Girl and Boy's sexual and marital relationship. During Boy's very first encounter with Girl, who had been injured in an accident, he recalls, "I saw you there on the stretcher, all unconscious – I said – well, to myself, more than anyone – 'That's the one; that's my destination'" (3: 480). At the hospital, Boy assumes another identity, claiming to be her brother so he could be by her bedside when she awakes. Is this an innocent gesture from a smitten boy or more of a thinly veiled social perversion masquerading as normative behavior? Is he more of an Imp of the Perverse? Boy displays what Robert F. Gross calls a "necrophiliac rapture" when gazing at the unconscious girl, and, in a gesture that hints at even more troubling behavior – incest – by admitting to Girl that "being your brother made it even more intense – made me hard" (3: 481). Albee does not develop Boy's actions but, as Gross suggests, "the implication is that the heterosexual idyll of Boy-meets-Girl is even more intense when you add suggestions of necrophilia and incest to spice it up."⁹ The broader point, Albee seems to be suggesting, is that Boy and Girl's acting in the present as if they are in some kind of Paradise is but another of the many illusions upon which they rely. Albee emphasizes the point when in the present action when the sexually obsessed Boy forces Girl to engaged in sexual activities she at first resists – he has to grab her wrists repeatedly until "*a slightly annoyed*" Boy gets his way and she allows "*herself to be dragged off*" where whatever sexual act they engage in "hasn't been done for centuries; three religions outlawed it in the Middle Ages!" (3: 478). When they re-enter the stage, the Girl is not pleased: "That wasn't funny! Well, certainly not as funny as you thought it was – was going to be" (3: 480). Even Albee's fleeting references to mother and motherhood are problematic. The Girl's giving birth was filled with her howling in intense pain and with blood flowing everywhere; Boy's attackers, trying to see a "Hopeless Mothers" concert call him a "motherfucker" (3: 464). Man cannot even remember his own mother. The serpent, we see, has been living all along in this self-constructed Garden of Eden. Albee could have entitled this play *After the Fall* or *Paradise Lost*.

The play shifts into another key as Man enters. It is a Pirandellian entry as he, like Himself in *The Man Who Had Three Arms*, addresses the audience directly, reminding us of the metatheatricality of *The Play About the Baby*. His is a curious monologue on various subjects, such as the scent of the Boy and Girl, "youngsmell" (3: 466); the time it takes to drive a car to and from a destination; a brief aside about "Reality determined by our experience of it?" (3: 466); and the baffling account of how, when he went to introduce his mother to some friends at a cocktail party, he could not "remember who she was" (3: 467). He connects his disconnection with his mother with the ineluctable passing of time and "dread" that comes to the individual as he or she approaches death. After the cocktail party encounter, his mother, we are told, "died three years later" (3: 467). Man's encounter with his mother is a painful reminder, in Albee's world, that people will die "from being forgotten" (3: 467). He brings his monologue to a philosophic close regarding how memories fade, our scents fade, and how "we *invent*, and then *reinvent*" our own realities. (3: 468). But then his tone of voice turns more ominous as the questions he raises become touchstones into the play: "Pay attention to this, what's true and what isn't is a tricky business, no? What's real and what isn't? Trick. Do you follow? Yes? No? Good. (*Shrugs*) Whichever" (3: 468). These are essentially the same questions lying at the heart of *Who's Afraid of Virginia Woolf?* and in so many other Albee plays. The questions are tactical at first, then metaphysical. With his commanding presence and confidence, Man's questions have the feel of a life-challenge to both the audience and, of course, Girl and Boy. The sense of Terror infiltrating the stage in *A Delicate Balance*, the epistemological questions animating the stage in *Tiny Alice*, and the sense of what truly constitutes the Real in *The Lady from Dubuque* reinvent themselves in *The Play About the Baby*.

Later, Man enters into another slightly bewildering monologue on various subjects, such as the musicality of plays, pretending to be blind while attending a Royal Academy exhibition where he informs the audience about a sculpture with a "bronze penis rubbed golden by the hundreds of years of Florentine men touching it – for good luck, for potency" (3: 479). The key shift occurs near the end of his speech, when his ramblings once again take on a more ominous tone. In reference to the young parents' love of their newborn, Man asks two foreboding questions: "I wonder how much they love it? How much they need it?" and then says to the audience, "Perhaps we should find out. As the lady said, stay tuned" (3: 479).

If Man's presence adds to the unreal ambience of the play, so, too, does Woman's. After addressing the audience about herself – she insists she is neither an actress nor a journalist but is here to assist Man. They form a mysterious team whose purpose Albee only slowly, by increments, reveals. Boy and Girl have no idea who these people are or why they have entered their world. Like Man, Woman launches into a long monologue about various topics, from being a good cook to notes on her former husband and former lovers, one of whom, a painter, committed suicide over their breakup. She mentions her less-than-successful interview with a famous novelist while being startled by the young couple romping naked back and forth during her speech, which ends with a tantalizing remark to the audience: "As for who I am and what I *do*, stay tuned" (3: 474). Throughout much of the play one couple holds center stage while the other couple remains off stage, their entrances and exits forming a contrapuntal structure within the drama.

As the action unfolds, each couple exchanges stories, reflections on the past, and, for the young couple, some of their fears come to the surface. For example, Girl reveals she has talked to a Gypsy about her future, which prompts Boy to warn that Gypsies make things disappear, like money – and babies. Talk of Gypsies, the fear of baby stealing, and the entering and exiting of strangers

(Man and Woman) create a felt tension, a sense of pending doom, the feeling that some catastrophe is about to occur. Talk of Gypsies and kidnapping triggers a primal fear in Girl, who suddenly associates Gypsies with Man and Woman: "Maybe they're Gypsies! Come to steal the baby!" (3: 486). As Girl races to check on her child, Boy, who still thinks more with his penis than his mind, appears to be at the very beginning of some degree of self-reflection, limited as it may be. Considering the possibility of losing their child to kidnappers, he says gently to no one in particular,

> If there's anybody out there wants to do this to us – to hurt us so – ask *why?* Ask what we've *done?* I can take pain and loss and all the rest *later* – I *think* I can, when it comes as natural as … sleep? But … now? We're *happy;* we love each other; I'm hard all the time; we have a baby. We don't even under*stand* each other yet! (3: 488)

Such insights were beyond the ken of Boy at the beginning of the play. Such insights will soon become more compelling when, after Girl and Boy listen to Man and Woman get into a heated exchange, Man announces the purpose of their visit: "We've come to take the baby" (3: 495) and Act 1 closes with Girl, hysterical, asking, "WHERE'S THE BABY?! WHAT HAVE YOU DONE WITH THE BABY?!" to which both Man and Woman reply, "*what* baby?" (3: 496).

Albee stages a fast-paced Act 2. Man heightens the Mysterious when talking about the "real or imagined baby" (3: 503). Man and Woman, at times, seem to be older versions of Boy and Girl. As we have now seen, Albee very much calls our attention to the very nature of identity, the role of truth and illusion, the passage of time, and the necessity of the scar, and a "broken heart" (3: 509). As Man says on more than one occasion, "Wounds, children; wounds. Without wounds what *are* you? You're too young for the batterings time brings us …" (3: 508). Albee also conflates memory, as Man and Woman lay claim to past events that only happened to Girl and Boy while, suddenly, reinventing the present to move plot and action to its climax. The characters sometimes repeat lines from Act 1. The Get the Guests finally transforms into Bringing Up Baby in this play, as the Man turns into a vaudeville actor, tosses the bundle (the baby) in the air, with Girl screaming, and then snaps open the blanket: "Shazaam! You see? Nothing! No baby! Nothing!" (3: 530). The child's very existence remains shrouded in mystery and thus is called into question by both Girl and Boy as well as the audience, an audience which from the very beginning realizes that bringing a literal, realistic approach to "interpreting" this drama is fruitless. For Albee has created a non-realistic dream glide, a play resistant to traditional notions of theatrical propriety. As Anne Paolucci observes, "the action is like events in a dream, where things happen without explanation, often with vivid clarity. We wake from such an experiences emotionally drained and with a sense of having experienced something more real than our structured daily existence."[10]

Questions of identity, "Time; time the great leveler" (3: 512), the role of truth and illusion, issues of memory and the misremembering of actual events, innocence and experience, and an overwhelming sense of loss underpin *The Play About the Baby*. Further, the source of loss, for Boy and Girl, may ultimately be from within themselves. All that is missing, for the present moment in their lives, are the "wounds" (3: 534) to which Man alludes, the emotional scarring that must be experienced through the messy and complex business of living itself.

In brief, Man and Woman have launched the young couple on their quest to experience pain, suffering, and loss. Following the elder couple's suggestions, Girl and Boy decide that, in keeping with the absurdist logic of the play, indeed, they do not have a child. It has been an illusion. At final curtain they hear the baby crying, which may or may not be but an imaginary child, a lie of the mind. But Girl and Boy understand now, for the first time, the profound wounding of the heart and spirit that they must experience before they may embark on whatever kind of regenerative quest they choose to partake in in the future.

The Goat or, Who Is Sylvia? (Notes Toward a Definition of Tragedy)

The Goat or, Who Is Sylvia? (Notes Toward a Definition of Tragedy) is, for many, Albee's most provocative play. When theatergoers settled into their seats at the John Golden Theatre in New York City on March 10, 2002, little did they know just how transgressive a play it would be. Albee astonished the audience. At the start, we see a wealthy couple, proud parents of their sensitive gay teenage son, in their upscale apartment. The play features Martin Gray, who just turned fifty, a successful architect and the youngest winner to the Pritzker Prize, the most prestigious award in his profession. He recently has been "chosen to design The World City, the two hundred billion dollar dream city of the future ... set to rise in the wheatfields of our Middle West" (3: 553). As the curtain opens, he is distracted but readying to be interviewed for the television series "People Who Matter" by long-time friend and producer, Ross Tuttle. Stevie Gray, his attractive, well-spoken, and intelligent wife, is happily arranging flowers in their living room. Stevie adores and loves her husband of twenty-two years and, by outward appearances, theirs is an ideal marriage.

However, this is an Edward Albee play and, as seen in so many of the earlier plays, such as one also featuring the interaction of humans and animals, *Seascape*, marriages are problematic at best, and too often lead to a kind of spiritual-death-in-life existence for husbands and wives. Hence Albee + Marriage = Trouble. So it is hardly surprising in *The Goat*, moments after the action begins, that Stevie drops a line adumbrating the holy storm that is about to shatter all that is whole about this family: "The old foreboding? The sense that everything going right is a sure sign that everything's going wrong, of all the awful to come? All that?" (3: 542). Indeed, Martin by the end of Scene 1 confides to Ross that he is in love with another woman, Sylvia, who is a goat. A stunned and holier-than-thou Ross betrays his friend, mailing Stevie a letter about her husband's involvement in this taboo subject. The audience watches an ideal family implode in the final two scenes of this one-act tragedy, climaxing when Stevie returns home with the slaughtered sacrificial animal whose throat has been slashed and whose blood drenches both the dead animal and her executioner. While other American dramatists have also explored bestiality – Rochelle Owen's *Futz* (1965) comes to mind (and of course there is Woody Allen's popular 1972 film *Everything You Always Wanted to Know About Sex (But Were Afraid to Ask)* that features a scene in which Gene Wilder is in love with a sheep) – Albee's is the first play in the history of American drama to feature both a man in love with a goat and goatricide.

The Goat or, Who Is Sylvia? is, on one level, a play about bestiality. About ten minutes into the performance Martin tells his wife, "I've fallen in love! … Her name is Sylvia! … She's a goat" (3: 546–547). Stevie, not surprisingly, does not take him seriously and dismisses the baffling remark. But soon she and the audience realize just how disarmingly honest Martin, who until now has kept his affair a secret, is in disclosing his trespass. Upon first gazing at the goat, Martin relates how he was overwhelmed by a passion and love the likes of which he never experienced, even with his beloved wife: "I didn't know *what* it was – what I was feeling. It was … it wasn't like anything I'd felt before; it was … so … amazing, so … extraordinary! There she was, just looking at me, with those *eyes* of hers, and …" (3: 567). He cries out to Ross, "Yes! Yes! I am! I'm in love with her. Oh, Jesus! Oh, Sylvia! Oh, Sylvia!" (3: 568). When Martin shows Ross her photograph, his friend's response is unambiguous: "THIS IS A GOAT! YOU'RE HAVING AN AFFAIR WITH A GOAT! YOU'RE FUCKING A GOAT!" To which Martin, replies, "Yes" (3: 570). Many startled theatergoers at the John Golden Theatre that night shared Ross's visceral response, as will Stevie and Billy in the scenes that follow.

Of course *The Goat or, Who Is Sylvia?* is much more than a play about a "Goat fucker!" (3: 572). Its central subject lies elsewhere. Albee himself explains the point during an interview with Stephen Bottoms:

> That play isn't about goat-fucking. What I wanted to do is not just sit there being judges of the characters. I wanted people to go to that play, and imagine themselves in the situation, and really think hard about how they would respond if it was happening to them. That's really what I am after. Put yourself there. "How the fuck would I react? Why am I making this judgment about those people? Because I probably wouldn't make it if it was happening to me."[11]

This is Albee's invitation to challenge American cultural normative expectations about what it means to enter into a loving relationship whose very existence moves the play from its comedic opening to its tragic ending. If we accept Albee's claim, perhaps *The Goat* is less about bestiality just as, say, Paula Vogel's *How I Learned to Drive* (1997) is hardly about another cultural taboo, pedophilia. Rather, both plays explore the fundamental nature of love, proscribed societal notions of acceptable behavior, its affect on the Self and the Other, and the complex relationship between perceived cultural constructions of victim and victimizer. Albee invites audiences to rethink the very nature of love and the various ways in which societies, ancient and contemporary, define what is and is not morally acceptable behavior. As the playwright observes, "Every civilization sets quite arbitrary limits to its tolerances. The play is about a family that is deeply rocked by an unimaginable event and how they solve that problem. It is my hope that people will think afresh about whether or not all the values they hold are valid."[12] In this context, and regardless of the values put to the test in this drama, Martin is right when he notes that the Eumenides "don't stop" (3: 552).

As mentioned, *The Goat or, Who Is Sylvia?* is, for many, Albee's most provocative play, and we can take "provocative" in the broadest definitional sense. For Albee has produced a work intended to cause a reaction, perhaps in anger, disgust, or shock, and it is certainly a play that invites audiences to think more carefully about the implications of a man having an affair with an animal. Not surprisingly, "Provocative" also may be associated with, in certain contexts, behavior that is likely to arouse sexual desire.

The central subject of *The Goat*, we realize, has less to do with bestiality and more to do with the nature of sexual desire, the clash of urban and pastoral worlds, and the primal need for companionship and love in various provocative manifestations: in Martin's obsession and multiple sexual encounters with a female goat; in Martin's recounting of an adult getting an erection while holding his newborn baby, the implication being this is in reference to himself and his son Billy; in Stevie's perfectly understandable meltdown that animates Scene 2; in the brief moment when the son passionately kisses his father, which Albee calls a "*sexual kiss*" (3: 615) and which raises another tabooed subject – homosexual incest; and in Stevie's bloody – and provocative – revenge that closes the play. Perhaps such action explains the broad range of audience response to the play, which drew both praise and scorn, and which won numerous major awards for best new play of the year in 2002 (Tony, New York Drama Critics Circle, Drama Desk, and Outer Critics Circle). As one reviewer put it during the play's Washington, D.C., run in 2005, "Albee recalls that theatergoers sometimes walked out during performances of the play. Most commonly it happened not while goat love was being discussed but during a fleeting homoerotic sequence. 'Goats are okay as long as they are the right sex,' Albee concludes dryly. 'But don't try it with a guy.'"[13]

Many critics have noted Albee's allusion to Shakespeare's *The Two Gentlemen of Verona*, whose song about the beautiful and faithful Silvia serves as a possible touchstone into some of Albee's larger concerns. Shakespeare writes,

> Who is Silvia? What is she,
> That all our swains commend her?
> Holy, fair, and wise is she;
> The heaven such grace did lend her,
>   That she might admired be.   (IV, ii, 39–43.)

Albee parodies the first two lines, as Stevie reflects,

> Who is Sylvia.
> What is she
> That all our goats commend her ...   (3: 584)

Albee does not develop the allusion to Shakespeare's song, but the parallels of the celebration of a pure love in the song mirror Martin's primal and immediate attraction to the goat, whose eyes transfix him upon their first meeting. The final two stanzas to the song, in other words, capture the emotional attachment and pure love Martin has for Sylvia:

> Is she kind as she is fair?
> For beauty lives with kindness.
> Love doth to her eyes repair,
> To help him of his blindness;
>   And, being help'd, inhabits there.
>
> Then to Silvia let us sing,
> That Silvia is excelling;
> She excels each mortal thing

Upon the dull earth dwelling.
　　To her let us garlands bring.　　　　(IV, ii, 44–53)

If *The Two Gentlemen of Verona* is a comedy dramatizing betrayals and love, *The Goat or, Who Is Sylvia?* lays claim to similar issues. Of course in Shakespeare's play, harmony, order, and, above all, love ultimately return to their rightful place in the social order, whereas in Albee's play, disharmony, disorder, and shattered love reign supreme by the final curtain.

Albee also tantalizes readers with another subtitle in the published version of his play: *(Notes Toward a Definition of Tragedy)*. If the play hardly fulfills (nor should it have to) all of characteristics of Aristotelean tragedy, there is enough of a postmodernist version of loss in *The Goat* to move audiences "toward a definition of tragedy." While it may be an exaggeration to call Martin a tragic hero, and he hardly exudes the stubborn pride (hubris) of a Kreon in Sophocles' *Antigone* (441 BC) or a Willy Loman in Arthur Miller's *Death of a Salesman* (1949), he does display his own version of a fatal flaw or error of judgment (hamartia), experiences a profound reversal of fortune (peripeteia), and certainly discovers that his fall to the bottom of fortune's wheel has been brought about by his own actions. But he does not come to some epiphanic moment in which he experiences catharsis, purgation, and a coming to consciousness. Nor do his actions somehow affect the nation, although, as J. Ellen Gainor suggests, his planned World City introduces an ecological/environmental clash of the rural versus the urban that will affect the polis.[14]

The repartee between Martin and Stevie in Scene 2 sparkles in both text and performance. When Stevie announces, "I think we 'd better talk about this. If I'm going to kill you I need to know exactly why – all the details" (3: 582), Martin obliges, explaining how, in looking for a second home for the family in the country-side nearby, he met his future lover, Sylvia, who "was looking at me with those eyes of hers and … I melted, I think" (3: 597). Moments later he adds, "And there was a connection there – a communication – that, well, an epiphany, I guess comes closest, and I knew what was going to happen" (3: 599). Martin also explains that he sought professional help but therapy only exacerbated his loneliness, for all the other patients were unhappy and wanted to be cured, whereas he could not understand "what was wrong with … with … being in love … like that" (3: 589). Martin's sense of isolation and aloneness only increases so that, finally, pressed by his friend, he confides in Ross as a form of emotional release. Of course this turns out to be a fateful decision. For Ross betrays his friend twice – first in sending the letter about Sylvia to Stevie, and second in telling her where she can find her rival. Throughout Scene 2 both Stevie and the audience are struck by the specificity with which Martin chronicles his beastly affair in ways distantly reminiscent of the specificity with which

Martha recalls what her imaginary son looked like as a baby in *Who's Afraid of Virginia Woolf?* In a momentary exchange between father and son – "Billy *(really sad)*: Oh, Dad! Martin: Poor Dad?" – Albee seems to be alluding to a fellow playwright whose title and subtitle foreshadow part of Martin's marital fate: Arthur Kopit's *Oh Dad, Poor Dad, Mama's Hung You in the Closet and I'm Feelin' So Sad: A Pseudoclassical Tragifarce in a Bastard French Tradition* (1960).

Martin's revelations devastate Stevie. For her, it is the ultimate, to borrow Susan Sontag's phrase, "negative epiphany."[15] The stage directions ascribed to Stevie capture the emotional hemorrhaging she experiences. "*Grotesque incomprehension*" (3: 596) as well as "*Hideous enthusiasm*" (3: 597) inform her body language until she reaches a breaking point and "*howls three times, slowly, deliberately; a combination of rage and hurt*" (3: 599). Moreover, once the reality of her situation sets in, she knows a kind of spiritual death awaits: "I realized – probably in the way if you suddenly fell off a building – oh, shit! I've fallen off a building and I'm going to die; I'm going to go splat on the sidewalk" (3: 580). Suddenly her ideal marriage becomes as problematic, indeed, tragic as any marriage depicted in the Albee canon. Stevie, we realize, has been on top of fortune's wheel in her twenty-two years of marriage only to find herself on the bottom of fortune's wheel when least expected:

> Something can happen that's outside the rules, that doesn't relate to The Way The Game Is Played. Death before you're ready to even think about it – that's part of the game. A stroke that leaves you sitting looking at an eggplant the week before had been your husband – that's another. Emotional disengagement, gradual, so gradual you don't even know it's happening, or sudden – not very often, but occasionally – that's another. You've read about your spouses – God! I hate that word! – "spouses" who all of a sudden start wearing dresses – Yours, or their own collection – wives gone dyke ... but if there's one thing you *don't* put on your plate, no matter how exotic your tastes may be is ... bestiality. (3: 581)

Stevie's reactions throughout Scene 2 intensify as she symbolically shatters expensive vases, the outer manifestation of her inner turmoil and rage. Above all, she experiences a profound sense of loss. A broken spirit, not broken vases, begins to inhabit the stage. As Stevie says to her husband in a hard, low voice, "Because you've broken something and it can't be fixed!" (3: 604). Thus Stevie sets her sights on getting what from her point of view will be revenge and justice: "You have brought me down, you goat-fucker; you love of my love! You have brought me down to *nothing! (Accusatory finger right at him)* You have brought me down, and, Christ!, I'll bring you down with me!" (3: 605). This is what Albee in *Who's Afraid of Virginia Woolf?* calls "total war."

Albee releases his postmodern Furies at the end of the play. Stevie seeks justice through revenge. In the closing moments, a sense of myth, ritual, violence, and sacrifice coalesce with Stevie's bloody entrance in which she drags her slain rival's body across the stage. A visually arresting scene, her homecoming moves the play toward a new definition of tragedy. Sylvia's crime? "She loved you … you say. As much as *I* do" (3: 622), Stevie utters quietly in her last lines. Perhaps her choice of the present tense hints at the possibility of reconciliation – Stevie does not say "As much as *I* did" but "as *I* do" – yet a bleaker reading of the ending is probably more in accord with the playwright's vision.

There is an overwhelming sense that this marriage is forever broken. These are characters whose lives are as shattered as the vases littering a home that lies in "*ruins*" (3: 606). Martin cannot fathom why anyone would slit the innocent goat's throat. By the final curtain, he is a defeated, shell-shocked, and sobbing man. His apologies at the end seem empty, emanating from a voice drained of its timbre. At the start of the play, Martin was at the pinnacle of his career, a celebrated professional whose future surely brimmed with more and greater dazzling successes. By play's end, he is reduced by his Medea to a conquered man set adrift in a world devoid of authentic meaning and discernible borders. The road map to The Future City has been lost. The goat may have lost its physical life, but it is, Albee implies, even worse for her human counterparts. Just as Martin had crushed his wife's spirit, so Stevie has succeeded in crushing her husband's. Stevie in one sense emerges victorious – the adulterous couple has been vanquished, her victory total. Yet her victory comes at a tragic price. She is now the image of a woman whose vitality has been leeched from her very being. While Sylvia's blood has literally been drained out of a slit throat and drips off of her conqueror's arms, Stevie's blood, Albee suggests, has been spiritually drained from her. A once vital woman, Stevie is now a woman whose vitality is nowhere in evidence. In a play animated by full, raw emotion, she is by the final curtain an emotionless woman filled with emptiness. A victim of a well-meaning but wayward husband, Stevie faces a future whose only certainty is its uncertainty. Billy faces a new world in which it is very possible he becomes a cosmic waif, drifting with little or no clear purpose. His may be a plea for the restoration of a whole, loving family, but since he, too, is reduced to a note toward a definition of tragedy, his future world seems as unstable and mutable as his present world. The Billy of *Who's Afraid of Virginia Woolf?* could always escape; he could always walk away to deliver another telegram. Billy (the goat, or, if you prefer, the kid) of *The Goat or, Who Is Sylvia?*, by contrast, cannot escape from the sins of an immediate past that have been foisted upon him. By play's end, Billy must be a lighter shade of Gray.

The beautiful messy inconclusiveness of the play's ending does not necessarily preclude a return to order, but the likelihood of such a return seems remote, if not impossible. To some, Sylvia has been transformed from mere goat to scapegoat, as Boróka Prohászka Rád suggests, "the foreigner who is sacrificed in order to save the still indispensable member of the community." But, unfortunately for this twenty-first century family, *The Goat or, Who is Sylvia? (Notes Toward a Definition of Tragedy)* may turn "into a playful mockery of its own subtitle, subverting the idea of a single scapegoat and dispersing the role of the tragic victim onto all three of the Grays."[16] Albee leaves Martin, Stevie, and Billy to face the Void with little or no sense of moral direction or family unity. The family's last name – Gray – is all too fitting, for they inhabit a world that is neither black nor white but gray, symbolically that ineffable "color" of human experience in which behavioral borders, cultural hegemony, and, above all, familial love must be called into question. The answers to such questions will vary for each member of the audience, but it is clear that Albee's play achieves what great theater does: it provokes an audience to think, to respond, to become emotionally involved in a spectacle whose various and controversial subject matters have a purchase on our consciousness. Still, the closing lines of the play, voiced by a son who gets no reaction from his parents – "Dad? Mom?" (3: 622) – must, for now, go unanswered.

Chapter 9

A Theater of Loss

Occupant

When I met Edward Albee for the first time, in 1980, he had just published "Louise Nevelson: The Sum and the Parts," an introduction to *Louise Nevelson: Atmospheres and Environments*. Nevelson, one of the most revered sculptors of the twentieth century, is the central subject of *Occupant*, the playwright's homage to his dear friend. Soon after her death, in April 1988 at age eighty-eight, Albee recalled that Nevelson was "a talker of incomparable talent."[1] In this two-character play, spotlighting an interview with The Man and Nevelson, we learn much about both the public persona and the private sensibility of this incomparably talkative artist. The play opened with preview performances on February 5, 2002, at the Signature Theatre in New York City. Anne Bancroft played the lead. However, Bancroft came down with pneumonia and had to withdraw from the show, "so the production never officially opened" (3: 624). Finally, on June 5, 2008, the play enjoyed its premiere at the Signature, with Mercedes Ruehl delivering a powerful performance as Louise Nevelson. The action unwinds within a minimalist set whose platforms, with black wooden furniture, appear as imagistic allusions to Nevelson's signature sculptural style. Toward the play's end, wood sculptures slowly appear, and finally the whole back stage "*is filled with her art work*" (3: 690). It is an appropriate bit of visual theatricks.

The plot and action of *Occupant* is, for Edward Albee, refreshingly straightforward, despite the fact that the character of Nevelson comes back from the dead some twenty years later to speak with the knowledgeable, if at times testy, even hostile, interviewer, simply called The Man. The play charts her upbringing, from her birth as Louise Berliawsky in Kiev, Russia, to Jewish parents in 1899, the family's immigration to the United States six years later, and her childhood insecurities to her ill-fated marriage to the wealthy New Yorker Charles Nevelson, the birth of her son, her subsequent divorce and abandoning her son for European travels, studies, and sexual affairs, and, finally, to her return to New York City. There her hard-earned and painstakingly slow rise, beginning in the 1950s, to prominence as a woman artist of singular talent emerged. (Financially struggling most of her life, Nevelson died with her estate worth an estimated $100 million.) The play spotlights, too, key emotional moments in the sculptor's life, moments that ultimately would give her the courage to be the fiercely independent artist whose flamboyant dress and deportment were as well known as her art work would finally become. As Albee said, "'She was always doing a performance. Nevelson in public was Nevelson in private, and even at home she never came downstairs without all the makeup.'"[2] Hence the attention-grabbing hats, jewelry, dresses, and, above all, sable eyelashes, costumes that came to visually define that public persona that was Louise Nevelson.

Albee's *Occupant*, like *The Lady from Dubuque* before it and *Me, Myself & I* after, raises broader questions about self-identity, and the various ways in which such identity is remembered, misremembered, and projected, both in terms of a public self and a private individual. In this regard, *Occupant* also raises fundamental epistemological questions about how the individual can accurately know what is knowable, and how can one find an appropriate vocabulary that adequately expresses meaning. Beyond the important question of "Who am I?" Albee's play asks, "How is social identity created, nurtured, preserved?" And "how does one construct a private self, a personal sense of identity that might complement the celebrity-hood that Nevelson achieved and reveled in?" In addressing such questions, Albee does not portray Nevelson as merely the absolutely determined-to-succeed woman that she was but also as a woman filled with self-doubt, self-disclosure, all-too-human frailty and fallibility. Albee succeeds in resurrecting a woman who has been dead for twenty years (the number of years being dead can be adjusted, the stage directions read, to the time of a new actual performance of the play) and reminding audiences of her remarkable life within the modern art world.

Nevelson enjoyed *Tiny Alice* and its unique set, which "with its specific construction of a miniature house onstage has been very important to the images in my work," she once observed. As Mel Gussow reports in his excellent biography on Albee, "Inspired by *Tiny Alice,* she created a series of small 'dream houses,' which led to the walk-in environment 'Mrs. N's Palace.' In the catalogue [*Atmospheres and Environments*], Albee wrote, 'Nevelson feels that she began making her "worlds" as an alternative space, so to speak – to create for herself a fathomable reality in the midst of the outside chaos. What has happened, of course, is that the private has become public, the refuge accessible to all.' Something similar could be said about Albee, himself."[3]

Something similar could be said about *Occupant* as well. For what Albee has staged is not merely a theatricalized biography. It is a play in which the private has become the public. The younger man, in his forties, animates this private/public dialectic by introducing Nevelson to a third actor in the play: the audience. Indeed, as Albee has done in so many of his plays, audience participation becomes an important element within the spectacle. Each character directly addresses the audience at times, involving them, if possible, as active participants in the dramatic experience. As the play unfolds, the interviewer asks the predicable question here, the unexpected query there, his emotional registers signified by the seemingly minor but telling stage directions noted before he delivers his lines. The Man often reacts positively, as noted from the following words Albee deploys: He *"laughs"* (3: 628, 630), and seems *"amused"* (3: 629), even *"genuine"* (3: 634); at other times he sports a *"slight smile"* (3: 640) and plays to the audience, *"mouth open in astonishment"* (3: 638). Soon his deportment is *"casual"* (3: 644). However, at other times Albee directs The Man to act more ambivalently: he *"sighs"* (3: 628) and acts as if he is *"placating"* Nevelson. Body language and verbal language inhabit the play space simultaneously as The Man appears *"apologetic"* (3: 637), then is seen *"gently needling"* (3: 629) the sculptor; at other moments he appears *"a little dubious"* (3: 635) as he, confused by Nevelson's response, tries *"to pin it down"* (3: 637). Some in the audience are not sure how to interpret the action when The Man simply *"shrugs"* (3: 646). Finally, Albee indicates through his stage directions some of The Man's negative (body) language: he is at one point *"mildly put out"* (3: 628), is seen as *"scoffing"* (3: 635) at his guest; after Nevelson fires back at one question, The Man holds his *"hand up, in surrender"* (3: 635), and moments later he *"shakes his head; grudgingly"* (3: 640). Minutes later his response to Nevelson is *"false"* (3: 646). Finally, some of his questions seem deliberately offensive, as he launches a *"new attack"* (3: 634) on the artist.

So while some reviewers found The Man unsatisfying, and his demeanor off-putting, his role is nonetheless important to play. For his shifts in emotional registers make this more than just a Q & A with a famous dead person, and such shifts reveal Albee's dramatic strategy. Albee writes a script filled with questions that allow Nevelson to shine, to star in her own show. She becomes the occupant of her own space. The Man knows when to press. He knows when to back off. He allows her the narrative space that gives the play its mimetic energy. By doing so, The Man generates a theatrical give-and-take that not only showcases Albee's linguistic dexterity but creates its own metadramatic tension within the play. As Anne Paolucci observes, "what we actually have is a fencing match" between the two characters.[4]

Louise Nevelson, of course, is the key interviewee. She forms the nerve center of *Occupant*. As in real life, the fictional Nevelson is an ambitious and ambiguous figure. She is, among other things, her own performance artist and costume designer. Theatergoers gaze upon a Nevelson dressed in Noh robes, a turban, and those conspicuous sable eyelashes. For some, she would make Dali's mustache and eyes seems prosaic. At times she addresses the audience directly, claiming more than once that The Man does not understand what he is talking about. At other times she opens up about deeply personal matters. What we are seeing is the growth of an artist as a young, then older, woman. She shares several transformative experiences that ultimately gave her the courage to pursue true art. For example, she reflects back to when she was a young girl and was transfixed by a horse and its unbridled freedom:

> I was coming home from school, and I was eleven maybe, and all of a sudden there was this huge black horse … running, alone, with no harness, or carriage. Maybe it'd broken away from the stable. And there it was – huge, bigger than any horse I'd ever seen. All black, and against the green everywhere - everything was in foliage, everything was in bloom – I was running home from school, and I ran to keep up with the horse, the … huge black horse. But I couldn't, of course; so I stopped and watched as long as I could … until it vanished. I've never forgotten that. Nothing has ever affected me like that. Ever. (3: 661–662)

From an eleven-year-old's viewpoint, the horse represented a kind of freedom, beauty, power, and strength, qualities the Nevelson would need later in life as she broke barriers in the male-dominated New York City sculpture world.

A second transformational experience for the sculptress came when she visited the Musee de L'homme in Paris, where she was stunned by the power of African sculpture, which "knocked Picasso out, and it knocked me out, too … Picasso's cubism and this so-called primitive art. These two things; *they* changed me, too" (3: 679). Like her childhood experience with the horse, her witnessing the art in Paris provided her with inspiring models, models that became equipment for living for her. It gave her the courage to realize that "it's all about the damn specialness you've felt about yourself ever since you were a little girl. You're special; you're talented; you are going to be somebody" (3: 681). Such experiences, moreover, highlight the importance Albee places on the metaphysical question, "Who Am I?" Artistically, this question of identity leads Nevelson toward greatness by creating a room of her own, or, if you prefer, a space of her own. In a gesture of self- assessment, she recognizes that "You're going to be your*self*. You're going to find out who that 'you' is – what that 'you' is – and you're going to … *occupy* that *space* … if it kills you" (3: 681).

Yet another transformative moment for Nevelson came at New York's Metropolitan Museum. She was, we hear, stunned by the sheer aesthetic beautify of "costumes for the Japanese Noh theatre!" To her, "each robe was a universe … Some of them had gold cloth with medallions, and the cloth was so finely woven that the likes of it I never saw before" (3: 677). Like the dark horse, Picasso, and the African art, the Japanese robes became garments she herself would embrace, the ultimate Nevelson costume, an extension of her very being. The robes were nothing less than epiphanic for her: "... Oh, my God, life is worth living if a civilization can give us this. And so I sat there and wept, and wept and sat. And I went home, and it gave me a whole new life" (3: 677). And, in Albee's play, it gave Nevelson a new-found sense of consciousness.

Galvanized by such self-awareness, Nevelson ushers the play toward its climax with the brief story about wood. With friends (like Albee himself), she collected wood throughout the city – "broken chairs, banisters, flat pieces, anything" (3: 689). These would become the materials she would use in her sculptures, of course, works of art that conferred upon its creator a fame and respect for which she worked a lifetime. Albee near the play's end slowly fills the stage with wooden sculptures, a visual reminder of his protagonist's contributions to modern art. As Nevelson puts it, "But if you finally come *into* yourself like I did, if you know the space you ... occupy ... well, then ... you go on ... You work harder than ever. You turn the world into one huge Nevelson. It was ... fucking ... wonderful" (3: 691).

Albee winds down the action by having Nevelson reflect on her dying and death. Her fame, we learn, follows her to her hospital room, where she lays dying of lung cancer. Her famous name has been placed on her door – in capital letters. Wanting her privacy, to die with dignity and respect, she orders the nurses to remove her name and in its place has her new name placed on her door: "Occupant" (3: 696).

Not surprisingly, *Occupant* drew mixed reviews. But Albee in this play once again shows his artistic courage to experiment with theatrical convention, to create new, inventive forms, and to challenge audiences, to make audiences work, to think, to reflect about a play that is ultimately about selected issues of a nation as reflected through the private anxieties of the individual. As Paolucci suggests, "*Occupant* is all about Nevelson, but it is also about the rest of us, as we struggle to find our own niche, as we lay down the road that will take us to what is our own space, our work-in-progress."[5] And this is why this play occupies an important, if relatively minor, place within Albee's oeuvre.

Knock! Knock! Who's There!?

Edward Albee has composed one of the longest plays in American dramatic history – *Who's Afraid of Virginia Woolf?* (257 pages in the revised 2005 Broadway revival edition) – and one the shortest as well – *Knock! Knock! Who's There!?*

He calls it his "one-page … frippery" (3: 7). The "Author's Note" preceding the play is longer than the play itself, which was first performed at the McCarter Theatre Center in Princeton, on October 25, 2003. Emily Mann directed and, in a delightful choice for casting, Bruce Webber, the *New York Times* theater critic, lent his voice to the tape recorded drama. For the set, Albee insists on a boarded up doorway placed somewhere in the theater: in a hallway near the restroom or in a remote part of the theater lobby. The plot and action are simple. The audience hears knocking, thumping sounds and the cries of a entrapped theater critic: "Help! Help! …. Is anyone there? …. Help! Someone's locked me in here! Let me out! … I'm a critic! Let me out! … Help!" (3: n.p.) Albee ends his script with a stage direction that reads, "*Repeat endlessly.*" As the dramatist explains, "the entire play should be performed over and over again whenever the theatre is accessible to the patrons" (3: n.p.).

For nearly six decades Albee and the theater critics had what could charitably be called a problematic relationship. Not surprisingly, Albee loves Beckett's famous line in *Waiting for Godot*, "crritic." To be sure, there are many Albeephiles who find much to praise in the latest Albee work, even if such praise might seem a bit of a reach. On the other hand, the Albeephobes have been voicing their displeasure with his works for his entire career. John Simon and Frank Rich, to cite but two theater critics, often appeared more as self-annointed hatchet men than reasonable and objective critics. The hostility of some critics became so intense by the 1980s that Albee, along with such fellow major American playwrights as Arthur Miller, David Mamet, Sam Shepard, and Tony Kushner, began staging their works abroad – in Vienna, London, Edinburgh – and in various cities around the United States that geographically and symbolically were as far from New York City Broadway critics as possible. Albee surely delighted in writing this forty-four-word play about a critic for whom there is No Exit.

At Home at the Zoo

For years Albee wanted to "flesh out" his brilliant first composition, *The Zoo Story*. Nearly five decades later, he did just that, creating a two-act version. He composed *Homelife* (Act 1) and then included *The Zoo Story* (Act 2), at first entitled *Peter and Jerry*, and finally re-christened *At Home at the Zoo*. As Albee explained in 2007, "There's a first act here somewhere which will flesh out Peter fully and make the subsequent balance better. Almost before I knew it, *Homelife* fell from my mind to the page … *intact*. There was the Peter I had always known – a full three-dimensional person and – wow! – here was Ann, his wife, whom I must have imagined deep down, forty-some years ago, but hadn't brought to consciousness."[6] In 2013, Albee pointed out to David Crespy and Lincoln Konkle that *The Zoo Story*

> Was my first play, and you don't necessarily get everything right in your first play ... I was aware by the time I had finished writing it that I had written a play about one and a half characters. Jerry is a three-dimensional person. Peter was not fleshed out sufficiently to be a fully dimensional character ... So what I did was write another forty-five minute play to be performed before *The Zoo Story* which introduces us to the character Peter and his wife Ann. It lets us understand a great deal about who he was so that we will understand more comprehensively about why he behaves the way he does to Jerry ....[7]

Today Albee does not permit *The Zoo Story* to be staged as a stand-alone play.

Albee also made minor changes to *The Zoo Story*: Peter's salary is adjusted, going from $18,000 to $200,000 a year; the allusion to Baudelaire remains but the second author changes from J. P. Marquand to Stephen King; references to "the Village" become "Greenwich Village"; there are a few minor changes to the stage directions; and he deletes a few lines – some really textured ones – during the climatic knifing scene. A curious change comes in the form of the character descriptions of Peter and Jerry; in the original *The Zoo Story*, such descriptions are richly symbolic pre-texts, brimming with allusions to their physical appearance and, more importantly (especially for directors, actors, and readers), their spiritual condition. In *Homelife*, Peter's description is reduced, though still telling; Jerry's remains the same, luckily. However, in Act 2, *The Zoo Story*, Albee minimizes much of the stage directions regarding the setting, which is disappointing. For audiences or readers familiar with the original 1959 play, the changes seem minor; but a new generation coming to the play for the first time misses out on the richly presented character and setting descriptions in the original that add to our better understanding of the clash of two worlds that so animate Peter and Jerry's fated and fatal encounter. The revisions are curious, if only because the original dazzles. Further, Albee omits the informative original "Preface," in which he, with humor, introduces the play and himself to the world. Revisions nonetheless made, the Hartford Stage Company premiered the play on June 6, 2004, with the New York City debut at the Second Stage Theatre following on November 11, 2007. While lacking the emotional and narrative energy of *The Zoo Story*, *Homelife* stands as a decorous and worthy first act of *At Home at the Zoo*. It fulfills, for many, what Albee observed as early as 2004: "I always thought that there was more to the character of Peter. He was seen by many audiences through the eyes of Jerry. I think people will find him now more sympathetic and understandable."[8]

Homelife, as its title implies, concerns Peter and his wife, Ann, within the comforts of their Upper East Side apartment in New York City. This is hardly the seedy apartment seen in, say, Suzan Lori-Parks' *Topdog/Underdog* (2001); rather, this is vintage Albeeland: a nicely furnished, neat apartment whose inhabitants are, if not rich, certainly well off, white, educated, comfortable. This setting underscores the symbolic logic of the play, for ultimately Albee, as he has done throughout his oeuvre, wants to upset the delicate balance of Peter and Ann's well-appointed and orderly home. Just as the set and setting are familiar Albee choices, so the plot unwinds in classic Albeean fashion. When theatergoers watch the opening moments of the play, they see a Peter, now slightly older (forty-five years old) than the original Peter, who is "bland; not heavy; pleasant, if uninteresting looking. Tidy; circumspect. Wears glasses to read" (n.p.). He is self-absorbed, reading a textbook that the publishing company for whom he works will soon bring out. His wife, Ann, thirty-eight years old, enters from the kitchen, towel in hand. Albee describes her as "Tall, a bit angular; pleasant looking, unexceptional" (n.p.). In her opening lines that foreshadow Jerry's impulse to communicate in *The Zoo Story*, she announces to a distracted Peter, "We should talk" (9). Indeed, in a distant way Ann is to Peter what Jerry will be to Peter later that afternoon: she is the feminized and much more in control, lucid, intelligent, and loving version of Peter's antagonist in *The Zoo Story*, the crazed one whose irrepressible impulse to communicate with Peter culminates in a ritualized suicide/murder. In *Homelife* her reflections on her own life – should she undergo a mastectomy? Have an affair? Are her own needs, sexual and otherwise, being satisfied? – lead to, for Peter, inconvenient, and then disturbing, questions about their marriage and the values underpinning their relationship. Thus their urbane apartment becomes a contestatory zone, where gentle and even humorous banter yields to deeper questioning about the complacency and normality of their bourgeois existence, which in turn leads to painful admissions on both their parts, culminating with Ann's completely uncharacteristic and surprising physical assault on Peter, the hard slap to the face completely unnerving him – and adumbrating his fatal encounter with Jerry hours later. On the brink of the abyss, of facing the Truth, Peter and Ann at play's end come to the Beckettian recognition that there is nothing to be done about their marriage, since the "safe" patterns of their past return and their impulse to live, to be, are (re)pressed back into the safe, predictable world where their lives will be, as Tolstoy writes in *The Death of Ivan Ilych (1886)*, "most simple and most ordinary and therefore most terrible."[9]

Albee works carefully to flesh out Peter. This is clearly a man who prefers the path of least resistance, who prefers not to get involved with the messy business of living itself. If Peter worries that his "penis seems to be … retreating" (29), it is emblematic of his stance toward the self and the other – to retreat from the difficult or complex situations, to retreat, indeed, from the realization that his marriage is veering toward stagnation. No wonder Ann calls him "Mr. Circumspection" (32). Or as Peter puts it, "I'm not a bad person, you know; my life may not be very exciting … no jagged edges …" (42). Ann presses, inquiring if Peter has the courage to face their marriage authentically, to acknowledge that perhaps his love is not enough, and to address her primal fears, to which he replies:

> I thought we both made a decision – when we decided to be together, or even before we knew each other – I thought we made a decision, *must* have made one, that what we wanted was a smooth voyage on a safe ship, a view of porpoises now and then, a gentle swell, bright clouds way off, a sense that it was a … familiar voyage, though we'd never take it before – a pleasant journey, all the way through. And that's what we're having …. (45)

Although Ann agrees, she clearly remains bothered by the status of their marriage. She yearns for wild passion, lust even. But in Bartleby-like fashion, Peter prefers not to. There is more than a hint of Tobias from *A Delicate Balance* and Charlie from *Seascape* here.

The source of his sexual reluctance, we soon learn, stems from a formative encounter he had a quarter of a century earlier with a young woman at college, where in an arranged fraternity sex party he was to make love to her. To Peter's surprise, she preferred anal sex, which became so rough and bloody that she had to seek medical aid. Peter, traumatized by the violent encounter, vowed never to harm a woman again: "So … so I've been careful never to hurt anyone – to hurt *you*; you being everyone for so long now" (52). So the one time he gave into what Ann craves – where two individuals "become animals, *strangers*, with nothing less than impure simple lust for one another" (47) – was such a negative experience that Peter has been, by his own admission, "too careful … too gentle …." (53), not only in his intimate life, but in his entire life. Peter is, we see, hardly equipped to take the "disorder," "chaos," and "madness" (55) Ann wants to embrace.

Kindness and cruelty – the teaching emotion – is not limited to *The Zoo Story*. They also reveal themselves, however briefly, in *Homelife*: after hearing about Peter's college sex encounter, Ann voices her own personal frustrations and looks Peter "*in the face, smiles, slaps him hard. His mouth opens in astonishment; she kisses his cheek where she slapped him*" (55). Here is a momentary breakthrough, what in *The Zoo Story* Jerry calls "contact." For a precious few moments Peter and Ann let their emotional guards down, embrace "the chaos! The madness!" (56). They fantasize about devouring their birds, their girls, and even themselves. Just when the audience might expect some epiphanic, life-changing moment, however, Albee subverts that moment. In its place, we see a Beckett-like ending in which Ann repeats her opening-scene activity – "I think I'll try doing the spinach again" (57) and Peter regains circumspection and retreats into the spiritual inertia that defines his very existence. He prepares to read again – this time in the park, where he will soon meet Jerry. Honest communication between this couple proves to be too much, and they retreat into their deadening habits once again, the momentary glimpse of passion fading along with any hope of some kind of spiritual rejuvenation. Ann knows too well that "there's nothing to be done" (42). They are married, do love each other, but live if not in parallel worlds, in worlds more separated than they realize. Ann emerges as another strong, independent, intelligent Albee woman, though it is, in Albee's world, preordained that her search for raw, animal pleasure will go unfulfilled. Instead, many of the key issues in *The Zoo Story* reveal themselves in the prequel: loneliness in the midst of companionship; the inability to communicate honestly; and a sense of Terror in the common. The safe, predictable world of the well-meaning-yet lacking Peter, of course, will be forever shattered in the next hour or so when he retreats to Central Park and experiences the death-saturated world that is *The Zoo Story*.

Me, Myself & I

Fellow playwright and director, Emily Mann, commissioned Albee to stage *Me, Myself & I*, which was first presented at the Berlind Theater at the McCarter Theater Center in Princeton, New Jersey, on January 25, 2008 and, later, at Playwrights Horizons theater in New York City on September 12, 2010. Predictably, the play drew largely mixed to negative reviews, a pattern now long associated with most premieres of a new Albee play.[10] Although the two-act play lasts some two hours, it appears more as a vaudevillian, comedic, and absurdist sketch than a fully realized drama, but the repartee sparkles, and its broader familial and cultural concerns resonate. As he did in *The American Dream* nearly six decades earlier, Albee's language – the witty, fast-paced dialogues, filled with linguistic disconnects, humor, sarcasm, bafflement, and terror – animate the stage. The play concerns another disjointed Albee family: Mother, a self-absorbed matriarch who does not know which of her sons is which; her twenty-eight-year-old identical twins, the mean-spirited OTTO and the meek and confused otto, the palindromically named children adding to the confusion about identity that lies at the core of the play; Dr., Mother's physician boyfriend who moved in years earlier when the Man/Father, upon seeing his newly born offspring, abandoned the family; and Maureen, otto's attractive girlfriend whose distant cousin could be Shelly from Sam Shepard's *Buried Child* (1978).

Mother, who thinks one child loves her and the other does not, begins nearly all of her conversations with her children with such questions as "Who *are* you? Which one *are* you? ... I never know which one you are ... Are you the one who loves me?"[11] Indeed, the question of identity underpins the absurdist world this dysfunctional family inhabits. The domineering OTTO reinforces the point when announcing he has decided to move to China and to reimagine himself; he will, he claims, become Chinese. Moreover, he denies the existence of otto, which sends the "good" twin first into an emotional tailspin, then into an existentialist crisis about his very being in the world. Recounting gazing into the mirror, OTTO enjoys his life-altering moment: "I realized it *wasn't* my image I saw there; it was just like ... exactly like me ... but it *wasn't* me; it was someone else. It was me identically; it was my *real* identical twin" (66). Despite otto's desperate protests – "No! You're my *brother!*" (67) – OTTO confers upon his newly-minted imaginary brother both his "real" status in the world and his new name: *Otto*, the italics and Capital *O* distinguishing and distancing him from the disowned otto. As otto's sense of abandonment and confusion intensifies, he learns that his manipulative twin just seduced Maureen, who did not realize she was sleeping with OTTO. As the play draws to its close, otto still can't believe OTTO was "Fucking my Maureen!" (77).

As the play draws to a close, Albee spotlights its carnivalesque nature by having the Man/Father suddenly return home after twenty-eight years. With trumpets, bells, and whips sounding, the Man/Father bursts in riding a chariot – filled with sacks of emeralds – drawn by four big black panthers. "Hey, honey, I'm back! How ya doin'?" (73). This is *The American Dream* on steroids. The stage directions in Act 2, Scene 7 confirm the unreal texture of this play. The chariot is made of papier-mâché ("*or whatever*") and all the props are "*clearly fake*" (73). Upon learning that OTTO had arranged for the father's homecoming, the happy ending sign-prop turns to the "Former Happy Ending" back side, and the father charges off in the chariot. Nonsensical dialogues fill the stage in this madcap ending. Albee presents the "Conclusion" in which OTTO and otto acknowledge that now they are triplets, laugh and embrace each other. Moments later the play ends with Otto saying, "Well, I think the play's over. Let's go join the curtain call" (77).

Me, Myself & I, like *The Man Who Had Three Arms* and *The Play About the Baby* before it, radiates a Pirandellian texture. That is, this is very much a metatheatrical work, one calling attention to its art and artificiality. Characters sometime explain their actions to the audience, breaking through the invisible fourth wall of the theater repeatedly. This comes, as we have seen in several other Albee plays, from Albee's insistence that members of the audience become active participants in the spectacle, emotionally engaged participants. Even the minimalist set, which Albee states should contain "*no naturalistic enclosures*" (6), calls attention to the fact that this is a nonrealistic staged experience that invites the audience to raise, among other points, epistemological questions about the very nature of reality and the ways in which the individual knows what's knowable. Albee, in to his eighties when he staged what was to be his last play, still demonstrates his ongoing willingness to examine the very nature of dramatic mimesis and to challenge traditional notions of theatrical conventions.

Albee deploys the language of the absurd. Characters constantly ask questions, do not always understand, give nonsensical responses. The disconnect between word, body gesture, and meaning fills the stage. For *Me, Myself & I* involves, like Shepard's *True West*, a search for the Real, a search for meaning in a world lacking authentic connections, genuine human relationships, and felt love. A sense of abandonment and loss of innocence infiltrates the stage. Albee establishes the point early on with an allusion to James Agee's poem "Knoxville: Summer of 1915," a poem about a caring, loving family whose child experiences the warmth and innocence – but yearns for answers to the Sophoclean fundamental question, "Who am I?" Indeed, the Sophoclean question lies at the nerve center of *Me, Myself & I*, but within a world shorn of the caring, loving, warmth, and innocence embedded in Agee's reflective poem, a poem which often moved Albee to tears. Depending on how one wishes to view the play, it's possible to construct a reading in which the three Ottos, in their search for self-identity, are really *one* person, each staged character reflecting differing aspects of a single individual. Austin and Lee in Shepard's play may be two separate brothers, but then again Shepard creates the possibility that they simply represent a split personality of a signal figure that so appeals to Shepard (and Arthur Miller for that matter). In any event, the symbolic incoherence of the action, plot, and ending of *Me, Myself & I*, then, functions as a metaphor for characters' struggles to find order, meaning, and moral purpose in a world devoid of these very qualities.

Part III

Dialogues

Chapter 10

Critical Reception

The only detectable consistency in Albee scholarship is its lack of consistency. Any review of six decades of books, articles, and reviews reveals the balkanization of Albee criticism, the Albeephobe's attack countered by the Albeephile's defense. Indeed, ever since *The Zoo Story*, each new Albee play has produced nothing less than divided loyalties. Such varied audience responses come from the productions themselves, for Albee delights in challenging the orthodox aesthetics of Broadway and in refusing to repeat dramatic formulas that might raise his reputation in commercial and, perhaps, critical terms. Still, whether praising or attacking Albee, critics acknowledge the playwright's unmistakable influence on contemporary American drama. Albee, we see, reinvented the American stage beginning in 1959 by carrying on the moral seriousness of American drama established by Susan Glaspell, Eugene O'Neill, Tennessee Williams, and Arthur Miller.

There has been, broadly speaking, an overall shift in the tenor of Albee scholarship. After Albee fell out of favor with his increasing difficult plays in the 1970s and 1980s, since the 1990s to the present Albee has enjoyed the restoration of his reputation. Today, he has been rightfully accorded many accolades testifying to his brilliance. At the time of his death in 2016, he was *the* elder statesman of the American stage. He has influenced a host of younger playwrights, from Adrienne Kennedy, Sam Shepard, Terrence McNally, and David Mamet to Paula Vogel, Sarah Ruhl, and Amy Herzog, to name but a few.

There is no shortage of books on Albee, some of which I spotlight here. The Belgium critic Gilbert Debusscher' s *Edward Albee: Tradition and Renewal* (1967), the first book on the playwright, places Albee in a useful historical context, citing him as the American playwright most worthy of carrying on the legacies on O'Neill, Miller, and Williams. According to Debusscher, Albee assimilated rather than copied the French avant-garde style in the early plays but produced a distinctly American cadence. Examining the plays through *Malcolm*, Debusscher claims that Albee is technically sound but often lapses into " 'theater for theater's sake.'" Debusscher concludes that Albee is a nihilist: "Albee's work contains no positive philosophical or social message. His theatre belongs in the pessimistic, defeatist or nihilistic current."[1] Subsequent studies challenge such conclusions. Nelvin Vos's slender volume, *Eugene Ionesco and Edward Albee: A Critical Study* (1968), focuses on Ionesco's absurdism and the ways in which it differs from Albee's.

Four books on Albee appeared in 1969, and the British critic Christopher Bigsby's remains the best. His *Albee* locates Albee's impulse to dramatize the human need "to break out of his self-imposed isolation" and establish "contact with his fellow man," to experience a "revival of love." Bigsby concludes that Albee explores the "source of a limited but genuine hope" in human encounters.[2] Ruby Cohn's *Edward Albee* is a brief but substantive study. Albee, for Cohn, is obsessed with stripping away illusions in human experience: "Whereas Sartre, Camus, Beckett, Genet, Ionesco, and Pinter represent that reality in all its alogical absurdity, Albee has been preoccupied with illusions that screen man from reality."[3] Michael E. Rutenberg's *Edward Albee: Playwright in Protest* investigates Albee's sociopolitical quarrels with American culture. This book also contains two informative interviews with Albee. Such statements as Albee "is into what is happening" make this study very much a product of the 1960s.[4] Still, this well-documented study is useful enough. Richard Amacher's *Edward Albee* explicates the plays, making good connections between Greek drama and Albee. In his revised version (1982), Amacher covers the plays through *Lolita*.

The 1970s saw its share of new books on Albee. Ronald Hayman's *Edward Albee* (1971) discusses the plays through *All Over*. With no introduction or conclusion Hayman presents detailed plot summaries. Anne Paolucci's *From Tension to Tonic: The Plays of Edward Albee* (1972) is an insightful, provocative book filled with references to Dante and Pirandello. For Paolucci, Albee "is the only one of our playwrights who seems to have accepted and committed himself to serious articulation of the existential questions of our time."[5] Though published years ago, her insights remain surprisingly fresh today and the book remains an important one. In 2010, Paolucci revisits Albee in her *Edward Albee (The Later Plays)*, an excellent study that covers the most of Albee's latest plays. Albee wrote her a personal letter, praising her illuminating study. Foster Hirsch's *Who's Afraid of Edward Albee?* (1978) argues largely from a psychological perspective, citing Albee's homosexuality as influencing his characterizations. He also finds the playwright's career in a state of decline. Anita Maria Stenz's *Edward Albee: The Poet of Loss* (1978), a solid psychological reading of the characters, discusses the plays through *Seascape*. Her central thesis is on target: there is in an Albee play, she argues, a moral obligation to live with awareness.

A number of edited collection of critical essays on Albee are available for students and scholars. The best one to date is Stephen Bottoms's *The Cambridge*

Companion to Edward Albee (2005), which contains fourteen essays from leading theater scholars. The volume also includes a fresh interview with the playwright. Other useful collections are *Edward Albee: A Collection of Critical Essays*, edited by C. W. E. Bigsby (1975); *Edward Albee: Planned Wilderness*, edited by Patricia De La Fuente (1980); *Edward Albee: An Interview and Essays*, edited by Julian Wasserman (1983); *Critical Essays on Edward Albee*, edited by Philip Kolin and J. Madison Davis (1986); *Edward Albee: Modern Critical Views*, edited by Harold Bloom (1987); and *Edward Albee: A Casebook*, edited by Bruce J. Mann (2003). The Kolin and Davis volume contains thirty-nine essays, by far the most of any of the collected essays. The quality of thought in these collections remains impressive, despite the fact that many of them first appeared years ago. Complementing these collections are special issues of journals devoted to Albee: Norma Jenckes edited a special edition of the journal *American Drama* (Spring 1993) and Anne Paolucci's *PSA: The Official Publication of the Pirandello Society of America 8* (1992), which features essays on Albee and Pirandello. For a more recent special journal partially devoted to Albee, readers may consult guest editor Lenke Németh's "Edward Albee's 'Late-Middle' Period," in the *Hungarian Journal of English and American Studies* (Spring 2009); the five essays are outstanding. The other half of the journal is devoted to American theater history. Readers will also enjoy Philip Kolin's *Conversations with Edward Albee* (1988), which contains twenty-seven interviews.

C. W. E. Bigsby's *A Critical Introduction to Twentieth-Century American Drama*, Vol. 2 (1984) is essential reading. He relies extensively on Albee's unpublished materials. Bigsby's sense of social history and existentialism enhances his illuminating study. Albee has tackled, Bigsby rightly concludes, "issues of genuine metaphysical seriousness in a way that few American dramatists before him have claimed to do, and done so, for the most part, with a command of wit and controlled humour which has not always characterized the work of O'Neill, Miller and Williams. He has set himself the task of probing beneath the bland surface of contemporary reality and created a theatre which at its best is luminous with intelligence and power."[6] Bigsby revisits Albee in an eloquent and insightful chapter on Albee in his *Modern American Drama, 1945–1990* (1992), a volume that was also updated under the title *Modern American Drama, 1945–2000* (2001). For many, Bigsby's many books on various aspects of an ongoing narrative history of American drama in general, and Albee in particular, are the best there are.

Gerry McCarthy's *Edward Albee* (1987) discusses Albee's key themes and techniques, and is especially rewarding on matters of stage and performance on the plays through *The Lady from Dubuque*. Matthew Roudané explores Albee in *Understanding Edward Albee* (1987), a reading of the plays through *The Man Who Had Three Arms*, and in *"Who's Afraid of Virginia Woolf?": Necessary Fictions, Terrifying Realities* (1990), a concentrated book on Albee's masterwork. Roudané also revisits Albee in editors Don B. Wilmeth and Christopher Bigsby's *The Cambridge History of American Theatre*, Vol. III (2000). Stephen J. Bottoms also focuses on Albee's most well-known play in his excellent *Albee: "Who's Afraid of Virginia Woolf?"* (2000), which is part of Cambridge University Press's "Plays in Production" series.

There is only one biography on Albee, and it is outstanding. Mel Gussow's *Edward Albee: A Singular Journey* (1999) is as authoritative as it is readable. "As Albee looks to his future," speculates Gussow, "the new plays and continuing revivals, the reinterpretations and the reevaluations, the mystery of his birth and his sense of abandonment remain."[7]

For more international perspectives, readers may consult Helmut M. Braem's *Edward Albee* (1968), which provides a useful European vantage point (written in German), as do Liliane Kerjan's *Edward Albee* (1971) and her *Le Théâtre d'Edward Albee* (1979) (written in French). Two scholars from Spain are worth noting. Alberto Mira published a Spanish edition of *Who's Afraid of Virginia Woolf?*, entitled *Quién teme a Virginia Woolf?* (1997), which features an extensive introduction and useful bibliographies (written in Spanish). Ana Antón-Pacheco's *El Teatro de los Estados Unidos: Historia y Crítica* (2005) has an outstanding chapter on Albee (written in Spanish). Finally, a scholar from India, Rana Nayar, published *Edward Albee: Towards a Typology of Relationships* (2003) (written in English).

Four bibliographic reference books are available to help students and scholars become familiar with the extant Albee scholarship. Richard E. Amacher and Margaret Rule's *Edward Albee: At Home and Abroad* (1973), Richard Tyce's *Edward Albee: A Bibliography* (1986), and Charles Lee Green's *Edward Albee: An Annotated Bibliography, 1968–1977* are all very useful. However, the most thorough book is Scott Giantvalley's *Edward Albee: A Reference Guide* (1987), with nearly 3,000 entries within its 459 pages. Matthew Roudané's *American Drama: Contemporary Authors Bibliographic Series* (1989) contains an excellent chapter on Albee by Anne Paolucci and Henry Paolucci. Readers will also find that Barbara Lee Horn's *Edward Albee: A Research and Production Sourcebook* (2003) is filled with helpful information, including an informative chapter on Albee's life. Also extremely useful is Phyllis T. Dircks's *Edward Albee: A Literary Companion* (2010), which provides very useful "factual and interpretive material."[8]

Some more recent books on Albee are outstanding and highly recommended. Few American dramatists have directed as many of his own plays as has Albee. Thus Rakesh H. Solomon's *Albee in Performance* (2010) is a welcome and original book, one that "examines how this major American playwright transformed written drama into dynamic performance as he staged major professional productions of a representative spectrum of his works."[9] This study really gives one an appreciation of all the complex directorial choices that Albee makes while staging his plays. Toby Zinman's *Edward Albee* (2008) is a refreshing and highly intelligent read of Albee's plays through 2004. "The dangers of safety are examined in each of Albee's plays," Zinman explains, "which reveal, in dazzlingly different ways, how crucial it is to live honorably – true to oneself, true to one's art, true to one's ethical and philosophical beliefs."[10] This is an excellent book. Readers will enjoy David Crespy's *Richard Barr: The Playwright's Producer* (2013), which traces Barr's (and Clinton Wilder's) great influence on Albee throughout their careers.

Readers will also enjoy the many books that contain single chapters on Albee. David Krasner's *American Drama 1945–2000: An Introduction* (2006) and his edited collection, *A Companion to Twentieth-Century American Drama* (2005), immediately come to mind, as do Marc Robinson's *The American Play, 1787–2000* (2009), Kerstin Schmidt's *The Theater of Transformation: Postmodernism in American Drama* (2005), and Walter A. Davis's *Get the Guest: Psychoanalysis, Modern American Drama, and the Audience* (1994). Readers may also wish to consult Don B. Wilmeth and Christopher Bigsby's edited book, *The Cambridge History of American Theatre, Vol. III* (2000) and Matthew Roudané's *American Drama since 1960: A Critical History* (1996).

Looking to future research on Albee, readers should consult the website for the Edward Albee Society. A number of leading Albee scholars got together and formed the Society in 2013. There readers will find links to the Society's *New Perspectives in Edward Albee Studies*, a new book series. Here is a list of the forthcoming volumes: Volume #1– *Edward Albee and Absurdism* (2016) edited by Michael Y. Bennett; Volume #2 – *Edward Albee and Sexuality/ Gender* (2017) edited by John M. Clum and Cormac O'Brien; Volume #3 – *Edward Albee as a Theatrical and Dramatic Innovator* (2018) edited by David A. Crespy; Volume #4 – *Edward Albee's Influence on American Drama* (2019) edited by Natka Bianchini; and Volume #5 – *Edward Albee's Own Influences* (2020) edited by [TBD]. These collections of critical essays promise to be a welcome addition to Albee scholarship. As the Society notes in its webpage:

> Published by Brill, under their Brill I Rodopi imprint, *New Perspectives in Edward Albee Studies* – a publication of The Edward Albee Society – is a book series meant to provide an outlet for scholarship and criticism on, or related to, Edward Albee and his works. Annual volumes feature original, academic essays and review-essays centered around a special

topic. Each volume is edited by a different Editor. The book series welcomes and encourages different critical and theoretical scholarly approaches to Albee studies. In keeping with Albee's own view that drama is literature, *New Perspectives in Edward Albee Studies* is also very interested in essays that examine Albee's plays as dramatic literature.

The future of Albee scholarship, indeed, looks very bright.

Epilogue: Final Curtain

> To all of you who have made my being alive so wonderful, so exciting and so full, my thanks and all my love.
>
> *–Edward Albee*

Albee wrote the epigraph above before undergoing heart surgery in 2012. He instructed that the message be released upon his death, and that note was used in many obituaries here and abroad in September of 2016. Despite the subject matter of his plays, the message reveals Albee's compassion for embracing his very being in the world, his compassion for those he admired, and his moral optimism.

Albee's commitment to dramatic excellence yielded numerous accolades. He was, for many, the preeminent playwright of the postwar American theatre. The distinguishing marks of Albee's dramas lie in his unique uses of language, dramatic form, and characters who struggle with the self and the other. Although he shows, in the some two dozen plays he wrote, a rich variety of performative styles and cultural concerns, his focus is often the American family – and more specifically often husbands and wives – whose competing narratives animate the stage. Victims and victimizers, the pursued and the pursuer vie for a metaphorical, psychological, and spiritual space in his plays. Meanwhile, options slowly diminish. There are no real survivors, no remissions of pain. Spaces open up which prove unbridgeable. Necessity rules. Irony is constantly reborn from the frustrated desires of those who obey compulsions they would wish to resist. And yet there is a fractured poetry, there is an energy and a passion to the lives of those whose demons he stages. There is an intensity, a resonance, and a power which lifts them above their social insignificance, just as the plays themselves never compromise with the banality of surfaces.

Poetry, Robert Frost writes, "ends in a clarification of life – not necessarily a great clarification, such as sects or cults are founded on, but in a momentary stay against confusion."[1] Perhaps Albee's most important contribution to contemporary American theater lies in his ability to present the kind of clarification Frost envisioned. When he is at his best, Albee produces in certain characters and, ideally, in the audience "a momentary stay against confusion," a still point in the messy business of living that paves the way for the possibility of existing with a heightened sense of self-responsibility. Heated repartee, sexual tensions, indecisiveness, death, a preoccupation with vital lies, a withdrawal from meaningful human encounters, indifference – these are the issues that Albee mines, but not from the position of a nihilist. Rather, Albee explores these issues because they can trigger in his plays catharsis, personal growth, and an ultimately life-giving experience for his characters and audiences. He pinpoints the value of writing this kind of drama:

> Many people at the colleges I visit ask me over and gain, "Why do you ask such tough questions and why do your plays seem so difficult or depressing?" Or "Why don't you write happy plays?" About what, happy problems? But I keep reminding them that drama is an attempt to make things better. Drama is a mirror held up to them to show the way they do behave and how they don't behave that way any longer. If people are willing to be aided in the search for total consciousness by not only drama but all the arts – music and painting and all the other arts give a unique sense of order – then art is life-giving. Art gives shape to life; it increases consciousness.[2]

To understand the role of death in Albee's theater, paradoxically enough, is to understand the compassion, the affirmation, the optimism of his world view. The plays are death-saturated because the presence of death, once internalized, shapes the quality of human existence. The playwright emphatically states his views with respect to his preoccupation with death:

> As opposed to the slaughter in Shakespeare, the tuberculosis and consumption in Chekhov, the death-in-life in Beckett? Is that what you mean? There are only a few significant things to write about: life and death; and the fact that people avoid thinking about death – and about *living*. I think we should always live with the consciousness of death. How else can we possibly participate in living life fully?[3]

Since *The Zoo Story*, Albee has always brought such a vision to the design of each new play.

Albee remained one of the most influential and controversial American dramatists. He and his fellow playwrights saw "in the theatre a living art in which actors and audience inhabit the same time, breathe the same air, see on the stage, and reflect in themselves, a sense of community always under threat but always yearned for."[4] He was responsible for introducing, and never really abandoning, European absurdist influences within a uniquely American context; for revitalizing the American theater through clever dialogue; and for exploring the human soul-scape in images as powerful as those of Eugene O'Neill, Tennessee Williams, and Arthur Miller. In brief, Albee reinvented the American stage at a time when its originality and quality seemed to be fading. He continued to be a major spokesperson for the moral seriousness of American theater. Above all, he had the artistic instinct and courage to stage significant, universal public issues and private tensions of the individual and a culture thinking in front of themselves.

Five years before his death, Albee said of Richard Barr, the legendary producer of most of Albee's works, that he was "a man who understood that in the battle for the life of the serious arts in our country, caution and compromise are the twin handmaidens of disaster."[5] Albee, himself, threw caution and compromise out the window for his entire career. Lucky for us, for he left contemporary audiences throughout the world with a remarkable number of plays that present "a personal, private yowl" that "has something to do with the anguish of us all."[6]

Notes

Preface

1 Albee has also composed several adaptations over his long career, but none since 1981. I have omitted discussion of these adaptations mainly because Albee concedes that, whatever their merits or inadequacies, they are merely ways to polish his craft, to hone his technique, to concentrate on dramatic voice.

2 Matthew Roudané, "Albee on Albee," *RE: Artes Liberales* 10 (Spring 1984), p. 8.

Chapter 1 Life

1 Edward Albee, "*Exorcism* – the Play O'Neill Tried to Destroy," Foreword, *Exorcism: A Play in One Act*, Eugene O'Neill (New Haven: Yale University Press, 2012), pp. viii–ix.

2 Personal conversation with Albee, October 31, 1985.

3 Eric Olsen, *The Last Word: Edward Albee*. Video. New York Times.com. No date.

4 Lincoln Konkle, *Thornton Wilder and the Puritan Narrative Tradition* (Columbia: University of Missouri Press, 2013), p. 247. Konkle offers a detailed and insightful account of Wilder's influence on the young Albee in his book.

5 Edward Albee, "*Exorcism* – the Play O'Neill Tried to Destroy," ed., p. vii.

6 Mel Gussow, *Edward Albee: A Singular Journey* (New York: Simon & Schuster, 1999), p. 22.

7 Walter Wager, ed., *The Playwrights Speak* (New York: Delta, 1968), p. 27.

8 Wager, p. 40.

9 Edward Albee, *The Plays* Vol. 1 (New York: Coward, McCann, and Geohegan, 1981), p. 7.

10 Christopher Bigsby, "'Better alert than numb': Albee since the Eighties," in Stephen Bottoms, ed., *The Cambridge Companion to Edward Albee* (Cambridge: Cambridge University Press, 2005), p. 148.

Chapter 2 Overview

1 Steven Price, "Fifteen-Love, Thirty-Love: Edward Albee," in David Krasner, ed., *A Companion to Twentieth-Century American Drama* (Oxford: Blackwell, 2005), p. 253.

2 Matthew Roudané, "An Interview with Edward Albee," *Southern Humanities Review* 16 (1982), pp. 41, 43.

3 Anne Paolucci, *From Tension to Tonic: The Plays of Edward Albee* (Carbondale: Southern Illinois University Press, 1972), p. 4.

4 Roudané, "Albee on Albee," p. 1.

5 Robert Brustein, *The Theatre of Revolt* (Boston: Little, Brown, 1964), p. 363.

6 Antonin Artaud, *The Theatre and Its Double*, trans. Mary Caroline Richards (New York: Grove, 1958), p. 41.

7 Matthew Roudané, "A Playwright Speaks: An Interview with Edward Albee," in Philip C. Kolin and J. Madison Davis, eds., *Critical Essays on Edward Albee* (Boston: Hall, 1986), p. 195.

8 Roudané, "A Playwright Speaks," p. 194.

9 Mike Boehm, "Edward Albee, Three-Time Pulitzer Prize Winning Playwright and Author of *Who's Afraid of Virginia Woolf?*, Dies at 88," *Los Angeles Times*, Thursday, September 22, 2016. Electronic edition, no page.

10 C. W. E. Bigsby, *A Critical Introduction to Twentieth-Century American Drama, Vol. 2* (Cambridge: Cambridge University Press, 1984), p. 327.

11 Julian Beck, "Storming the Barricades," in Kenneth H. Brown, ed., *The Brig* (New York: Hill and Wang, 1965), pp. 7, 9, 18.

12 Roudané, "Albee on Albee," p. 4.

13 Digby Diehl, "Edward Albee," *Transatlantic Review* 13 (1963), p. 72.

14 Roudané, "A Playwright Speaks," p. 198.

15 Albert Camus, *The Myth of Sisyphus and Other Essays* (New York: Vintage, 1955), p. 10.

16 Edward Albee, *The Zoo Story and the American Dream* (New York: Signet, 1960), p. 54.

17 Saul Bellow, *Henderson the Rain King* (Greenwich: Fawcett Crest, 1959), p. 68.

18 Toby Zinman, *Edward Albee* (Ann Arbor: University of Michigan Press, 2008), p. 1.

19 Albee, *The Plays*, Vol. 1 (New York: Coward, McCann, and Geohegan, 1981), p. 10.

Chapter 3 Contexts

1 Mas'ud Zavarzadeh, *The Mythopoeic Reality* (Urbana: University of Illinois Press, 1976), pp. 18, 38.

2 Roudané, "Albee on Albee," pp. 5–6.

3 Christopher Bigsby, "Introduction," in Bigsby, ed., *Edward Albee: A Collection of Critical Essays* (Englewood Cliffs: Prentice-Hall, 1975), p. 4.

4 Matthew Roudané, "An Interview with Arthur Miller," in Roudané, ed., *The Collected Essays of Arthur Miller* (London: Bloomsbury, 2015), p. 370.

5 Daniel Blum, *Theatre World: Season 1962–1963*, Vol. 19 (New York: Chilton Books, 1963), p. 6.

6 Jack Poggi, *Theater in America: The Impact of Economic Forces, 1870–1960* (Ithaca: Cornell University Press, 1968), pp. 46–49.

7 Mark Kennedy, "Broadway's Attendance, Box Office Figures Hit Record Highs," *The Atlanta Journal-Constitution* (May 28, 2015), Sec. C, p. 3.

Chapter 4 Ritualized Forms of Expiation

1 Roudané, "A Playwright Speaks," p. 199.

2 Alice Griffin, "Edward Albee," in *TheaterPro.com: An eMagazine of Theater in New York And London*. No date or page.

3 David A. Crespy, *Richard Barr: The Playwright's Producer* (Carbondale: Southern Illinois University Press, 2013), p. 80.

4 Alan Prince, "An Interview with John Barth," *Prism* (1968), p. 62.

5 Paolucci, *From Tension to Tonic*, p. 40.

6 See Edward Albee, "How *The Zoo Story* Became a Two-Act Play," in *At Home at the Zoo* (New York and London: Overlook Duckworth, 2011), n.p.

7 Roudané, "A Playwright Speaks," p. 199.

8 Bigsby, *A Critical Introduction*, p. 258.

9 Roudané, "An Interview with Edward Albee," p. 38.

10 Camus, *The Myth of Sisyphus and Other Essays*, p. 10.

11 Edward Albee, *The Plays*, Vol. 1 (New York: Coward, McCann, and Geohegan, 1981), p. 10.

12 Samuel Beckett, *Waiting for Godot* (New York: Grove, 1954), p. 58.

13 Roudané, "Albee on Albee," p. 4.

14 Michael E. Rutenberg, *Edward Albee: Playwright in Protest* (New York: Avon, 1969), p. 220.

15 Roudané, "A Playwright Speaks," p. 197.

16 Roudané, "Interview with Edward Albee," p. 43.

17 Gussow, *Edward Albee*, p. 99.

18 Zinman, p. 26.

19 See Gilbert Debusscher, *Edward Albee: Tradition and Renewal*, trans. Anne D. Williams (Brussels: Center for American Studies, 1967), p. 24.

20 *The Collected Plays of Edward Albee, Vol. 1*, lists the premiere as May 16, 1960, but April 15, 1960 is the correct date.

21 Edward Albee, quoted in Gussow, p. 135.

22 See Martin Esslin, *The Theatre of the Absurd* (Woodstock: The Overlook Press, 1969).

23 Gussow, p. 135.

24 C. W. E. Bigsby, *Albee* (Edinburg: Oliver and Boyd, 1969), p. 30.

25 Debusscher, p. 33.

26 Edward Albee, *Fam and Yam: An Imaginary Interview, in The Sand Box and The Death of Bessie Smith* (New York: Signet, 1963), p. 85. All further references are to this edition and will be cited parenthetically in the text.

27 Gussow, p. 97.

28 Roudané, "An Interview with Arthur Miller," p. 361.

29 Roudané, "A Playwright Speaks," pp. 195–196.

30 Edward Albee, *The Zoo Story and The American Dream* (New York: Signet, 1960), pp. 53–54.

31 Anne Paolucci, "Albee and the Restructuring of the Modern Stage," *Studies in American Drama, 1945-Present* 1 (1986), pp. 14–15.

32 Susan Sontag, *On Photography* (New York: Farrar, Straus, 1977), p. 19.

33 "Gussow, Albee: Odd Man in On Broadway," *Newsweek*, February 4, 1963, p. 51.

34 Albee, *The Zoo Story* and *The American Dream*, p. 54.

Chapter 5 Challenging Broadway

1 Albee, *The Plays*, Vol. 1, p. 10.

2 Walter A. Davis, *Get the Guests: Psychoanalysis, Modern American Drama, and the Audience* (Madison: University of Wisconsin Press, 1994), p. 242.

3 "Blood Sport," *Time*, October 26, 1962, p. 84.

4 Harold Bloom, ed., *Edward Albee: Modern Critical Views* (New Haven: Chealsea House, 1987), pp. 6, 8.

5 Roudané, "An Interview with Edward Albee," p. 38.

6 Edward Albee, *Who's Afraid of Virginia Woolf?* (New York: Atheneum, 1962), p. 155.

7 Stephen J. Bottoms, *Albee: "Who's Afraid of Virginia Woolf?"* (Cambridge: Cambridge University Press, 2000), pp. 15–33.

8 Roudané, "An Interview with Edward Albee," p. 38.

9 Digby Diehl, "Edward Albee Interviewed," in Philip C. Kolin, ed., *Conversations with Edward Albee* (Jackson: University Press of Mississippi, 1988), p. 22.

10 Virginia Woolf, *To the Lighthouse* (New York and London: Harcourt Brace Jovanovich, 1955), p. 268.

11 William Flanagan, "The Art of the Theatre IV: Edward Albee: An Interview," in *Conversations with Edward Albee*, p. 52.

12 René Girard, *Violence and the Sacred*, trans. Patrick Gregory (Baltimore: Johns Hopkins University Press, 1977), p. 31.

13 Patricia De La Fuente, "Edward Albee: An Interview," in *Conversations with Edward Albee*, pp. 152–153.

14 Press conference transcript, Billy Rose Theatre, New York City, March 22, 1965. Quoted here from Richard E. Amacher, *Edward Albee*, rev. ed. (Boston: Twayne, 1982), pp. 119–120.

15 See John M. Clum, "'Withered Age and Stale Custom': Marriage, Diminution, and Sex in *Tiny Alice, A Delicate Balance,* and *Finding the Sun,*" in *The Cambridge Companion to Edward Albee*, pp. 59–74.

16 Mary E. Campbell, "The Tempters in Albee's *Tiny Alice*," *Modern Drama* 13 (1970), p. 25.

17 Edward Albee, *Tiny Alice* (New York: Atheneum, 1965), p. 138.

18 Anita Marie Stenz, *Edward Albee: The Poet of Loss* (The Hague: Mouton, 1978), p. 62.

19 Camus, *The Myth of Sisyphus and Other Essays*, p. 10.

20 Thomas P. Adler, "Art or Craft: Language in the Plays of Albee's Second Decade," in Patricia De La Fuente, ed., *Edward Albee: Planned Wilderness* (Edinburg, TX: Pan American University Press, 1980), p. 55.

21 Press conference transcript, Amacher, p. 119.

22 Jean-Paul Sartre, from *Existentialism Is a Humanism, Existentialism*, ed. Robert C. Solomon (New York: Modern Library, 1974), pp. 204–205.

23 Saul Bellow, *Him with His Foot in His Mouth and Other Stories* (New York: Harper & Row, 1984), p. 36.

24 Roudané, "Albee on Albee," p. 4.

25 Personal interview with the author, September 23, 1980, Berkeley, CA.

26 William Barrett, *What Is Existentialism?* (New York: Grove, 1964), pp. 58–59.

27 Barrett, p. 59.

28 T. S. Eliot, *The Complete Poems and Plays* (New York: Harcourt Brace, 1971), p. 120.

29 Barrett, p. 59.

30 Paolucci, *From Tension to Tonic*, p. 110.

31 M. Gilbert Porter, "Toby's Last Stand: The Evanescence of Commitment in *A Delicate Balance*," *Educational Theatre Journal* 31 (1979), p. 403.

32 Virginia I. Perry, "Disturbing Our Sense of Well-Being: The 'Uninvited' in *A Delicate Balance*," in *Edward Albee: An Interview and Essays*, Julian N. Wasserman, ed., Lee Lecture Series, University of St. Thomas, Houston, TX (Syracuse: University of Syracuse Press, 1983), p. 59.

33 Roudané, "Albee on Albee," p. 4.

34 Eliot, p. 126.

35 Thomas P. Adler, "Albee's 3 ½: The Pulitzer Plays," in *The Cambridge Companion to Edward Albee*, p. 82.

36 Given how precise Albee is with his grammar and language, it was surprising to find a mechanical error near the very start of the play. He forgets the apostrophe in the contraction of the word "that's" (2: 273). In the first edition published in 1969 by Atheneum, the punctuation is correct. The error in the present edition is an absolute rarity within Albee's texts.

37 Roudané, "Albee on Albee," pp. 3–4.

38 Personal conversation with Professor Baotong Gu, Department of English, Georgia State University, Atlanta, on July 20, 2016. I also wish to thank Professor Douglas Reynolds, Department of History at Georgia State, for his insights on Mao Tse-Tung.

Chapter 6 "The greatest sin in living is doing it badly – stupidly, or as if you weren't really alive"

1 Bigsby, *A Critical Introduction*, p. 318.

2 Elisabeth Kübler-Ross, *On Death and Dying* (New York: Macmillan, 1970), p. 160.

3 Bigsby, *A Critical Introduction*, p. 314.
4 Roudané, "An Interview with Edward Albee," p. 41.
5 Henry James, *The Ambassadors* (New York: Norton, 1964), p. 132.
6 Bigsby, *A Critical Introduction*, p. 318.
7 Camus, *The Myth of Sisyphus and Other Essays*, p. 5.
8 Carl G. Jung, "Archetypes of the Collective Unconscious," in William J. Handy and Max R. Westbrook, eds., *Twentieth Century Criticism* (New York: Free Press, 1974), p. 215.
9 Jung, p. 217.
10 Jung, p. 216.
11 Jung, p. 230.
12 Albee, *The Plays, Vol. 1*, p. 10.
13 Roudané, "Albee on Albee," p. 4.
14 Ken Kesey, *One Flew Over the Cuckoo's Nest* (New York: Signet, 1962), p. 13.
15 Gussow, p. 295.
16 Gussow, p. 297.
17 Roudané, "An Interview with Edward Albee," pp. 33–34.
18 Gussow, p. 297.
19 T. S. Eliot, *The Wasteland in Selected Poems* (New York: Harcourt, Brace and World, Inc., 1977), p. 53.
20 Roudané, "An Interview with Edward Albee," p. 35.
21 Linda Ben-Zvi, "'Playing the Cloud Circuit': Albee's Vaudeville Show," in *The Cambridge Companion to Edward Albee*, pp. 178–181.
22 Roudané, "An Interview with Edward Albee," p. 35.
23 Roudané, "A Playwright Speaks," p. 197.
24 Hilton Als, "He Said, She Said," *The New Yorker*, October 20, 2003, p. 33.
25 Philip C. Kolin, "Edward Albee's *Counting the Ways*: The Ways of Losing Heart," in *Edward Albee: An Interview and Essays*, p. 125.

Chapter 7 A Quest for Consciousness

1 Roudané, "An Interview with Edward Albee," p. 40.
2 Roudané, "An Interview with Edward Albee," p. 40.
3 Kübler-Ross, p. 112. Albee told me that her book influenced his conception of *The Lady from Dubuque*.
4 Personal conversation with Albee, November 18, 1988.
5 Roudané, "Albee on Albee," pp. 1–2.
6 Thomas P. Adler, "*The Man Who Had Three Arms*," *Theatre Journal* 35 (1983), p. 124.
7 Roudané, "Albee on Albee," p. 2.
8 Roudané, "A Playwright Speaks," p. 198.
9 See Rakesh Solomon, *Albee in Performance* (Bloomington: Indiana University Press, 2010).

10 Sheridan Morely, "Chance Discovery," *Spectator* (London), May 26, 2001, pp. 63–64.

11 See Zinman, p. 107.

12 Anne Paolucci, *Edward Albee (The Later Plays)* (New York: Griffon House Publications, 2010), p. 121.

13 Matthew Roudané, "Shepard on Shepard: An Interview," in Roudané, ed., *The Cambridge Companion to Sam Shepard* (Cambridge: Cambridge University Press, 2002), p. 79.

14 Albert Camus, *The Myth of Sisyphus* (Paris: Gallimard, 1942), p. 18.

15 Zinman, p. 115.

16 Edward Albee, quoted in Gussow, p. 351.

17 Rakesh H. Solomon, "Albee Stages *Marriage Play:* Cascading Action, Audience Taste, and Dramatic Paradox," in *The Cambridge Companion to Edward Albee*, p. 172.

18 Edward Albee, *New York Magazine*, November 15, 1993, p. 74.

Chapter 8 As I Lay Dying

1 Christopher Bigsby, "'Better Alert Than Numb': Albee since the Eighties," in *The Cambridge Companion to Edward Albee*, p. 148.

2 Edward Albee, "Introduction," in *Three Tall Women* (New York: Dutton, 1994), n.p. All further references to this "Introduction" are to this edition and will be cited parenthetically in the text.

3 Brenda Murphy, "Albee's Threnodies: *Box-Mao-Box, All Over, The Lady from Dubuque* and *Three Tall Women*," in *The Cambridge Companion to Edward Albee*, p. 106.

4 Paolucci, *Edward Albee (The Later Plays)*, p. 108.

5 Barbara Lee Horn, *Edward Albee: A Research and Production Sourcebook* (Westport: Praeger, 2003), pp. 50–51. See also Phyllis T. Dircks, *Edward Albee: A Literary Companion* (Jefferson and London: McFarland, 2010), pp. 82–83.

6 Zinman, p. 128.

7 Zinman, pp. 127–128.

8 Gussow, p. 348.

9 Robert F. Gross, "Perversity and Loss in *The Play About the Baby*," *Hungarian Journal of English and American Studies* 15, No. 1 (Spring 2009), p. 126.

10 Paolucci, *Edward Albee (The Later Plays)*, p. 74.

11 Stephen Bottoms, "Borrowed Time: An Interview with Edward Albee," in *The Cambridge Companion to Edward Albee*, p. 243.

12 Edward Albee, from inside dust jacket cover, *The Goat or, Who Is Sylvia?* (New York: Overlook Press, 2003).

13 Chip Crews, "Getting Edward Albee's 'Goat,'" *Washington Post*, Sunday, March 13, 2005, p. 2.

14 J. Ellen Gainor, "Albee's *The Goat*: Rethinking Tragedy for the 21st Century," *The Cambridge Companion to Edward Albee*, pp. 208–209.

15 Susan Sontag, *On Photography* (New York: Farrar and Straus, 1977), p. 19.
16 Boróka Prohászka Rád, "Transgressing the Limits: *The Goat or, Who is Sylvia*," *Hungarian Journal of English and American Studies* 15, No. 1 (Spring 2009), p. 151.

Chapter 9 A Theater of Loss

1 Dorothy Rabinowitz, "The Art of the Feud," *New York Magazine*, September 25, 1989, p. 88.
2 Gussow, p. 334.
3 Gussow, pp. 334–335.
4 Paolucci, *Edward Albee (The Later Plays)*, p. 151.
5 Paolucci, *Edward Albee (The Later Plays)*, p. 155.
6 Edward Albee, "How *The Zoo Story* Became a Two-Act Play," in *At Home at the Zoo* (New York and London: Overlook Duckworth, 2011), n.p. All further references are to this edition and will be cited parenthetically in the text.
7 Crespy, David and Lincoln Konkle, "A Conversation with Edward Albee," in Haley Gralen, ed., *Text &Presentation, 2013: The Comparative Drama Series 10* (Jefferson and London: McFarland & Company, 2013), p. 14.
8 Jason Zinoman, "On Stage and Off," *New York Times*, April 2, 2004, Section E, Column 3, p. 2.
9 Leo Tolstoy, *The Death of Ivan Ilych and Other Stories* (New York: Signet, 1977), p. 104.
10 For an excellent analysis of the play, see Boróka Prohászka Rád, "Discourses of the I: The Panic of Identity in Edward Albee's *Me, Myself & I*," *Acta Universitatis Sapientiae Philologica* 8, No. 1 (2016), pp. 29–39.
11 Edward Albee, *Me, Myself & I* (New York: Dramatists Play Service, 2011), pp. 6–7. All further references are to this edition and will be cited parenthetically in the text.

Chapter 10 Critical Reception

1 Debusscher, pp. 82–83.
2 Bigsby, *Albee*, pp. 9, 96.
3 Ruby Cohn, *Edward Albee* (Minneapolis: University of Minnesota Press, 1969), p. 6.
4 Michael E. Rutenburg, *Edward Albee: Playwright in Protest* (New York: Drama Book Specialists, 1969), p. 16.
5 Paolucci, *From Tension to Tonic*, p. 3.
6 Bigsby, *A Critical Introduction*, p. 328.
7 Gussow, p. 404.
8 Dircks, p. 1.
9 Solomon, *Albee in Performance*, p. 3.
10 Zinman, p. 9.

Epilogue

1 Robert Frost, *Complete Poems of Robert Frost* (New York: Holt, Rinehart, 1964), p. vi.
2 Roudané, "A Playwright Speaks," pp. 194–195.
3 Roudané, "A Playwright Speaks," p. 195.
4 Christopher   Bigsby,   *Twenty-First   Century   American   Playwrights* (Cambridge: Cambridge University Press, forthcoming).
5 Edward Albee, "Foreword," in Crespy, p. x.
6 Edward Albee, "Preface," *The Zoo Story* and *The American Dream* (New York: Signet, 1960), p. 54.

Further Reading

The following bibliography provides selected published works by and about Edward Albee.

Readers may also consult the Edward Albee Society's website, which is an excellent source for ongoing updates about all things Albee.

Plays

The Collected Plays of Edward Albee Volume 1. New York: Overlook Duckworth, 2004. Includes *The Zoo Story*; *The Death of Bessie Smith*; *The Sandbox*; *The American Dream*; *Who's Afraid of Virginia Woolf?*; *The Ballad of the Sad Café*; *Tiny Alice*; *Malcolm*.

The Collected Plays of Edward Albee Volume 2. New York: Overlook Duckworth, 2005. Includes *A Delicate Balance*; *Everything in the Garden*; *Box* and *Quotations from Chairman Mao Tse-Tung*; *All Over*; *Seascape*; *Listening*; *Counting the Ways*; *The Lady from Dubuque*.

The Collected Plays of Edward Albee Volume 3. New York: Overlook Duckworth, 2005. Includes *Lolita*; *The Man Who Had Three Arms*; *Finding the Sun*; *Marriage Play*; *Fragments*; *Occupant*; *The Play About The Baby*; *Knock! Knock! Whos There!?*; *The Goat or, Who is Sylvia?*

At Home at the Zoo. New York: Overlook Duckworth, 2011.

Me, Myself & I. New York: Dramatists Play Service, 2011.

Essays

Stretching My Mind: The Collected Essays 1960 to 2005. New York: Carroll & Graf, 2005.

Interviews

Crespy, David and Lincoln Konkle. "A Conversation with Edward Albee," Haley Gralen, ed. *Text & Presentation, 2013: The Comparative Drama Series 10*. North Carolina: McFarland & Company, 2013, pp. 7–13.

Kolin, Philip C., ed. *Conversations with Edward Albee*. Jackson and
    London: University Press of Mississippi, 1988.

Bibliographies

Amacher, Richard E. and Margaret Rule. *Edward Albee at Home and
    Abroad: A Bibliography*. New York: AMS Press, 1973.
Giantvalley, Scott. *Edward Albee: A Reference Guide*. Boston: G. K. Hall, 1987.
Green, Charles Lee. *Edward Albee, an Annotated Bibliography, 1968–1977*.
    New York: AMS Press, 1980.
Tyce, Richard. *Edward Albee: A Bibliography*. Lanham: Scarecrow, 1987.

Books

Amacher, Richard E. *Edward Albee*. Rev. ed. Boston: Twayne, 1982.
Antón-Pacheco, Ana. *El Teatro de los Estados Unidos: Historia y Crítica*.
    Madrid: Langre, 2005.
Bigsby, C. W. E. *Albee*. Edinburgh: Oliver & Boyd, 1969.
Bigsby, C. W. E., ed. *Edward Albee: A Collection of Critical Essays*. Englewood
    Cliffs: Prentice-Hall, 1975.
Bigsby, C. W. E. *A Critical Introduction to Twentieth-Century American Drama,
    Vol. 2*. Cambridge: Cambridge University Press, 1984.
Bigsby, C. W. E. *Modern American Drama, 1945–2000*. Cambridge: Cambridge
    University Press, 2001.
Bloom, Harold, ed. *Edward Albee: Modern Critical Views*. New Haven: Chelsea
    House, 1987.
Bottoms, Stephen, *Albee: "Who's Afraid of Virginia Woolf?"*
    Cambridge: Cambridge University Press, 2000.
Bottoms, Stephen ed. *The Cambridge Companion to Edward Albee*. Cambridge:
    Cambridge University Press, 2005.
Braem, Helmut M. *Edward Albee*. Hanover: Friedrich Verlag Velber, 1968.
Cohn, Ruby. *Edward Albee*. Pamphlets on American Writers No. 77.
    Minneapolis: University of Minnesota Press, 1969.
Crespy, David A. *Richard Barr: The Playwright's Producer*. Carbondale: Southern
    Illinois University Press, 2013.
Davis, Walter A. *Get the Guests: Psychoanalysis, Modern American Drama, and
    the Audience*. Madison: University of Wisconsin Press, 1994.
Debusscher, Gilbert. *Edward Albee: Tradition and Renewal*. Trans. Anne
    D. Williams. Brussels: American Studies Center, 1967.
De La Fuente, Patricia, ed. *Edward Albee, Planned Wilderness: Interviews, Essays,
    and Bibliography*. Edinburg, TX: Pan American University, 1980.
Dircks, Phyllis T. *Edward Albee: A Literary Companion*.
    Jefferson: McFarland, 2010.

Dutton, Richard. *Modern Tragicomedy and the British Tradition.*
  Norman: University of Oklahoma Press, 1986.
Gussow, Mel. *Edward Albee: A Singular Journey.* New York: Simon &
  Schuster, 1999.
Hayman, Ronald. *Edward Albee.* New York: Ungar, 1971.
Hirsch, Foster. *Who's Afraid of Edward Albee?* Berkeley: Creative Arts
  Book, 1978.
Horn, Barbara Lee. *Edward Albee: A Research and Production Sourcebook.*
  Westport: Praeger, 2003.
Jenckes, Norma, ed. *American Drama: Edward Albee*, Spring 1993. [Special
  edition of journal.]
Kerjan, Liliane. *Edward Albee.* Paris: Éditions Seghers, 1971.
Kolin, Philip, ed. *American Playwrights since 1945: A Guide to Scholarship,
  Criticism, and Performance.* Westport: Greenwood Press, 1989.
Kolin, Philip C. and J. Madison Davis, eds. *Critical Essays on Edward Albee.*
  Boston: G. K. Hall, 1986.
Krasner, David. *American Drama 1945–2000.* Oxford: Blackwell Press, 2006.
Krasner, David, ed. *A Companion to Twentieth-Century American Drama.*
  Oxford: Blackwell Press, 2005.
Mann, Bruce J., ed. *Edward Albee: A Casebook.* New York: Garland, 2001.
McCarthy, Gerry. *Edward Albee.* New York: St. Martin's Press, 1987.
Mira, Alberto, ed. *Quién teme a Virginia Woolf?* Madrid: Catedra Letras
  Universales, 1997.
Nayar, Rana. *Edward Albee: Towards a Typology of Relationships.* New
  Delhi: Prestige, 2003.
Németh, Lenke, ed. *Hungarian Journal of English and American Studies,* 15,
  Spring 2009. [Special issue of journal contains six essays on Albee's
  "Late-Middle Period."]
Paolucci, Anne. *From Tension to Tonic: The Plays of Edward Albee.*
  Carbondale: Southern Illinois University Press, 1972.
Paolucci, Anne. *Edward Albee (The Later Plays).* Middle Village, New York:
  Griffon House, 2010.
Roudané, Matthew. *Understanding Edward Albee.* Columbia: University of South
  Carolina Press, 1987.
Roudané, Matthew, ed. *American Drama: Contemporary Authors Bibliographic
  Series*, Vol. 3. Detroit: Gale, 1989.
Roudané, Matthew. *"Who's Afraid of Virginia Woolf?": Necessary Fictions,
  Terrifying Realities.* Boston: Twayne, 1990.
Roudané, Matthew, ed. *Public Issues, Private Tensions: Contemporary American
  Drama.* New York: AMS Press, 1993.
Roudané, Matthew. *American Drama since 1960: A Critical History.*
  Boston: Twayne, 1996.
Roudané, Matthew, with Martin Middeke, Peter Paul Schnierer, and Christopher
  Innes, eds. *The Methuen Drama Guide to Contemporary American
  Playwrights.* London: Bloomsbury, 2014.

Rutenberg, Michael E. *Edward Albee: Playwright in Protest.*
    New York: Avon, 1969.
Schmidt, Kerstin. *The Theater of Transformation: Postmodernism in American Drama.* New York and Amsterdam: Rodopi, 2005.
Solomon, Rakesh H. *Albee in Performance.* Bloomington: Indiana University Press, 2010.
Stenz, Anita Maria. *Edward Albee: The Poet of Loss.* The Hague: Mouton, 1978.
Vos, Nelvin. *Eugene Ionesco and Edward Albee: A Critical Essay.* Grand Rapids: W. B. Eerdmans, 1968.
Wasserman, Julian N., ed. *Edward Albee: An Interview and Essays.* Lee Lecture Series, University of St. Thomas, Houston. Syracuse: Syracuse University Press, 1983.
Wilmeth, Don B. and Christopher Bigsby. *The Cambridge History of American Theatre*, Vol. III. Cambridge: Cambridge University Press, 2000.
Zinman, Toby. *Edward Albee.* Ann Arbor: University of Michigan Press, 2008.

Index